MATCH
DIARY 2001

EDITOR: Chris Hunt
ART EDITOR: David Houghton
ASSISTANT EDITOR: Ian Foster
SUB-EDITOR: James Bandy

CONTRIBUTING EDITOR: Hugh Sleight
GROUP ART DIRECTOR: Darryl Tooth
CONTRIBUTORS: Richard Adams, Kevin Pettman, Martin Barry,
Kev Hughes, Bev Ward, Giles Milton, Phil Smith, Katherine Hannah,
Becky Booth, Calum Booth, Leyton Edwards, Phil Bagnall, Dawn Brown

A 'MILE AWAY CLUB' PRODUCTION
First published in Great Britain in 2000 by Hayden Publishing Ltd.
Copyright Emap Active Ltd 2000,
Colour Origination: Gildenburgh Reprographics
Printed and bound in Italy by LEGO, Vicenza.
ISBN 0 9533683 4 3
MATCH MAGAZINE, Bretton Court, Bretton,
Peterborough PE3 8DZ, England

MATCH DIARY 2001

Christy Whelehan

NAME ~~Christy John Whelehan~~

ADDRESS The bungalow west berks golf club chaddleworth Newbury berkshire RG 20 7DU

STICK YOUR PHOTO HERE

TELEPHONE NUMBER 01488 638 723

MOBILE PHONE NUMBER 07778 78 00 96

E-MAIL ADDRESS kim_whelehan@talk21.com

BIRTHDAY 21st May 1991

THE BEST TEAM IS Liverpool

FAN CLUB MEMBERSHIP NUMBER

THE BEST PLAYER IS Michael Owen

PREMIERSHIP WINNERS 2001 Manchester United

FA CUP WINNERS 2001 Liverpool

LEAGUE CUP WINNERS 2001 Liverpool

CHAMPIONS LEAGUE WINNERS 2001 Bayern Munich

UEFA CUP WINNERS 2001 Liverpool

SIGNATURE Christy Whelehan

MONDAY 1

○ NEW YEAR'S DAY

TUESDAY 2

○ BANK HOLIDAY IN SCOTLAND

Ⓑ **JONATHAN GREENING** *born 1979, Scarborough, England*

WEDNESDAY 3

★ *MATCH on sale*

THURSDAY 4

FRIDAY 5

SATURDAY 6

Ⓑ **ATTILIO LOMBARDO** *born 1966, St Maria La Fossa, Italy*

SUNDAY 7

FOOTY ANAGRAM
This red-hot striker has a crisp shot.

Answer for the last week in December 2001: HASSAN KACHLOUL

THIS WEEK IN 1994...

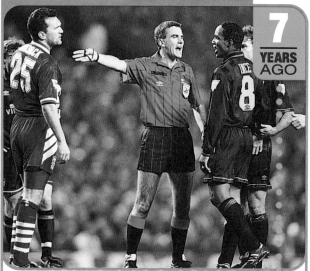

7 YEARS AGO

THE FOOTBALL TIMES

2 YEARS AGO...

JANUARY 4, 1999: Arsenal go two goals down at Second Division Preston in the FA Cup but scrape a goal back through Boa Morte before half-time. Emmanuel Petit inspires the comeback by scoring twice and Marc Overmars completes a 4-2 win.

5 YEARS AGO...

JANUARY 6, 1996: Liverpool cruise past Rochdale in the Third Round of the FA Cup with a 7-0 win at Anfield. Stan Collymore grabs a hat-trick and Ian Rush comes off the bench to notch his 42nd goal in the FA Cup, a new competition record.

10 YEARS AGO...

JANUARY 1, 1991: Paul Gascoigne becomes the first player to be sent-off in a live televised match while playing for Tottenham against Man. United in 1991.

24 YEARS AGO...

JANUARY 3, 1977: The fastest-ever own goal in English football is scored by the Torquay defender Pat Kruse, who heads past his own 'keeper just six seconds after the kick-off against Cambridge United.

38 YEARS AGO...

JANUARY 5, 1963: Due to freak weather, the FA Cup Third Round is delayed for an incredible two months. The conditions are so bad that the games aren't played until March 11, 1963. Referees said there was snow chance of playing until it cleared!

Liverpool grab late equaliser in controversial 3-3 classic

ANFIELD WAS IN SHOCK ON January 4, 1994 – their old rivals Man. United had scored three goals in the opening 25 minutes and Liverpool were heading for a thrashing. The home defence had crumbled under intense pressure from The Red Devils. Steve Bruce powered a header past Grobbelaar, while Giggs and Irwin added to the early onslaught as shots came at the Liverpool 'keeper from every angle. But with pride and honour at stake, Liverpool were forced to fight back. Nigel Clough was having a tough time settling in on Merseyside, but he clawed his team back with two stunning strikes before half-time. Graeme Souness's team continued to press United back and finally got their just reward when defender Neil Ruddock equalised to the delight of a rapturous Anfield crowd. To add controversy to the game it was then claimed that Grobbelaar had been paid £125,000 to throw the match, but he was later acquitted of the charges in court.

Complete history of Liverpool v Man. United

	LIVERPOOL WINS	DRAWS	MAN. UNITED WINS
League	44	42	48
FA Cup	2	4	8
League Cup	3	0	1
Other	0	3	1
Total	49	49	58

Last five meetings
(up to the end of 1999-2000 season)

1 FA PREMIERSHIP MARCH 4, 2000
Man. United 1 *(Solskjaer 45)*
Liverpool 1 *(Berger 27)*

2 FA PREMIERSHIP SEPTEMBER 9, 1999
Liverpool 2 *(Hyypia 23, Berger 68)*
Man. United 3 *(Carragher ogs 3, 44, Cole 18)*

3 FA PREMIERSHIP MAY 5, 1999
Liverpool 2 *(Redknapp pen 69, Ince 89)*
Man. United 2 *(Yorke 23, Irwin pen 56)*

4 FA CUP JANUARY 24, 1999
Man. United 2 *(Yorke 88, Solskjaer 90)*
Liverpool 1 *(Owen 3)*

5 FA PREMIERSHIP SEPTEMBER 24, 1998
Man. United 2 *(Irwin pen 19, Scholes 79)*
Liverpool 0

Last time Liverpool beat Man. United

FA PREMIERSHIP DECEMBER 17, 1995
Liverpool 2 *(Fowler 45, 87)*
Man. United 0

"MY CLUB DEBUT!"

JOE COLE

WEST HAM DEBUT: January 2, 1999
GAME: West Ham 1 Swansea 1
ATTENDANCE: 26,039
MATCHFACTS RATING: 6/10

Cole made his debut in the FA Cup Third Round, replacing Hartson after 65 minutes with West Ham trailing 1-0. The young midfielder brought an extra level of skill to the game and while Dicks levelled the scores with four minutes left, it was the new boy Cole who caught the eye.

MONDAY
8

TUESDAY
9

★ *MATCH on sale*

WEDNESDAY
10

THURSDAY
11

B **EMILE HESKEY** *born 1978, Leicester, England*

FRIDAY
12

B **RICHARD RUFUS** *born 1975, Lewisham, England*

SATURDAY
13

B **MARK BOSNICH** *born 1972, Fairfield, Australia*

SUNDAY
14

B **RUEL FOX** *born 1968, Ipswich, England*

THE EYES HAVE IT
Who is this Turkish delight?

Last week's answer: MICHAEL OWEN

THIS WEEK IN 1997...

4 YEARS AGO

Middlesbrough docked three points for refusing to play

ON JANUARY 14, 1997 MIDDLESBROUGH WERE FINED £50,000 and docked three points for refusing to play their Premier League fixture against Blackburn. Bryan Robson claimed Boro were unable to field a team because of an incredible injury list and an outbreak of flu within the club. His mistake was to call the fixture off without consulting the Football Association. Robson did not have the authority to change the fixture and the FA had to take action. It was a disaster for Middlesbrough, who were already fighting relegation. The points deduction left them four points adrift at the bottom of the Premiership and they never recovered. To rub salt into the wound, it was the deducted three points that relegated Boro because they were only two points from safety at the end of the season. The club might have felt robbed, but they definitely won't be doing it again!

Football's bad luck tales – ten of the worst!

IPSWICH TOWN: Lost in three consecutive play-off semi-finals, but finally ended their jinx last year!

RUUD VAN NISTELROOY: Close to a dream move to Man. United, then collapsed with a knee injury!

STUART PEARCE: Recovered at top speed from a broken leg playing for West Ham in 1999, only to suffer another one straight away. In typical Psycho style, Pearce thought he was fit to play on!

STEVE MORROW: After winning the League Cup with Arsenal in 1993, Tony Adams dropped Morrow during the celebrations and broke the midfielder's arm. He was never the same player after that!

RONALDO: Big Ron recovered from a serious knee injury after World Cup '98, got himself fit, then did the same thing in his first game back playing for Inter Milan. Faces a battle to get back to his best!

HAMILTON ACADEMICAL: Docked 15 points by the Scottish FA in 1999-2000 after the players went on strike because they hadn't been paid. The Accies couldn't recover the points and were relegated!

ENGLAND: Cheated out of a semi-final place in the 1986 World Cup by Diego Maradona's handball!

MIDDLESBROUGH: In 1997, Boro lost both of the Cup Finals and got relegated from the Premiership!

STEVENAGE: The Vauxhall Conference side celebrated when they won promotion to Division Three in 1996 but were refused a place in the Football League because their ground wasn't up to scratch!

NEWCASTLE UNITED: Reached two Cup Finals in two years, 1998 and 1999, but lost them both!

THE FOOTBALL TIMES

8 - 14 JANUARY

2 YEARS AGO...
JANUARY 8, 1999: Brian Kidd is named Manager Of The Month for December, the first honour he has won since taking over from Roy Hodgson at Blackburn Rovers.

4 YEARS AGO...
JANUARY 8, 1997: Kevin Keegan resigns as Newcastle United manager. The move is completely unforeseen and shocks the Geordie fans. John Toshack is an early candidate for the high-profile position.

6 YEARS AGO...
JANUARY 10, 1995: In a transfer market sensation, Man. United manager Alex Ferguson signs Newcastle United striker Andy Cole for £7 million, a British record.

8 YEARS AGO...
JANUARY 10, 1993: Norwich lose 1-0 at Sheffield Wednesday and fail to return to the top of the Premier League. The result also means that, despite being second, they have a negative goal difference.

19 YEARS AGO...
JANUARY 9, 1982: Only eight fixtures survive the bitterly cold conditions that have swept the nation. Amazingly, three of these ties are in Scotland!

HAPPY BIRTHDAY...
EMILE HESKEY

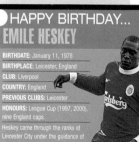

BIRTHDATE: January 11, 1978
BIRTHPLACE: Leicester, England
CLUB: Liverpool
COUNTRY: England
PREVIOUS CLUBS: Leicester
HONOURS: League Cup (1997, 2000), nine England caps.

Heskey came through the ranks at Leicester City under the guidance of Martin O'Neill and made his dream move to Liverpool in March 2000. The powerful striker proved himself at international level when he caused havoc against Argentina and Kevin Keegan rewarded the striker with a place in his squad for Euro 2000.

MONDAY 15

TUESDAY 16

★ MATCH on sale

WEDNESDAY 17

THURSDAY 18

FRIDAY 19

SATURDAY 20

SUNDAY 21

B **JERMAINE PENNANT** born 1983, Nottingham, England

B **STEFFEN FREUND** born 1970, Brandenburg, Germany

B **NICKY BUTT** born 1975, Manchester, England   B **WILLEM KORSTEN** born 1975, Boxtel, Holland

CODE BREAKER
Can you crack the secret code to name this Premiership star?

Last week's answer: MUZZY IZZET

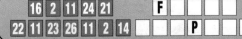

THIS WEEK IN 1997...

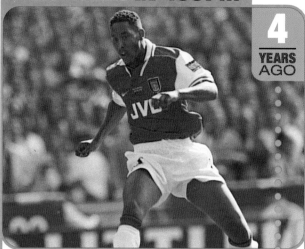

4 YEARS AGO

Arsenal swoop to bring young French star Anelka to Highbury

ARSENAL ANNOUNCED A CONTROVERSIAL DEAL TO BRING Paris St Germain's Nicolas Anelka to Highbury on January 15, 1997. The French club said Arsenal had made an illegal approach to steal their exciting 17-year-old striker. But Arsene Wenger was determined to get his man and Anelka signed for a bargain £500,000. The young Frenchman helped The Gunners to secure the League and FA Cup double in his first season in England. In the next campaign, 1998-99, Anelka showed his immense talent by netting 17 goals to become Arsenal's top scorer. However, things turned sour in the summer of 1999 when he demanded a transfer from Highbury. After months of failed negotiations, he signed for Real Madrid in a £23 million deal, but only after falling from hero to zero status with the Arsenal fans.

Ten dodgy football transfers

1. CHRIS SUTTON – Blackburn to Chelsea: Gianluca Vialli paid £10 million for Sutton, thinking he would be the regular scorer Chelsea needed, but the striker only managed three goals all season.

2. ESTEBAN FUERTES – Colon De Sante Fe to Derby: The £2.3 million hitman returned to Argentina only two months after joining Derby because his passport turned out to be a forgery. Dodgy eh?

3. STEPHANE GUIVARC'H – Auxerre to Newcastle: The French striker did nothing in the 1998 World Cup, but Newcastle still paid £3.5 million for him. Lasted three months before being sold to Rangers.

4. KEVIN DAVIES – Southampton to Blackburn: The striker only scored twice after his £7.25 million move to Ewood Park, but he was transferred back to The Dell and started banging in the goals again.

5. LES FERDINAND – Newcastle to Tottenham: His £6 million switch saw a return of just 12 goals in 46 league games after a series of injuries. Sir Les is still looking to play a full season with Spurs.

6. LEE SHARPE – Man. United to Leeds: Earned a packet at Leeds after his £4.5 million transfer, but was not part of David O'Leary's plans when he took over as boss, so Sharpey was on his way again.

7. MARCO BOOGERS – Sparta Rotterdam to West Ham: Arrived for £1 million but turned out to be hopeless in front of goal. He was rumoured to have lived in a caravan during his brief spell in London!

8. MASSIMO TAIBI – Venezia to Man. United: Arrived for a whopping £4.5 million and gave people hope that Man. United wouldn't win the league for once. Loaned to Reggina after some terrible gaffs.

9. DARKO KOVACEVIC – Red Star Belgrade to Sheffield Wednesday: Wasn't that bad for Sheffield Wednesday, but couldn't settle in Yorkshire. Now cracking in the goals for Italian giants Juventus.

10. STAN COLLYMORE – Liverpool to Aston Villa: A great talent, but developed depression after his £7 million move from Liverpool. It didn't help when John Gregory made him train on his own, though.

THE FOOTBALL TIMES

15-21 JANUARY

2 YEARS AGO...

JANUARY 19, 1999: Roberto Di Matteo's 90th minute goal against Coventry ensures Chelsea stay top of the Premiership – two points ahead of Man. United. Di Matteo added to Leboeuf's 25-yard effort after Darren Huckerby put Coventry 1-0 ahead.

3 YEARS AGO...

JANUARY 17, 1998: Barnsley, rooted to the bottom of the Premiership, give their hopes of survival a lift with a 1-0 victory over fellow strugglers Crystal Palace. Ashley Ward's first-half strike gives The Tykes only their sixth win of the season.

13 YEARS AGO...

JANUARY 17, 1988: Colin Moynihan, England's sports minister, says that UEFA should wait until after the 1988 European Championships before deciding whether to allow English clubs back into Europe after they were banned for crowd violence.

18 YEARS AGO...

THIS WEEK IN 1983: Watford manager Graham Taylor says he will run in the London Marathon to raise money for a new stand at Vicarage Road. Taylor's gruelling training schedule for the event involves a six o'clock start every morning.

22 YEARS AGO...

THIS WEEK IN 1979: Trevor Francis is rumoured to be leaving Birmingham City for £1 million. Nottingham Forest are ready to break the British transfer record fee for the star striker, reports MATCH.

HAPPY BIRTHDAY...
NICKY BUTT

BIRTHDATE: January 21, 1975
BIRTHPLACE: Manchester, England
CLUB: Man. United
COUNTRY: England
PREVIOUS CLUBS: None
HONOURS: Premier League (1996,1997,1999), FA Cup (1996, 1999), European Cup (1999), eight England caps.

A firm favourite with manager Alex Ferguson and the Old Trafford crowd, Butt played a vital role in United's 1999 European Cup Final, filling the void left by the suspended Roy Keane and Paul Scholes. He's yet to establish himself for England, but still has plenty of time to impress.

B **FRANK LEBOEUF** *born 1968, Marseille, France*

★ *MATCH on sale*

B **ANDREI KANCHELSKIS** *born 1969, Kirovograd, Ukraine*

B **FRANCIS JEFFERS** *born 1981, Liverpool, England*

SHARP SHOOTER
Which England striker has the middle name Ivanhoe?

Last week's answer: FRANK LAMPARD

THIS WEEK IN 1926...

75 YEARS AGO

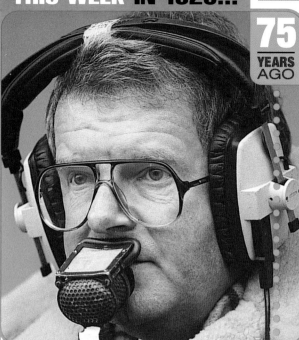

Britain hears the first ever live football commentary on radio

THE GAME BETWEEN SHEFFIELD UNITED AND ARSENAL at Highbury on January 22, 1926 was the first match to be broadcast live on radio. One commentator described the action, while another yelled out where it was happening on the pitch. This brought football to a mass audience, instead of just people who could afford to go to the games themselves. After 75 years of live commentary on the radio, it's still going strong and personalities like John Motson, Barry Davies and Alan Green have turned commentary into an art form.

The best of football commentators and pundits – think before you speak!

"What I said to them at half-time would be unprintable on the radio." **GERRY FRANCIS**

"I wouldn't say David Ginola is the best left-winger in the Premiership, but there are none better." **RON ATKINSON**

"What will you do when you leave football, Jack – will you stay in football?" **STUART HALL**

"For those of you watching in black and white, Spurs are in the all-yellow strip." **JOHN MOTSON**

"I honestly believe we can go all the way to Wembley, unless somebody knocks us out." **DAVE BASSETT**

"Mark Hughes at his very best – he loves to feel people right behind him." **KEVIN KEEGAN**

"That's football, Mike. England have had no chances and scored twice." **TREVOR BROOKING**

"Both sides have scored a couple of goals and both sides have conceded a couple of goals." **PETER WITHE**

"And with four minutes gone, the score is already 0-0." **IAN DARKE**

"I don't think there's anybody bigger or smaller than Maradona." **KEVIN KEEGAN**

THE FOOTBALL TIMES

3 YEARS AGO...
THIS WEEK IN 1998: Arsenal's all-time leading goalscorer Ian Wright tells MATCH that he intends to pursue a career as a TV interviewer. Well, Wrighty was never short of something to say, was he?

5 YEARS AGO...
THIS WEEK IN 1996: Blackburn striker Alan Shearer is on Inter Milan's shopping list, reports MATCH, but he's only rated third behind Ivan Zamorano and Ronaldo.

7 YEARS AGO...
JANUARY 28, 1994: Graeme Souness is sacked as manager of Liverpool. While the former Rangers boss managed to win the FA Cup for The Reds only two years earlier, Souness never really lived up to the high standards he set himself as a player.

21 YEARS AGO...
THIS WEEK IN 1980: Mike Channon sets a goalscoring record for Southampton, reports MATCH. He grabs his 161st goal for the club in an impressive 4-1 league win against Manchester City and goes on to score 185 league goals for The Saints.

92 YEARS AGO...
JANUARY 23, 1909: Newcastle United's Albert Shepherd promises he'll leave the field early if he scores a hat-trick against Notts County in Division One. And true to his word, after Shepherd smashes home four goals, he gets an early bath all to himself with 10 minutes still on the clock!

"MY RED CARD DAY!"
EMMANUEL PETIT

DATE: January 24, 1999
GAME: Wolves 1 Arsenal 2
SENT-OFF: 87 mins
OFFENCE(S): Foul, dissent
REFEREE: Steve Dunn (Bristol)

Petit was booked for a foul on Wolves midfielder Carl Robinson after 23 minutes of this FA Cup tie. Then, with only three minutes left, a decision went against Arsenal and the Frenchman screamed and gestured at the referee's assistant, leading to a second yellow card for dissent.

22 - 28 JANUARY

★ MATCH on sale   **B** **JOHN COLLINS** *born 1968, Galashiels, Scotland*

B **STEVE HARPER** *born 1974, Easington, England*   **B** **TIM FLOWERS** *born 1967, Kenilworth, England*

B **KEVIN CAMPBELL** *born 1970, Lambeth, England*

FOOTY ANAGRAM
This Belgium international striker was born in Croatia.

Last week's answer: EMILE HESKEY

BORN KARPU STAR

THIS WEEK IN 1994...

7 YEARS AGO

Liverpool go back to the boot room to appoint Roy Evans

LIVERPOOL WENT BACK TO THEIR ROOTS AND APPOINTED stalwart coach Roy Evans as their new manager on January 31, 1994. He replaced former Kop favourite Graeme Souness, who resigned after his disastrous 33 months in charge produced only one trophy, the FA Cup in 1992. The final straw was a hugely embarrassing home defeat by Bristol City, when the dismayed fans called for Souness to be dismissed – something that had never happened before at Anfield. The appointment of Evans heralded a return to the old Liverpool style and many hoped it would lead to the old success. Souness had made many changes in a short space of time, like demolishing the famous 'boot room' and creating a poor Liverpool squad of overpaid and under-achieving players. So while Evans was delighted at getting the chance to prove himself as manager, he still faced a tough task to rebuild the squad and challenge fierce rivals Man. United.

The ten longest-serving managers
in the Premiership

Roy Evans lasted five years as the Liverpool boss, which is pretty good these days. But which top-flight managers have been in the hot-seat the longest?

	MANAGER	CLUB	DATE APPOINTED
1.	ALEX FERGUSON	Man. United	November 1986
2.	BRYAN ROBSON	Middlesbrough	May 1994
3.	HARRY REDKNAPP	West Ham United	August 1994
4.	GEORGE BURLEY	Ipswich Town	December 1994
5.	PETER REID	Sunderland	March 1995
6.	JIM SMITH	Derby County	June 1995
7.	ALAN CURBISHLEY	Charlton Athletic	June 1995
8.	ARSENE WENGER	Arsenal	September 1996
9.	GORDON STRACHAN	Coventry City	November 1996
10.	GIANLUCA VIALLI	Chelsea	February 1998

THE FOOTBALL TIMES

1 YEAR AGO...
JANUARY 31, 2000: Alan Shearer scores twice against his old club Blackburn to put Newcastle into the quarter-finals of the FA Cup. If they can beat Tranmere Rovers it'll be another Wembley trip for The Magpies.

2 YEARS AGO...
JANUARY 29, 1999: Manchester City, led by Joe Royle, begin to climb Division Two in search of a play-off spot with a 1-0 win away at Stoke City. The victory stretches City's unbeaten run to seven games.

7 YEARS AGO...
FEBRUARY 2, 1994: Newcastle United sign Norwich City winger Ruel Fox in a £2.25 million deal. Along with the likes of Chris Sutton, Fox is one of a host of Norwich stars who helped The Canaries finish third in the Premiership in 1993.

18 YEARS AGO...
THIS WEEK IN 1983: Andy McCulloch, the Sheffield Wednesday striker, struggles to make the FA Cup Third Round replay at Southend because of a bruised foot. But MATCH has a different story, saying the injury isn't in his foot at all, it's a nasty boil on his backside – that's gotta hurt!

49 YEARS AGO...
FEBRUARY 2, 1952: When Wolves start the game at Anfield, the Liverpool team move to positions that make a mockery of their shirt numbers. It takes Wolves ten minutes to work out what's happening, by which time they've conceded two goals!

"MY CLUB DEBUT!"
JODY MORRIS

CHELSEA DEBUT: February 4, 1996
GAME: Chelsea 5 Middlesbrough 0
ATTENDANCE: 21,060

Jody Morris made his Chelsea debut after coming on as a 72nd minute substitute for John Spencer. The Blues were already 5-0 up with Gavin Peacock scoring a hat-trick. Ruud Gullit produced a brilliant passing display to tear Boro apart as Morris soaked up the atmosphere of a jubilant Stamford Bridge.

29 JANUARY – 4 FEBRUARY

MATCH 5 - 11 FEBRUARY

 MONDAY 5

Ⓑ **BILLY DODDS** *born 1969, New Cumnock, Scotland*   Ⓑ **GIOVANNI VAN BRONCKHORST** *born 1975, Rotterdam, Holland*

 TUESDAY 6

★ *MATCH on sale*

 WEDNESDAY 7

Ⓑ **BRIAN DEANE** *born 1968, Leeds, England*

 THURSDAY 8

 FRIDAY 9

 SATURDAY 10

FEBRUARY 6, 1996

 SUNDAY 11

Ⓑ **NICK BARMBY** *born 1974, Hull, England*   Ⓑ **STEVE McMANAMAN** *born 1972, Liverpool, England*

THE EYES HAVE IT
Who is this Premier goal king?

Last week's answer: BRANKO STRUPAR

THIS WEEK IN 1998...

3 YEARS AGO

Owen becomes the youngest player to appear for England

AFTER SHOWING SCINTILLATING FORM FOR LIVERPOOL IN the Premier League, Glenn Hoddle selected Michael Owen to play for England in the friendly against Chile on February 11, 1998. This made him the youngest England player of the century at 18 years and 59 days old, and he soon adapted to the speed of international football. Despite his encouraging performance in an experimental side, the Liverpool star couldn't get on the scoresheet against Chile, who won the game courtesy of two goals from their own star Marcelo Salas. But it didn't take Owen long to get off the mark. The talented striker broke another record by scoring in only his third international against Morocco, making him the youngest player ever to score for England.

If you're good enough,
it doesn't matter how old you are...

RYAN GIGGS was even younger than Owen when he made his debut for Wales aged 17 years and 332 days old. But Ryan Green, 106 days younger than Giggsy, is the youngest Wales player ever.

CAMPBELL BUCHANAN was only 14 years old when he played for Wolves against WBA in 1942.

PAUL ALLEN became the youngest player to appear in an FA Cup Final when West Ham played Arsenal in 1980. Allen was only 17 years and 256 days old, but helped The Hammers to a 1-0 win.

NORMAN WHITESIDE, playing for Man. United in 1983, became the youngest player to score in the FA Cup Final aged 18 years and 18 days. He's also the youngest player to appear in the World Cup.

NEIL McBAIN became the oldest player to appear in an English league match in 1947. McBain was the 52-year-old manager of New Brighton but couldn't stop his team losing 3-0 to Hartlepool.

HARRY REDKNAPP had to play in midfield when he was manager of Bournemouth because of an injury crisis – his first league match for six years. He helped Bournemouth to win the match 3-1!

THE FOOTBALL TIMES

5 - 11 FEBRUARY

3 YEARS AGO...
THIS WEEK IN 1998: The Irish Football Association warns Wimbledon they would not be welcome in Dublin after continued speculation that the London club may be looking to build a new home in Ireland.

5 YEARS AGO...
THIS WEEK IN 1996: Arsenal manager Bruce Rioch refuses to sign a new deal, reports MATCH. The Gunners are linked with moves for England's Terry Venables and Grampus Eight boss Arsene Wenger.

8 YEARS AGO...
THIS WEEK IN 1993: As a joke, Tranmere Rovers give Italian side Pisa a blow-up sheep after their Anglo-Italian Cup meeting in 1993. Bizarrely, Pisa put the 'gift' in their trophy cabinet, thinking it's a serious gesture from the Tranmere pranksters!

13 YEARS AGO...
FEBRUARY 6, 1988: Vinnie Jones gets to grips with a young Paul Gascoigne playing for Tottenham. And anyone who's seen the pictures will feel sorry for poor Gazza, as he proves a real handful for Big Vinnie.

14 YEARS AGO...
THIS WEEK IN 1987: Tony Cottee tells MATCH he wants to break up the England partnership of Gary Lineker and Peter Beardsley after he scores his 23rd goal of the season for West Ham in the League Cup quarter-final against Tottenham.

▶ HAPPY BIRTHDAY...
STEVE McMANAMAN

BIRTHDAY: February 11, 1972
BIRTHPLACE: Liverpool, England
CLUB: Real Madrid
COUNTRY: England
PREVIOUS CLUBS: Liverpool
HONOURS: FA Cup (1992), League Cup (1995), European Cup (2000), 29 England caps.

Liverpool fans were heartbroken when Macca left for Spain in 1999, but the England star was seeking a new challenge away from Anfield. In the game of his life in May 2000, he scored in the Champions League Final, a 3-0 win over Valencia, to help Real lift the trophy in his first season.

MONDAY 12

TUESDAY 13

★ *MATCH on sale*

WEDNESDAY 14

THURSDAY 15

FRIDAY 16

Ⓑ **JAMIE POLLOCK** *born 1974, Stockton, England*

SATURDAY 17

SUNDAY 18

Ⓑ **GARY NEVILLE** *born 1975, Bury, England*   Ⓑ **KEITH GILLESPIE** *born 1975, Larne, Northern Ireland*

CODE BREAKER
Can you crack the secret code to name this Premiership star?

Last week's answer: ANDY COLE

16	7	1	6	25	16	2

		I				

21	16	7	5	6	18

						T

THIS WEEK IN 1998...

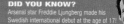

3 YEARS AGO

Gullit sacked as manager of Chelsea as Vialli takes control

WHEN RUUD GULLIT ARRIVED AT STAMFORD BRIDGE, HE might have been near the end of his playing career, but he still set the Premiership alight with his vision and pinpoint passing. As a player Gullit had won almost every trophy possible with both club and country, and he was one of the Premiership's first big-name foreign signings. When he was promoted to manager following the departure of Glenn Hoddle, the news was met with unbridled joy by the Chelsea fans, and despite some mediocre league form, The Blues won the FA Cup in 1997. By the New Year, backroom battles and the Dutchman's self-centred attitude had become too much for chairman Ken Bates, who was well-known for wielding the axe on his previous managers. On February 12, 1998 Bates announced that Ruud Gullit's time at Chelsea was up and Gianluca Vialli was promoted to player-manager.

GETTING THE BOOT – IT'S EASILY DONE
TOP MANAGERIAL SACKINGS FROM THE CRAZY WORLD OF TOP-FLIGHT FOOTY!

1.	JOHN BARNES	Celtic	Player disputes and losing to Rangers cost him dear!
2.	RUUD GULLIT	Chelsea	Disagreed with Ken Bates – a terrible mistake!
3.	RUUD GULLIT	Newcastle	The final straw was relegating Shearer to the bench!
4.	DAVE BASSETT	Nottingham Forest	The Forest board lost faith in the relegation expert!
5.	BARRY FRY	Barnet	Dismissed by Barnet and then Birmingham City!
6.	OSSIE ARDILES	Tottenham	Too attacking and couldn't pronounce 'Tottenham'!
7.	RON ATKINSON	Atletico Madrid	Fired after 96 days despite finishing third in league!
8.	MARK LAWRENSON	Oxford United	Complained about Oxford selling their best players!
9.	BOBBY ROBSON	Sporting Lisbon	Sacked after Sporting crashed out of the UEFA Cup!
10.	RON ATKINSON	Man. United	Got the boot after only three wins in 13 matches!

THE FOOTBALL TIMES

3 YEARS AGO...
THIS WEEK IN 1998: Trevor Sinclair signs for West Ham. During his time at QPR, top sides such as Man. United, Arsenal, Leeds and Blackburn all chased the goalscoring winger, but Harry Redknapp beat them all by securing his services for £2.3 million.

4 YEARS AGO...
THIS WEEK IN 1997: Gianluca Vialli's future at Chelsea is in doubt after he is dropped from the team to play Tottenham, reports MATCH. Vialli storms out of White Hart Lane before the end of the game!

10 YEARS AGO...
FEBRUARY 18, 1991: Roy Keane, playing for Nottingham Forest, almost causes a pitch invasion at St James' Park after making gestures to the Newcastle United crowd. The 19-year-old is hauled off immediately by his manager Brian Clough.

17 YEARS AGO...
FEBRUARY 14, 1984: Kevin Keegan says he'll retire as a player at the end of the season. He says the final straw was being beaten to the ball by Mark Lawrenson at Anfield – Lawro wasn't the fastest player!

48 YEARS AGO...
FEBRUARY 14, 1953: After scoring an extraordinary 46 goals in 30 games for Sheffield Wednesday, striker Derek Dooley breaks his leg. Doctors discover gangrene and cut it off – ouch! Due to the miracles of modern medicine, Joe Cole still has two legs after his minor break last season!

"MY RED CARD DAY!"
ROY KEANE

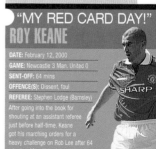

DATE: February 12, 2000
GAME: Newcastle 3 Man. United 0
SENT-OFF: 64 mins
OFFENCE(S): Dissent, foul
REFEREE: Stephen Lodge (Barnsley)

After going into the book for shouting at an assistant referee just before half-time, Keane got his marching orders for a heavy challenge on Rob Lee after 64 minutes. Man. United were already 1-0 down, but Keane's sending-off opened the floodgates and Newcastle won the match 3-0. Also booked in this bad-tempered match were Shearer, Cole, Stam (all dissent) and Paul Scholes (foul).

12 - 18 FEBRUARY

MONDAY
19

TUESDAY
20

★ *MATCH on sale*

WEDNESDAY
21

THURSDAY
22

B **SHAKA HISLOP** *born 1969, Hackney, England*

FRIDAY
23

B **GARETH BARRY** *born 1981, Hastings, England*

SATURDAY
24

SUNDAY
25

B **SHAUN GOATER** *born 1970, Hamilton, Bermuda*

SHARP SHOOTER
Who was the last English European Footballer Of The Year?

Last week's answer: RICHARD WRIGHT

THIS WEEK IN 1909...

92 YEARS AGO

Man. United move to their new Old Trafford stadium

MAN. UNITED BEGAN PLAYING FOOTBALL AT NORTH ROAD and then Bank Street in Clayton before arriving at Old Trafford on February 19, 1909. The new site was bought with a £60,000 grant from United's chairman, John Henry Davies, as well as funds from a local brewer. The new stadium was one of the most modern in the country, with a billiards room, massage rooms, a gymnasium and a plunge bath. There were 50,000 fans at the first game in the new ground, but United were beaten 4-3 by rivals Liverpool. Old Trafford was bombed during the Second World War and United were forced to play at Maine Road, home of old foes Manchester City. The ground re-opened in 1949 and was revamped for the World Cup in 1966.

Home sweet home!

Ipswich Town's Portman Road is the oldest ground in the Premiership – at 113 years old – and Sunderland's three-year-old Stadium of Light is the youngest. Man. United have the largest capacity in the Premiership and Southampton have the lowest.

CLUB	GROUND	MOVED IN	CAPACITY	RECORD
ARSENAL	Highbury	1913	38,500	73,295 (1935)
ASTON VILLA	Villa Park	1897	39,217	76,588 (1946)
BRADFORD CITY	Valley Parade	1903	21,634	39,146 (1911)
CHARLTON ATHLETIC	The Valley	1919	20,043	75,031 (1938)
CHELSEA	Stamford Bridge	1905	41,000	82,905 (1935)
COVENTRY CITY	Highfield Road	1899	23,650	51,455 (1967)
DERBY COUNTY	Pride Park	1997	33,597	33,378 (2000)
EVERTON	Goodison Park	1892	40,200	78,299 (1948)
IPSWICH TOWN	Portman Road	1888	22,600	38,010 (1975)
LEEDS UNITED	Elland Road	1919	40,204	57,892 (1967)
LEICESTER CITY	Filbert Street	1891	22,000	47,298 (1928)
LIVERPOOL	Anfield	1892	45,370	61,905 (1952)
MANCHESTER CITY	Maine Road	1923	33,000	84,569 (1934)
MAN. UNITED	Old Trafford	1909	68,500	76,962 (1939)
MIDDLESBROUGH	Riverside Stadium	1995	35,059	34,800 (2000)
NEWCASTLE UNITED	St James' Park	1892	36,834	68,386 (1930)
SOUTHAMPTON	The Dell	1898	15,000	31,044 (1969)
SUNDERLAND	Stadium Of Light	1998	48,000	42,192 (2000)
TOTTENHAM HOTSPUR	White Hart Lane	1900	36,236	75,038 (1938)
WEST HAM UNITED	Upton Park	1904	26,054	42,322 (1970)

THE FOOTBALL TIMES

2 YEARS AGO...
FEBRUARY 21, 1999: Henrik Larsson inspires Celtic to a 7-1 victory against Motherwell at Fir Park. The Swedish star scores four times, his third treble in four games, and tops the Scottish Premier League scoring charts with 30 goals.

5 YEARS AGO...
FEBRUARY 23, 1996: Newcastle sign David Batty from Blackburn Rovers in a £3.75 million deal. The transfer comes just one season after Blackburn won the Premier League in 1995 and the winning squad looks in danger of disintegrating.

8 YEARS AGO...
THIS WEEK IN 1993: The new generation of Man. United players is hailed in MATCH after they win the 1992 FA Youth Cup. The team of youngsters includes Nicky Butt, Gary Neville, Keith Gillespie, Ryan Giggs, Robbie Savage and David Beckham.

10 YEARS AGO...
FEBRUARY 20, 1991: Kenny Dalglish resigns as manager of Liverpool after a thrilling 4-4 FA Cup tie with Everton at Goodison Park. The football world is stunned as Kenny says he needs a rest from the pressures of management.

29 YEARS AGO...
FEBRUARY 21, 1972: Aston Villa fans are handed a treat when Brazilian club Santos, with their star player Pelé, visit Villa Park for a friendly match. An enthusiastic crowd sees the home team win 2-1 and, for once, Pelé doesn't get on the scoresheet.

HAPPY BIRTHDAY...
GARETH BARRY

BIRTHDATE: February 23, 1981
BIRTHPLACE: Hastings, England
CLUB: Aston Villa
COUNTRY: England
PREVIOUS CLUBS: None
HONOURS: Two England caps
After making his debut at the end of the 1997-98 season, Gareth Barry became a Villa regular after some solid performances at the heart of defence. Barry made an impressive debut for England against Ukraine and was one of the surprise names in Kevin Keegan's 22-man squad for Euro 2000.

MONDAY 26

B OLE GUNNAR SOLSKJAER *born 1973, Kristiansund, Norway*

TUESDAY 27

○ PANCAKE DAY

★ *MATCH on sale*

WEDNESDAY 28

THURSDAY 1

FRIDAY 2

B TREVOR SINCLAIR *born 1972, Dulwich, England*

SATURDAY 3

FEBRUARY 27, 1999

B EDGAR DAVIDS *born 1973, Paramaribo, Surinam*   B DARREN ANDERTON *born 1972, Southampton, England*

SUNDAY 4

○ WORTHINGTON CUP FINAL

FOOTY ANAGRAM
This Bantam loves his baked beans.

S A N E D A D W I N S

Last week's answer: KEVIN KEEGAN, 1979

THIS WEEK IN 1991...

10 YEARS AGO

Wing wizard Giggs makes an exciting debut for Man. United

THE OLD TRAFFORD CROWD GOT THEIR FIRST TASTE OF Ryan Giggs against Everton on March 2, 1991. He came on in the 35th minute for Denis Irwin, and while he couldn't stop Man. United losing 2-0, Alex Ferguson knew he had seen a future star. Before the season had ended, the 17-year-old was handed his first league start in the derby against Manchester City. The young Welshman repaid his manager's faith by scoring the only goal of the game. Ferguson kept his star away from the media and this clearly helped him to cope with the pressure. In his first full season, Giggs won the PFA Young Player Of The Year award and became the first player to retain the accolade the following year. In 1993 he helped Man. United to their first League crown for 26 years when the club lifted the first ever Premiership title. In his early years at United, Giggs was constantly compared to the mercurial George Best, but the wing wizard from Wales has become a legend in his own right after ten glorious years at Old Trafford.

The debuts of United legends

Ryan Giggs is now a veteran at Old Trafford after making his first team debut ten years ago against Everton. When did the Man. United legends first pull on the famous shirt?

DUNCAN EDWARDS	April 4, 1953 against Cardiff City, aged 16
BOBBY CHARLTON	October 6, 1956 against Charlton Athletic, aged 18
DENIS LAW	August 18, 1962 against West Bromwich Albion, aged 22
GEORGE BEST	September 14, 1963 against West Bromwich Albion, aged 17
BRYAN ROBSON	October 7, 1981 against Tottenham Hotspur, aged 24
MARK HUGHES	November 30, 1983 against Oxford United, aged 20
PETER SCHMEICHEL	August 17, 1991 against Notts County, aged 27
DAVID BECKHAM	September 23, 1992 against Brighton & Hove Albion, aged 17
ERIC CANTONA	December 6, 1992 against Manchester City, aged 26
ROY KEANE	August 15, 1993 against Norwich City, aged 22

THE FOOTBALL TIMES

26 FEBRUARY - 4 MARCH

2 YEARS AGO...
FEBRUARY 28, 1999: George Graham makes a move to sign the Ipswich Town coach Stewart Houston. Graham later installs Houston as his No. 2 at Spurs, reuniting their successful relationship while at Arsenal in the '80s and '90s.

4 YEARS AGO...
MARCH 2, 1997: Liverpool concede their first Premiership goal since New Year's Day when Ian Taylor's strike for Aston Villa secures all three points at Villa Park.

6 YEARS AGO...
MARCH 4, 1995: Andy Cole sets a new Premiership goalscoring record when he blasts five goals past a bewildered Ipswich at Old Trafford. Man. United make it an incredible two Premiership records in one afternoon by thrashing Ipswich 9-0.

10 YEARS AGO...
MARCH 2, 1991: Glasgow Rangers striker Mo Johnston misses an easy goalscoring opportunity in a game at Aberdeen. In his frustration he picks up a lump of dirt and throws it at the ground, pulling a muscle in his back. The bizarre accident causes him to miss the next two games – doh!

18 YEARS AGO...
THIS WEEK IN 1983: Swindon's teenage striker Paul Rideout reveals the reason why he has managed to double his goal tally for the season. He tells MATCH that his Dad advised him to start taking the club's penalties and nine of his 17 goals came from the spot. Nice one Dad!

FIRST VILLA GOAL!
JULIAN JOACHIM

DATE: February 28, 1996
GAME: Aston Villa 2 Blackburn 0
ATTENDANCE: 28,008
MATCHFACTS RATING: 7/10

Joachim marked his home debut for his new club with a smartly taken headed goal in the 55th minute. The new £1.5 million striker connected with Gary Charles's right-wing cross and left the 'keeper with no chance. When Southgate headed home a second goal on 71 minutes. When Joachim was substituted on 85 minutes he received a standing ovation from the Villa faithful after an impressive debut at his new footballing home.

MONDAY
5

TUESDAY
6

★ MATCH on sale

WEDNESDAY
7

B **RAY PARLOUR** born 1973, Romford, England

THURSDAY
8

B **JAMIE LAWRENCE** born 1970, Balham, England

FRIDAY
9

B **STEVE FROGGATT** born 1973, Lincoln, England

SATURDAY
10

MARCH 11, 1989

 B **MAURICIO TARICCO** born 1973, Buenos Aires, Argentina   B **PAVEL SRNICEK** born 1968, Bohumin, Czech Republic

SUNDAY
11

THE EYES HAVE IT
Who is this Wizard of Oz?

Last week's answer: DEAN WINDASS

THIS WEEK IN 1993...

8 YEARS AGO

San Marino collect their first ever World Cup qualifier points

ON THE MORNING OF MARCH 10, 1993 SAN MARINO HAD never scored any points in a World Cup qualifying match. But that changed by the end of the evening. The tiny nation knew they had to be at their best just to avoid a thrashing against Turkey. But the match turned out to be the greatest result in San Marino's history after a 0-0 draw! It might not compare with France's 3-0 win against Brazil in 1998 or England winning the World Cup in 1966, but the result was just as important to the jubilant San Marino fans. It got even better when they scored the fastest goal in World Cup history against England in November 1993, when Stuart Pearce's back-pass was turned home by striker Davide Gualtieri after just eight seconds!

Brain bustin' facts about San Marino!

Around 28,000 people live in San Marino – the size of a small town in most countries. England has a population of over 52 million, a few more players to choose from!

Despite its size, San Marino still has a capital city, also named San Marino, which has a population of 4,352 – but it's still more people than Wimbledon get at Selhurst Park!

San Marino have never qualified for the World Cup, but they always give 100 per cent!

On May 23, 2000 the new champions of the San Marino league were accepted into the UEFA Cup for the first time in the country's history – more record wins on the way!

San Marino were placed in the same qualifying group as Scotland, Latvia, Belgium and Croatia for the 2002 World Cup in Japan and North Korea – loads of goals there then!

They failed to pick up a point during the Euro 2000 qualifiers, letting in 43 goals. Their moment of glory came when their striker, Salva, scored in the 4-1 defeat by Austria!

THE FOOTBALL TIMES

5-11 MARCH

2 YEARS AGO...
THIS WEEK IN 1999: Gary McAllister tips Don Hutchison to be in the next Scotland squad because of his ability to get forward from midfield. It was a good tip as well, as England found to their cost at Wembley.

6 YEARS AGO...
MARCH 11, 1995: Tottenham march into the FA Cup semi-finals with a fine 2-1 win against Liverpool at Anfield. The Reds take an early lead, but goals from Sheringham and a curling effort from Jurgen Klinsmann give Tottenham a memorable Cup victory.

7 YEARS AGO...
MARCH 9, 1994: Peter Beardsley wins his 50th England cap after three years in the international wilderness. He has a great game in a 1-0 win against Denmark in which David Platt scores after 18 minutes.

17 YEARS AGO...
THIS WEEK IN 1984: Man. United striker Frank Stapleton tells MATCH he is not scared of Barcelona's Diego Maradona, who he is set to face in the quarter-finals of the Cup Winners' Cup. He was right to be confident – The Red Devils won 3-2!

114 YEARS AGO...
MARCH 5, 1887: Glasgow Rangers play in the English FA Cup for the last time, losing 3-1 to Aston Villa in the semi-final. It's thought Rangers lost because they ate a huge meal before the game! The 'keeper was said to have eaten all the pies and was at fault for all three of Villa's goals!

"MY CLUB DEBUT!"
EMILE HESKEY

LIVERPOOL DEBUT: March 11, 2000
GAME: Liverpool 1 Sunderland 1
ATTENDANCE: 44,693
MATCHFACTS RATING: 8/10

After completing his £11 million dream move to Anfield, Heskey began to repay his huge transfer fee with a display of enthusiasm and power. After only two minutes he earned a penalty after a strong run into the area was ended by Williams. Berger converted the spot-kick and Liverpool, with Heskey dominant, controlled the first half. Sunderland equalised with a penalty from Phillips, but Houllier and the Liverpool crowd left Anfield buzzing about their new signing.

MONDAY
12

TUESDAY
13

★ MATCH on sale

WEDNESDAY
14

Ⓑ **NICOLAS ANELKA** born 1979, Versailles-Yvelines, France   Ⓑ **MARK FISH** born 1974, Cape Town, South Africa

THURSDAY
15

Ⓑ **GIANLUCA FESTA** born 1969, Cagliari, Italy

FRIDAY
16

SATURDAY
17

MARCH 18, 1989

Ⓑ **LEE DIXON** born 1964, Manchester, England

SUNDAY
18

○ CIS SCOTTISH LEAGUE CUP FINAL

CODE BREAKER
Can you break the secret code to name this Premiership star?

23	18	19	26	22	5		F					
19	18	9	11	25	22	17			R			

Last week's answer: HARRY KEWELL

THIS WEEK IN 1872...

129 YEARS AGO

The first ever FA Cup Final is played at the Kennington Oval

THE FIRST FA CUP FINAL WAS HELD AT THE KENNINGTON cricket Oval on March 16, 1872. The final wasn't played at Wembley until 1923, when an estimated 250,000 people came to the stadium to watch the game, with half of them on the pitch! Only 15 teams entered the first FA Cup in 1872, including one team from Scotland and 13 from London. Wanderers FC beat the Royal Engineers 1-0 in the final after the Engineers were weakened by Lieutenant Cresswell's broken collar bone, even though Cresswell played on until the end as substitutes were not yet part of the game. The Wanderers retained the trophy in 1873 after beating Oxford University 2-0. The Engineers played in three of the first four FA Cup Finals and won at the third attempt against Old Etonians. In a five-year period in the early 1870s, the Engineers only lost three out of 86 matches. They scored 244 goals and conceded only 21. If only England could perform like that!

Top ten FA Cup Final winners

Man. United may not have defended the famous trophy last season, but they still top the all-time winners list. MATCH runs down the top ten winners of the FA Cup.

1.	MAN. UNITED	**1909**, 1948, 1963, 1977, 1983, 1985, 1990, 1994, 1996, 1999.
2.	TOTTENHAM HOTSPUR	**1901**, 1921, 1961, 1962, 1967, 1981, 1982, 1991.
3.	ARSENAL	**1919**, 1930, 1936, 1950, 1971, 1979, 1993, 1998.
4.	ASTON VILLA	**1887**, 1895, 1897, 1905, 1913, 1920, 1957.
5.	BLACKBURN ROVERS	**1884**, 1885, 1886, 1890, 1891, 1928.
6.	NEWCASTLE UNITED	**1910**, 1924, 1932, 1951, 1952, 1955.
7.	EVERTON	**1906**, 1933, 1966, 1984, 1995.
8.	LIVERPOOL	**1965**, 1974, 1986, 1989, 1992.
9.	WANDERERS FC	**1872**, 1873, 1876, 1877, 1888.
10.	WEST BROM	**1888**, 1892, 1931, 1954, 1968.

THE FOOTBALL TIMES

4 YEARS AGO...
MARCH 12, 1997: Stockport County beat Middlesbrough 1-0 in the second leg of the League Cup semi-final. However, Boro go through 2-1 on aggregate to their first Cup Final in their 121-year history.

5 YEARS AGO...
MARCH 18, 1996: Newcastle enjoy an emphatic 3-0 victory over West Ham at St James' Park. Les Ferdinand has a great game, hitting his 26th goal of the season to equal his best-ever record.

9 YEARS AGO...
MARCH 12, 1992: Liverpool's Wales striker Dean Saunders is suspended for three matches after television cameras show that he elbowed a Bristol Rovers player in an FA Cup Fourth Round clash.

17 YEARS AGO...
THIS WEEK IN 1984: Reading frontman Trevor Senior tells MATCH the reason for his success – he eats a ham omlette before every game. "Reading can't afford to give their players steak so I like a ham omlette instead," he explained. "It doesn't seem to be doing too badly for me!"

49 YEARS AGO...
MARCH 15, 1952: Fred Brown has a double nightmare while playing in goal for Aldershot Reserves against Millwall Reserves. He scores two identical own goals after twice hitting Millwall striker Jimmy Constantine on the back. The aim is to learn from your mistakes, Fred!

HAPPY BIRTHDAY...
LEE DIXON

BIRTHDATE: March 17, 1964
BIRTHPLACE: Manchester, England
CLUB: Arsenal
COUNTRY: England
PREVIOUS CLUBS: Burnley, Chester City, Bury, Stoke City
HONOURS: Division One (1989, 1991), Premier League (1998), FA Cup (1993, 1998) League Cup (1987, 1993), Cup Winners' Cup (1994), 22 England caps.

Arsenal snapped up Dixon from Stoke City for £350,000 when he was 24. Since then he's won every domestic honour possible with Arsenal and was rewarded for 13 years of service with a testimonial against Real Madrid.

MONDAY 19

○ ST PATRICK'S DAY HOLIDAY IN NORTHERN
IRELAND & REPUBLIC OF IRELAND

Ⓑ **MAGNUS HEDMAN** *born 1973, Stockholm, Sweden*

TUESDAY 20

★ *MATCH on sale*

Ⓑ **PAUL MERSON** *born 1968, Northolt, England*

WEDNESDAY 21

THURSDAY 22

FRIDAY 23

SATURDAY 24

MARCH 20, 1999

○ ENGLAND v FINLAND
○ SCOTLAND v BELGIUM
○ CYPRUS v REPUBLIC OF IRELAND
○ NORTHERN IRELAND v CZECH REPUBLIC
○ ARMENIA v WALES

Ⓑ **RAIMOND VAN DER GOUW** *born 1963, Oldenzaal, Holland*

SUNDAY 25

○ MOTHER'S DAY

SHARP SHOOTER
Which team scored the fastest goal in World Cup history in 1993?

Last week's answer: FABIEN BARTHEZ

THIS WEEK IN 1966...

35 YEARS AGO

Pickles discovers the stolen Jules Rimet trophy in a garden

THE JULES RIMET TROPHY WAS STOLEN FROM A STAMP exhibition in Westminster on March 20, 1966. The football world was thrown into panic as people asked what they would give to the new winners of the tournament in just three months time. The FA were left red-faced that the World Cup had been stolen in England, particularly when a hoax caller then demanded a £15,000 ransom. Fortunately, a heroic little dog called Pickles sniffed out the trophy in a South London garden while being taken for a walk by its owner! The black and white mongrel was foraging under some bushes and found the famous trophy in a parcel. To thank Pickles, the FA invited him to England's celebrations and gave its owner a £6,000 reward!

Top ten **weird World Cup facts!**

1. In the 1930 World Cup, the USA trainer ran onto the pitch, fell, smashed a bottle of chloroform and was carried off unconscious after smelling the fumes – he was replaced by the physiotherapist!

2. In 1934 and 1937, two World Cup qualifiers were officiated by a referee called Mr Frankenstein. Observers said he was a monster and would only referee matches if they were played late at night!

3. In December 1983, the USA camp suggested that all goalkeepers should wear helmets for the next World Cup. They said they were talking about soccer, but it sounds more like American football!

4. The highest attendance in the World Cup is 205,000, when Brazil met Uruguay on July 16, 1950!

5. The fastest sending-off in World Cup history occurred in 1986, when Uruguay's Jose Batista received his marching orders after just 55 seconds against Scotland – now that's an early bath!

6. Most teams have to rest people because of injuries or rotate the players in their squad, but when Brazil won the World Cup in 1962 they only used 12 players throughout the whole tournament!

7. A World Cup qualifier between Honduras and El Salvador got so heated it actually resulted in a war between the two countries. Wisely, the match referee declined to have anything to do with it!

8. The 1974 World Cup Final was delayed because the corner flags and halfway flags were missing!

9. Romania nearly missed out on the first World Cup in 1930, but they were a late arrival in Uruguay after King Carol insisted his country took part – he even picked the team for Romania's first game!

10. Brazil legend Jairzinho scored in every match of their triumphant 1970 World Cup campaign!

THE FOOTBALL TIMES

19 - 25 MARCH

2 YEARS AGO...

MARCH 21, 1999: Tottenham Hotspur beat Leicester 1-0 in the 1999 League Cup Final with a dramatic last-minute header from Allan Nielsen. The contest bursts into life when Justin Edinburgh is sent-off in the 63rd minute, but Spurs still win.

4 YEARS AGO...

MARCH 24, 1997: The match between Arsenal and Liverpool ends in controversy as referee Gerald Ashby awards a penalty even though Robbie Fowler insists that David Seaman didn't foul him. Seaman saves the weak spot-kick but Liverpool's Jason McAteer scores from the rebound.

10 YEARS AGO...

MARCH 23, 1991: Liverpool win 7-1 at Derby County with Beardsley, Rush and Barnes at their brilliant best. It's a big boost for The Reds' championship hopes as rivals Arsenal draw 0-0 with Norwich.

13 YEARS AGO...

MARCH 23, 1988: England draw 2-2 with Holland in a friendly at Wembley before the European Championships. Tony Adams has an eventful night, scoring for each team!

17 YEARS AGO...

MARCH 21, 1984: Liverpool smash four goals past Benfica away from home and romp to a 5-1 aggregate victory over the Portuguese team to earn themselves a place in the European Cup semi-final.

"MY RED CARD DAY!"

GILLES GRIMANDI

DATE: March 19, 2000
GAME: Arsenal 2 Tottenham 1
SENT-OFF: 85 mins
OFFENCE(S): Two fouls
REFEREE: Paul Durkin (Portland)

North London derbies are never quiet affairs and the tackles were flying in for this clash at Highbury. Amid a steady flow of yellow cards, Grimandi entered the book for a dangerous tackle on 37 minutes. He kept out of trouble until the 85th minute, when he went flying in on Sol Campbell. Referee Durkin judged it as a reckless challenge for a player that had already been booked and Grimandi had to go.

MONDAY 26

TUESDAY 27

★ MATCH on sale

Ⓑ **JIMMY FLOYD HASSELBAINK** *born 1972, Paramaribo, Surinam*

WEDNESDAY 28

○ ALBANIA v ENGLAND
○ SCOTLAND v SAN MARINO
○ ANDORRA v REPUBLIC OF IRELAND
○ BULGARIA v NORTHERN IRELAND
○ WALES v UKRAINE

THURSDAY 29

Ⓑ **MARC OVERMARS** *born 1973, Emst, Holland*

FRIDAY 30

SATURDAY 31

MARCH 28, 1992

SUNDAY 1

Ⓑ **STEVE WATSON** *born 1974, North Shields, England*   Ⓑ **CLARENCE SEEDORF** *born 1976, Amsterdam, Holland*

FOOTY ANAGRAM
This leggy striker is a real City boy.

| A | S | T | A | R | | E | N | O | U | G | H |

Last week's answer: SAN MARINO

THIS WEEK IN 1994...

7 YEARS AGO

Aston Villa beat Man. United to win their fourth League Cup

WHEN ASTON VILLA BEAT MAN. UNITED IN THE FINAL OF the League Cup on March 27, 1994 they joined Nottingham Forest and Liverpool as the only clubs to have won the trophy four times. Dean Saunders and Dalian Atkinson put The Villans 2-0 ahead, but Man. United pulled a goal back to set up a nailbiting finish. In the last minute, Man. United winger Andrei Kanchelskis handled a shot on his own goal line and became the first player to be sent-off in a League Cup Final. Saunders scored the resulting penalty to secure a 3-1 win and Villa returned to the West Midlands with the cup. It was a double blow for United as they'd been on course for the treble, but they still went on to win the League and FA Cup after this setback.

Who's won the most League Cup titles?

Liverpool and Aston Villa currently share the record of winning the League Cup five times, but some of England's leading clubs are hot on their heels.

LIVERPOOL	5-times winners	**1981**, 1982, 1983, 1984, 1995
ASTON VILLA	5-times winners	**1961**, 1975, 1977, 1994, 1996
NOTTINGHAM FOREST	4-times winners	**1978**, 1979, 1989, 1990
TOTTENHAM HOTSPUR	3-times winners	**1971**, 1973, 1999
LEICESTER CITY	3-times winners	**1964**, 1997, 2000
CHELSEA	2-times winners	**1965**, 1998
ARSENAL	2-times winners	**1987**, 1993
NORWICH CITY	2-times winners	**1962**, 1985
WOLVES	2-times winners	**1974**, 1980
MANCHESTER CITY	2-times winners	**1970**, 1976

THE FOOTBALL TIMES

26 MARCH – 1 APRIL

2 YEARS AGO...
MARCH 28, 1999: After a 3-1 victory over Poland at Wembley, part-time England boss and Fulham manager Kevin Keegan says he may be able to take the national job full-time – it's music to the FA's ears.

3 YEARS AGO...
MARCH 29, 1998: Paul Gascoigne makes his debut for Middlesbrough in the League Cup Final. He gives his loser's medal to Craig Hignett, who played in most of the games up to the final – what a hero!

8 YEARS AGO...
MARCH 31, 1993: England take a huge leap towards qualifying for the 1994 World Cup Finals with a win over Turkey in Izmir. Despite a hostile atmosphere, England successfully defend a 2-0 half-time lead.

22 YEARS AGO...
MARCH 28, 1979: Nottingham Forest thrash Chelsea 6-0. Forest's star striker Trevor Francis doesn't score, but midfield dynamo Martin O'Neill bags an emphatic hat-trick – absolutely magnificent!

96 YEARS AGO...
MARCH 29, 1905: The FA Cup semi-final replay between Aston Villa and Everton takes place at Trent Bridge (the cricket ground!). In a thrilling game, Villa progress to the final with a hard-fought 2-1 win.

"MY FIRST CAP!"
ROBBIE FOWLER

ENGLAND DEBUT: March 27, 1996
GAME: England 1 Bulgaria 0
ATTENDANCE: 29,708
MATCHFACTS RATING: N/A

Robbie Fowler had already scored 25 goals for Liverpool when he made his England debut in March 1996. Terry Venables brought him on as a substitute for Teddy Sheringham after 76 minutes and the striker clearly enjoyed the moment. England won the friendly courtesy of Les Ferdinand's goal after just six minutes.

MONDAY 2

TUESDAY 3

⭐ *MATCH on sale*

WEDNESDAY 4

THURSDAY 5

FRIDAY 6

SATURDAY 7

SUNDAY 8

Ⓑ **TEDDY SHERINGHAM** *born 1966, Highams Park, England*

Ⓑ **JOHN HARTSON** *born 1975, Swansea, Wales*

SHARP SHOOTER

Who's this Premiership new boy who loves his fruit cordial?

Last week's answer: SHAUN GOATER

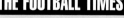

THIS WEEK IN 1993...

8 YEARS AGO

Players are warned about over-exuberant celebrations

WHETHER IT'S DOWN THE LOCAL PARK OR IN THE WORLD Cup Final, scoring a goal is a truly great feeling – the rush of blood, the tingling of goose bumps under the skin and the crazy urge to celebrate like a lunatic! However, on April 2, 1993, the FA decided that professional players should control themselves when they score. Goal celebrations were getting more ridiculous by the week and the FA said this over-exuberance could wind-up opposing fans enough to encourage crowd violence. Whether this is right or not is open to debate, but the ruling hasn't made much of an impact, even though the referees try and split up the kissing and cuddling as much as possible now! After years of polite clapping and shaking of hands, Cameroon's ageing Roger Milla did a dancing jig with the corner flag in the 1990 World Cup and the post-goal ritual became an art, with players even practising celebrations in training. It seems that every goal brings a new celebration, except from good old Alan Shearer who has promised never to deviate from his usual one-hand salute!

Great goal celebrations!

RYAN GIGGS, Man. United: In the FA Cup semi-final replay with Arsenal in 1999, extra-time was fast running out. But Ryan Giggs scored a wonder goal, ripped off his shirt off and swung it around his head like a crazed lunatic, revealing a rather hairy chest that he really should have kept covered up!

TEMURI KETSBAIA, Newcastle: The Georgian striker didn't get many first-team chances in 1997-98, so when he did score he kicked the advert hoardings in celebration. Strange, but very entertaining!

ALAN SHEARER, Newcastle: His celebration after scoring against former club Blackburn in the FA Cup in 2000 was remembered for not being his usual one-hand salute. Instead, he dived along the pitch and then pretended to be Robin Hood, shooting an arrow into the crowd. He later apologised!

FABRIZIO RAVANELLI, Middlesbrough: His debut hat-trick on the first day of the 1996-97 season against Liverpool saw a whole new craze in England. It involved lifting your shirt over your head and pointing your arms. White vests are optional, but it helps if you're not built like Jimmy 'Five Bellies'!

PAUL GASCOIGNE, England: Gazza's goal against Scotland in Euro '96 was remembered as much for the celebration as his fantastic strike (see the picture above!). He sprawled on the Wembley turf while Teddy Sheringham squirted water in his mouth, re-enacting the infamous 'dentist's chair' scene!

FRANK SINCLAIR, Chelsea: When Sinclair scored on the opening day of the 1997-98 season at Coventry he pulled his shorts down and danced in joy – he was reprimanded for his actions though!

THE FOOTBALL TIMES

2 - 8 APRIL

1 YEAR AGO...

THIS WEEK IN 2000: Blackburn striker Egil Ostenstad tells MATCH he's confident the club's new manager Graeme Souness is the man to turn the club's fortunes and lead them back to the Premiership.

3 YEARS AGO...

APRIL 3, 1998: Sunderland take a step closer to the Premiership after beating Tranmere 2-0 to put pressure on Division One leaders Nottingham Forest. Early goals from Kevin Phillips and Nicky Summerbee are enough to secure all three points.

3 YEARS AGO...

APRIL 4, 1998: Bradford record their first ever league victory at Carrow Road as Norwich are beaten 3-2. The Bantams strike three times in an amazing three minute spell either side of half-time, but The Canaries battle back to 3-2.

6 YEARS AGO...

APRIL 5, 1995: Leeds thump relegated Ipswich 4-0 in the Premiership at Elland Road. Striker Tony Yeboah grabs a first-half hat-trick as he completes a goalscoring feat of ten goals in ten games.

14 YEARS AGO...

THIS WEEK IN 1987: Ruud Gullit scores his 100th league goal as Dutch side PSV Eindhoven close the gap on leaders Ajax to just one point at the top of the league. Gullit has already decided to join AC Milan for £5.8 million in the close season.

"MY CLUB DEBUT!"
JON HARLEY

CHELSEA DEBUT: April 5, 1998
GAME: Derby 0 Chelsea 1
ATTENDANCE: 30,062
MATCHFACTS RATING: 7/10

Jon Harley got his chance with injuries to regular full-backs Graeme Le Saux and Celestine Babayaro. He certainly made a good impression on his debut and set up the goal that won Chelsea the match. He sent a fine curling cross into the area and onto the head of Mark Hughes, who looped the ball over 'keeper Hoult into the net. Harley was substituted after 83 minutes for Newton, but had proved he was a competent deputy for established internationals in defence.

MONDAY 9

ⓑ **ROBBIE FOWLER** born 1975, Liverpool, England

TUESDAY 10

★ MATCH on sale

ⓑ **ROBERTO CARLOS** born 1973, Sao Paulo, Brazil

WEDNESDAY 11

ⓑ **MALCOLM CHRISTIE** born 1979, Peterborough, England

THURSDAY 12

ⓑ **LUCAS RADEBE** born 1969, Johannesburg, South Africa

FRIDAY 13

○ **GOOD FRIDAY**

SATURDAY 14

SUNDAY 15

CODE BREAKER
Can you crack the secret code to name this Premiership star?

| 17 | 14 | 9 | 22 | 17 | | | | I |
| 15 | 14 | 7 | 7 | 12 | | | | Y |

Last week's answer: JOHN ROBINSON

DID YOU KNOW?
Shaka Hislop was a Spurs fan, but he didn't
see them play much growing up in Trinidad!

THIS WEEK IN 1988...

13 YEARS AGO

Shearer becomes youngest player to score a hat-trick

ON HIS FULL LEAGUE DEBUT AGED JUST 17 YEARS AND
240 days, Alan Shearer scored a hat-trick for Southampton against
Arsenal on April 9, 1988. It made him the youngest player to score
a hat-trick in the First Division (before it became the Premier League
in 1992). It was an impressive achievement for the striker, against an
Arsenal defence which included established internationals including
David O'Leary, Tony Adams and Kenny Sansom. The Gunners were
on a good run and their next game was the League Cup Final against
Luton, but they were shocked at the youngster's sensational debut
hat-trick and lost the game 4-2. It was a great boost for Shearer, who
got an instant rise in his weekly pay packet, and the leading clubs in
England took an immediate interest in the promising centre-forward.

Hat-trick facts – three out of three ain't bad!

In 1992, **ERIC CANTONA** became the first player to score a hat-trick in the new Premier League when
Leeds smashed five goals past Tottenham at Elland Road. He moved to Man. United later that year!

GEOFF HURST is still the only player to score a hat-trick in a World Cup Final. His famous trio of goals
helped England to beat West Germany 4-2 in the 1966 final at Wembley, their greatest ever triumph!

Super striker **DIXIE DEAN** scored an extraordinary 37 hat-tricks during his 12-year Everton career!

STAN MORTENSEN is the only player to have scored a hat-trick in an FA Cup Final. Mortensen,
playing up front for Blackpool, scored his record tally in 'Pool's classic 4-3 win over Bolton in 1953!

Middlesbrough legend **GEORGE CAMSELL** scored a total of nine hat-tricks in the 1926-27 season!

The term **'HAT-TRICK'** comes from cricket. It was first used to describe what happened when a bowler
took three consecutive wickets with three balls. If he performed this feat he was bought a new hat!

THE FOOTBALL TIMES

2 YEARS AGO...

APRIL 14, 1999: Ryan Giggs scores an
unbelievable goal in Man. United's FA Cup
semi-final replay at Villa Park. Giggsy picks
up the ball in his own half, dribbles past
the entire Arsenal defence and hits an
unstoppable shot past David Seaman.

4 YEARS AGO...

THIS WEEK IN 1997: Dennis Bergkamp
pleads with Arsenal to sign his Holland
team-mate Marc Overmars from Ajax,
reports MATCH. "I have recommended him
to Arsenal and I'll just have to hope now."
You see Dennis, dreams can come true!

6 YEARS AGO...

THIS WEEK IN 1995: Bob Wilson tells
MATCH how Gary Lineker is progressing
at the BBC. "He's doing his homework in
radio," said Wilson. "Footballers make
good panellists but few make presenters –
we'll just have to wait and see with Gary."

8 YEARS AGO...

THIS WEEK IN 1993: Southend's Stan
Collymore is attracting interest from a host
of Premiership clubs. MATCH reports that
Everton boss Howard Kendall has been to
watch the striker and Nottingham Forest
are also said to be interested in Collymore.

10 YEARS AGO...

APRIL 14, 1991: An inspired Tottenham
team beat Arsenal 3-1 in the 1991 FA Cup
semi-final at Wembley. Paul Gascoigne
fires in a cracking free-kick from 30 yards
and Gary Lineker grabs a brace of goals.

"MY RED CARD DAY!"

ROY KEANE

DATE:	April 14, 1999
GAME:	Man. United 2 Arsenal 1
SENT-OFF:	73 mins
OFFENCE(S):	Two bookable offences
REFEREE:	David Elleray (Harrow)

Both sides made sure this match, the
last ever FA Cup semi-final replay,
would live long in the memory.
Amid a host of bookings,
Keane was cautioned after
33 minutes for a late tackle.
With the score at 1-1, he received his
marching orders for a second bad
challenge. But United held on, with
Schmeichel saving a last-minute
penalty and Giggs scoring his wonder
goal to win the tie in extra-time.

○ EASTER MONDAY

★ *MATCH on sale*   Ⓑ **ANDY CAMPBELL** *born 1979, Middlesbrough, England*

Ⓑ **RIVALDO** *born 1972, Recife, Brazil*

Ⓑ **BILLY McKINLAY** *born 1969, Glasgow, Scotland*   Ⓑ **DION DUBLIN** *born 1969, Leicester, England*

SHARP SHOOTER
From which team did Dennis Bergkamp and Kanu join Arsenal?

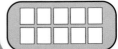

Last week's answer: DAVID BATTY

THIS WEEK IN 2000...

1 YEAR AGO

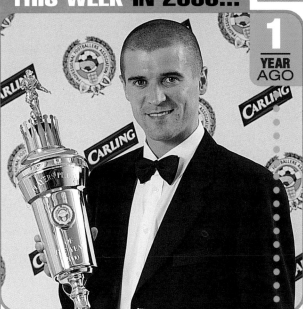

Roy Keane is named Football Writers' Player Of The Year

AT THE END OF 1998-99, DESPITE MAN. UNITED WINNING the unprecedented treble, both Player Of The Year awards were given to Tottenham's David Ginola. Alex Ferguson disagreed, believing his captain Roy Keane should have won the honours. Keane was again the favourite for the award last year after his commanding displays in the Premiership and Champions League. His vital goals helped United to another Premiership title and his anchoring of the midfield allowed the team to play their exciting, attacking football. Despite some tough competition from Harry Kewell and Kevin Phillips, Keane deserved to win the 2000 Football Writers' Player Of The Year award. He was also named the PFA's Player Of The Year, which was voted for by fellow Premiership players. By winning both awards, Keane joined a unique club – only nine players have ever won both awards in the same year.

Award-winning players of the past 10 years

YEAR	FOOTBALL WRITERS' PLAYER OF THE YEAR	PFA PLAYER OF THE YEAR
1990	John Barnes (Liverpool)	David Platt (Aston Villa)
1991	Gordon Strachan (Leeds United)	Mark Hughes (Man. United)
1992	Gary Lineker (Tottenham Hotspur)	Gary Pallister (Man. United)
1993	Chris Waddle (Sheffield Wednesday)	Paul McGrath (Aston Villa)
1994	Alan Shearer (Blackburn Rovers)	Eric Cantona (Man. United)
1995	Jürgen Klinsmann (Tottenham Hotspur)	Alan Shearer (Blackburn Rovers)
1996	Eric Cantona (Man. United)	Les Ferdinand (Newcastle United)
1997	Gianfranco Zola (Chelsea)	Alan Shearer (Newcastle United)
1998	Dennis Bergkamp (Arsenal)	Dennis Bergkamp (Arsenal)
1999	David Ginola (Tottenham Hotspur)	David Ginola (Tottenham Hotspur)
2000	Roy Keane (Man. United)	Roy Keane (Man. United)

THE FOOTBALL TIMES

16 - 22 APRIL

2 YEARS AGO...

APRIL 17, 1999: Blackburn surrender a 3-1 lead at The Dell as Southampton score two late goals. The result sends Rovers into the Premiership's bottom three and the club stare relegation in the face.

5 YEARS AGO...

APRIL 19, 1996: A lorry carrying 4,000 brand new Newcastle United away shirts is held up by three masked men on its way to a delivery. The hijackers are caught soon afterwards. Some people can't wait!

8 YEARS AGO...

APRIL 18, 1993: Arsenal beat Sheffield Wednesday 2-1 in the 1993 League Cup final, but midfielder Steve Morrow breaks his arm in the midst of the celebrations and leaves Wembley in an ambulance.

10 YEARS AGO...

APRIL 20, 1991: Nottingham Forest thrash Chelsea 7-0, with two goals apiece from Stuart Pearce and Roy Keane. The Blues' experienced boss Bobby Campbell says Pearce's performance is the finest individual display he has ever seen.

92 YEARS AGO...

APRIL 17, 1909: Fans invade the pitch at Hampden Park demanding to know why no extra time is being played after Rangers draw 1-1 with Celtic in the 1909 Scottish Cup Final. Bizarrely, the match officials don't know what to do, so neither side wins the cup and the tie is not replayed.

FIRST HAMMERS GOAL!

MICHAEL CARRICK

DATE: April 22, 2000
GAME: West Ham 5 Coventry 0
ATTENDANCE: 24,719
MATCHFACTS RATING: 7/10

Michael Carrick was only playing for West Ham because fellow young star Joe Cole had broken his leg. But just six minutes into his second Premier League start, the elegant midfielder collected a pass from Paolo di Canio and hammered a low 30-yard shot past goalkeeper Magnus Hedman. It capped a tremendous performance by the young prodigy, who adapted superbly to the pace and skill of the game. West Ham romped home 5-0 and Carrick looked like an old pro.

MONDAY
23

B DARREN HUCKERBY *born 1976, Nottingham, England*

TUESDAY
24

★ MATCH on sale   B STEFAN SCHNOOR *born 1971, Neumunster, Germany*   B DOMINIC MATTEO *born 1974, Dumfries, Scotland*

WEDNESDAY
25

⚬ REPUBLIC OF IRELAND v ANDORRA

THURSDAY
26

FRIDAY
27

SATURDAY
28

SUNDAY
29

B CLAUS JENSEN *born 1977, Nykobing, Denmark*

FOOTY ANAGRAM
This striker has a fiery temperament.

MARY SLOT CLONE

Last week's answer: INTER MILAN

36 YEARS AGO

Stanley Matthews bows out of football at the age of 50

SIR STANLEY MATTHEWS PLAYED IN A SPECIAL BENEFIT match on April 28, 1965 to commemorate his retirement from football. A team of international stars including Alfredo di Stefano, Lev Yashin and Ferenc Puskas flew in to honour one of the greatest footballers the world has ever seen. Matthews played his last competitive game in February 1965 – five days after his 50th birthday – when he helped Stoke City beat Fulham 3-1. Dubbed the 'Wizard Of The Dribble' for his awesome ability to leave defenders standing, he first appeared for home-town club Stoke in 1932 at the age of 17. He also played for Blackpool, where his superb display in the 1953 FA Cup Final brought him his one and only winners' medal. Matthews became the first ever winner of the European Player of the Year award in 1956 and won the last of his 54 England caps in 1957 at the age of 42, some 23 years after his international debut! Sir Stanley Matthews remains the only player in England to have been knighted while still playing football.

The oldest England players ever!

Sir Stanley Matthews played his last game for his country at the grand old age of 42. MATCH looks at the oldest England players ever, with David Seaman still going strong!

NAME	LAST GAME FOR ENGLAND	AGE
SIR STANLEY MATTHEWS	May 15, 1957 v Denmark	42 years, 103 days
PETER SHILTON	July 7, 1990 v Italy	40 years, 292 days
LESLIE COMPTON	November 22, 1950 v Yugoslavia	38 years, 71 days
STUART PEARCE	September 8, 1999 v Poland	37 years, 138 days
DAVID SEAMAN	June 20, 2000 v Romania	36 years, 275 days*
JESSIE PENNINGTON	April 10, 1920 v Scotland	36 years, 230 days
SAM HARDY	April 10, 1920 v Scotland	36 years, 228 days
TOM FINNEY	October 22, 1958 v USSR	36 years, 200 days
TED HUFTON	May 15, 1929 v Spain	36 years, 171 days
SAM CHEDGZOY	October 22, 1924 v Ireland	35 years, 268 days

*This was not David Seaman's final game for England.

THE FOOTBALL TIMES

2 YEARS AGO...
APRIL 28, 1999: David Seaman wins his 50th cap for England when Kevin Keegan's team draw 1-1 in Hungary. The Arsenal 'keeper won his first cap in 1989 against Saudi Arabia and never looked back.

3 YEARS AGO...
APRIL 26, 1998: Leicester win 4-0 away at Derby in the Premiership. All four goals are scored in the first 15 minutes, all are headers and all come from crosses. Emile Heskey (2), Muzzy Izzet and veteran Ian Marshall score the goals for The Foxes.

16 YEARS AGO...
APRIL 24, 1985: Liverpool win 1-0 away at Panathinaikos in the second leg of the European Cup semi-final. Mark Lawrenson scores the crucial goal to make it 5-0 on aggregate. The win books Liverpool's place in the final against Italian giants Juventus.

20 YEARS AGO...
APRIL 25, 1981: Stockport County are made to play with nine men and without their manager after part of the squad is delayed by snow on the way to the match at Bury. The missing men don't arrive until half-time, but Stockport still triumph 1-0!

51 YEARS AGO...
APRIL 26, 1950: Jimmy Dunn, the Leeds right-back, hits a long clearance towards the Blackburn goal which bounces through the legs of two defenders and into the net! It was Dunn's first and only goal for the club and one of the luckiest strikes ever.

"MY FIRST CAP!"
KEVIN PHILLIPS

ENGLAND DEBUT: April 28, 1999
GAME: Hungary 1 England 1
ATTENDANCE: 20,000
MATCHFACTS RATING: 7/10

Kevin Phillips deservedly won his first cap after firing Sunderland to the top of the First Division. He started in the attack with Alan Shearer, who put England ahead in the 22nd minute from the penalty spot. only for Hrutka's free-kick to level the match late in the second-half. Phillips made an encouraging international debut, despite being substituted in the 83rd minute, and showed glimpses of what he was doing week in, week out for his club.

MONDAY
30

TUESDAY
1

★ MATCH on sale

B **OLIVER BIERHOFF** *born 1968, Karlsruhe, Germany*

WEDNESDAY
2

B **DAVID BECKHAM** *born 1975, Leytonstone, England*

THURSDAY
3

FRIDAY
4

SATURDAY
5

○ **LAST WEEKEND OF 2000-2001 NATIONWIDE LEAGUE SEASON**

SUNDAY
6

THE EYES HAVE IT
Who is this £7.5 million sinner turned Saint?

Last week's answer: STAN COLLYMORE

THIS WEEK IN 1999...

2
YEARS
AGO

THE FOOTBALL TIMES

2 YEARS AGO...

MAY 1, 1999: For the Premiership clash between Liverpool and Tottenham, Stephen Lodge becomes the first referee to be wired up to his assistants via a headset.

4 YEARS AGO...

MAY 2, 1997: Chelsea's Gianfranco Zola is named the 1997 Football Writers' Player of the Year. It completes a hat-trick of awards for foreign stars after Eric Cantona (1996) and Jürgen Klinsmann (1995) were named winners in the previous two years.

8 YEARS AGO...

MAY 2, 1993: Man. United secure their first league title for 26 years as Oldham beat second-placed Aston Villa 1-0. Alex Ferguson becomes the first manager to win the league in England and Scotland.

16 YEARS AGO...

MAY 1, 1985: England grind out a 0-0 draw in the World Cup qualifier against Turkey to put them top of their group with a game in hand over Northern Ireland.

50 YEARS AGO...

MAY 3, 1951: Newcastle United return home triumphant with the FA Cup five days late! The team had a league match at Wolves on Wednesday night, so the loyal Geordie fans had to wait for their heroes!

Football mourns the death of England hero Sir Alf Ramsey

THE ONLY ENGLAND MANAGER TO WIN THE WORLD CUP died on May 1, 1999 and messages of respect arrived from around the world to honour one of the most innovative managers the game has ever seen. The teams that Sir Alf Ramsey named during the 1966 World Cup Finals were slated by the Press because they depended on a new system without wingers. But the 'Wingless Wonders', as the team soon became known, proved a handful for opposing sides who weren't familiar with the new system. In a twist of fate, Sir Alf died on the anniversary of his appointment as England boss – May 1, 1963. This was three years before the start of the tournament, but Ramsey was full of confidence at the time and told the Press: "England will win the World Cup in 1966." How's that for foresight? The greatest ever England manager could have won a fortune with his predictions, like choosing six random numbers on the National Lottery!

The tale of England's recent managers

BOBBY ROBSON (1982-1990) Cheated out of a semi-final place in 1986 by Diego Maradona's handball. Desperately close to a World Cup Final place in 1990 but lost to Germany on penalties.

GRAHAM TAYLOR (1990-1993) Had a fine reputation at club level, but failed miserably at Euro '92 and didn't even qualify for the World Cup in USA '94. Eventually hounded out of the job by the Press.

TERRY VENABLES (1994-1996) Came close to a place in the final of Euro '96, but England lost to Germany on penalties again. Created a good team, but left because of legal proceedings with Spurs.

GLENN HODDLE (1996-1999) Made good progress in France '98 until Argentina beat his side on penalties. The side was playing well under Hoddle but he was sacked for remarks about the disabled.

HOWARD WILKINSON (Temporary) Took over after Hoddle was sacked, but lost 2-0 to France in his only game in charge and wasn't offered the job on a full-time basis. Now England's U21 manager.

KEVIN KEEGAN (1999-present) Has impressed with his enthusiasm, but many believe he is tactically naive and he had no success at Euro 2000. Faces a difficult task to turn England into world-beaters.

"MY CLUB DEBUT!"

MICHAEL OWEN

LIVERPOOL DEBUT: May 6, 1997
GAME: Wimbledon 2 Liverpool 1
ATTENDANCE: 20,016
MATCHFACTS RATING: 7/10

Liverpool were heading for a 2-0 defeat at Selhurst Park when manager Roy Evans gave a debut to 17-year-old Michael Owen after 58 minutes. The youngster replaced winger Patrik Berger and was on the scoresheet within 16 minutes of his first Liverpool game. After a through ball from Bjornebye, Owen showed lightning pace to beat the chasing defenders and slot the ball beyond the reach of goalkeeper Neil Sullivan from just inside the 18-yard box.

MONDAY 7

○ WOMEN'S FA CUP FINAL
○ BANK HOLIDAY

TUESDAY 8

Ⓑ **CHRIS MAKIN** *born 1973, Manchester, England*

WEDNESDAY 9

★ *MATCH on sale* Ⓑ **DON HUTCHISON** *born 1971, Gateshead, England* Ⓑ **RICHARD JOBSON** *born 1963, Holderness, England*

THURSDAY 10

Ⓑ **DAVID WEIR** *born 1970, Falkirk, Scotland*

FRIDAY 11

○ FIRST LEG OF FA YOUTH CUP FINAL

SATURDAY 12

○ FA CUP FINAL

SUNDAY 13

CODE BREAKER
Can you crack the secret code to
name this Premiership star?

Last week's answer: KEVIN DAVIES

| 25 | 18 | 18 | | **L** | | |
| 6 | 21 | 14 | 5 | 3 | 18 | | | | **R** | | |

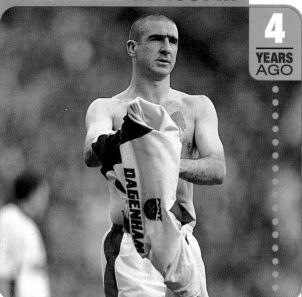

4 YEARS AGO

7 – 13 MAY

THE FOOTBALL TIMES

1 YEAR AGO...
MAY 13, 2000: Chasing a place in the Premiership, Barnsley put in an awesome display to beat Birmingham City 4-0 in the first leg of the play-off semi-final. Hignett and Shipperley add to Dyer's brace.

2 YEARS AGO...
MAY 12, 1999: On a tension-packed night, Blackburn draw 0-0 with Man. United at Ewood Park. But the point is not enough to survive the drop, and the champions of 1995 are relegated to the First Division.

7 YEARS AGO...
MAY 7, 1994: Everton escape from the jaws of relegation on the last day of the season, coming back from 2-0 down against Wimbledon at home to win 3-2. Graham Stuart is the saviour, scoring the winning goal in the 81st minute.

8 YEARS AGO...
MAY 9, 1993: Despite finishing a lowly sixth place in the Premiership, Liverpool hold a press conference to announce that Graeme Souness will remain as manager of the club for another three years.

11 YEARS AGO...
MAY 12, 1990: Ian Wright comes off the Crystal Palace bench to score against Man. United and force extra-time in the 1990 FA Cup Final. Wright puts Palace 2-1 up in extra-time, but Mark Hughes scores with seven minutes left to force a replay.

Eric Cantona says 'Au revoir' as he quits football at his peak

ERIC CANTONA PLAYED HIS LAST GAME FOR MAN. UNITED against West Ham on May 11, 1997. He had not told his manager or team-mates of his decision and the fans were blissfully unaware that this was the last time they would see the enigmatic Frenchman at Old Trafford. He announced his retirement seven days after guiding United to their fourth Premiership crown in five years. Alex Ferguson bought Cantona in November 1992 for the bargain price of £1 million. The striker had helped Leeds United to the First Division title in 1992 and Ferguson decided to build his team around the skilful playmaker. The result was spectacular – The Red Devils won England's first ever Premier League title six months later – their first league championship for 26 years. With Cantona at the heart of the team, United won four Premiership titles (1993, 1994, 1996 and 1997) and two 'doubles', by winning the FA Cup in 1994 and 1996. He retired from football at his peak, with United fans begging for more in the Theatre of Dreams.

Eric Cantona's career of highs and lows...

OCTOBER 1983	Makes first-team debut for his first professional club, French side Auxerre.
MAY 1985	Scores his first senior goal for Auxerre after doing a year's military service.
AUGUST 1987	Makes his first international appearance for France against West Germany.
SEPTEMBER 1988	Banned from international football after abusing the French national coach.
APRIL 1992	Lifts First Division title with Leeds in his very first season in English football.
MAY 1993	Wins the first ever Premier League with Man. United after playing a vital role.
MAY 1994	Wins the Premier League title, FA Cup and PFA Player Of The Year award.
JANUARY 1995	Kicks an abusive fan at Crystal Palace and gets banned for eight months.
MAY 1996	Captains United to another Premiership and FA Cup double after his ban.
MAY 1997	Retires from football after captaining United to their fourth Premiership title.

"MY RED CARD DAY!"
DON HUTCHISON

DATE: May 8, 2000
GAME: Leeds 1 Everton 1
SENT-OFF: 87 mins
OFFENCE(S): Foul, dissent
REFEREE: Andy D'Urso (Billericay)

Hutchison's second yellow card came in a heated match that set a new Premiership record of three dismissals and nine bookings. Referee Andy D'Urso sent Hutchison for an early bath when the Everton star kicked the ball away in despair after Stephen Hughes was harshly called back for fouling Lee Bowyer. Everton's Richard Dunne and Michael Duberry of Leeds also saw red.

MONDAY
14

TUESDAY
15

★ *MATCH on sale*

WEDNESDAY
16

○ **UEFA CUP FINAL**

THURSDAY
17

○ **SECOND LEG OF FA YOUTH CUP FINAL**

FRIDAY
18

Ⓑ **DENNIS BERGKAMP** *born 1969, Amsterdam, Holland*   Ⓑ **LEE HENDRIE** *born 1977, Birmingham, England*

SATURDAY
19

○ **LAST DAY OF 2000-2001 PREMIER LEAGUE SEASON**

SUNDAY
20

○ **LAST DAY OF 2000-2001 SCOTTISH PREMIER LEAGUE SEASON**

SHARP SHOOTER

Who won the PFA Player Of The Year award in 1995 and 1997?

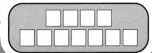

Last week's answer: LEE SHARPE

THIS WEEK IN 1993...

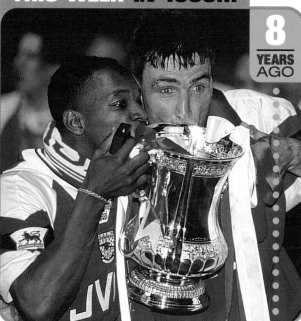

8 YEARS AGO

Arsenal become first team to win both domestic Cup titles

ARSENAL BECAME THE FIRST TEAM TO WIN BOTH OF THE Cup Finals in one season when they beat Sheffield Wednesday 2-1 in the FA Cup on May 20, 1993. It was a sickening blow for Wednesday, who had already lost to The Gunners in the Coca-Cola Cup Final just four weeks before. There was a 1-1 stalemate when the teams met in the final of the FA Cup, so they returned to Wembley in midweek for the replay. Ian Wright put Arsenal ahead after a clever one-two with Alan Smith, but Chris Waddle brought Sheffield Wednesday level in the second half to force extra-time. The scene was set for a penalty shoot-out until Andy Linighan headed the winner in injury-time. It was a proud achievement for manager George Graham, who became the first man to win the three major domestic honours – the League title, League Cup and FA Cup – as both a player and a manager.

George Graham's trophy haul

1964-65	Player	League Cup (Chelsea)
1969-70	Player	European Fairs Cup (Arsenal)
1970-71	Player	League Championship and FA Cup double (Arsenal)
1986-87	Manager	League Cup (Arsenal)
1988-89	Manager	League Championship (Arsenal)
1990-91	Manager	League Championship (Arsenal)
1992-93	Manager	League Cup (Arsenal)
1992-93	Manager	FA Cup (Arsenal)
1993-94	Manager	European Cup-Winners' Cup (Arsenal)
1998-99	Manager	League Cup winner (Tottenham Hotspur)

THE FOOTBALL TIMES

14 - 20 MAY

2 YEARS AGO...
MAY 16, 1999: Man. United overcome Tottenham Hotspur 2-0 to win their fifth Premiership title in seven years. Had Tottenham equalised, Arsenal would have been Champions after they beat Villa 1-0.

3 YEARS AGO...
MAY 17, 1998: Paul Gascoigne is spotted on a boozy night out in London after he'd promised to reform his ways. The England manager Glenn Hoddle says it's not certain he will be picked for his World Cup squad.

3 YEARS AGO...
MAY 16, 1998: Hearts beat Rangers 2-1 to lift the Scottish Cup. In Walter Smith's last season as manager, The Gers fail to win a trophy for the first time in 11 years after Celtic win the Premier League title.

19 YEARS AGO...
MAY 15, 1982: Liverpool win their 13th League championship title. Manager Bob Paisley is particularly pleased as the team were struggling in ninth place in January!

57 YEARS AGO...
MAY 20, 1944: Hibernian and Rangers draw the League Cup Final in Scotland. Bizarrely, the match is decided on who won the most corners! Hibs shade it 6-5!

HAPPY BIRTHDAY...
DENNIS BERGKAMP

BIRTHDATE: May 18, 1969
BIRTHPLACE: Amsterdam, Holland
CLUB: Arsenal
COUNTRY: Holland
PREVIOUS CLUBS: Ajax, Inter.
HONOURS: Dutch League (1990), Dutch Cup (1987, 1993), Cup Winners' Cup (1987), UEFA Cup (1992, 1994), Premiership (1998), FA Cup (1998).

Bergkamp controls the ball with astonishing ease and scores spectacular goals. He arrived at Arsenal in 1995, helped them to win the double in 1998 and was named PFA and Football Writers' Player Of The Year in the same year.

★ *MATCH on sale*

B **DANNY TIATTO** *born 1973, Melbourne, Australia*

◇ CHAMPIONS LEAGUE FINAL

B **STEPHEN GLASS** *born 1976, Dundee, Scotland*

◇ TENNENTS SCOTTISH CUP FINAL
◇ THIRD DIVISION PLAY-OFF FINAL

B **STEVE SEDGLEY** *born 1968, Enfield, England*

◇ SECOND DIVISION PLAY-OFF FINAL

B **LEE SHARPE** *born 1971, Halesowen, England*   B **PAUL GASCOIGNE** *born 1967, Gateshead, England*

FOOTY ANAGRAM
This Scots midfielder has a rough reputation.

Last week's answer: ALAN SHEARER

CRY RAGE BULI

THIS WEEK IN 1999...

2 YEARS AGO

THE FOOTBALL TIMES

21 - 27 MAY

1 YEAR AGO...

MAY 27, 2000: England earn a 1-1 draw with Brazil at Wembley ahead of the Euro 2000 finals. Liverpool's Michael Owen scores England's goal and gives a great all-round display to give Kevin Keegan a timely reminder of his ability and fitness.

3 YEARS AGO...

MAY 25, 1998: In a thrilling Division One play-off final, Charlton beat Sunderland 7-6 on penalties. Clive Mendonca scores the first hat-trick in play-off history and Sasa Ilic's penalty save is estimated to be worth around £10 million to the club.

4 YEARS AGO...

MAY 21, 1997: Watford's 19-year-old striker David Connolly becomes the youngest player ever to score a hat-trick for the Republic of Ireland as they beat Liechtenstein 5-0 to move into second place in their World Cup qualifying group.

7 YEARS AGO...

MAY 23, 1994: Everton 'keeper Neville Southall becomes the most-capped Welsh player when Wales beat Estonia 2-1 in a friendly. He wins his 74th cap on the night and beats Peter Nicholas's record.

19 YEARS AGO...

MAY 26, 1982: Aston Villa become the fourth English team to win the European Cup after beating Bayern Munich 1-0. Peter Withe's goal means the cup stays in England for a record sixth season.

Man. United clinch historic treble triumph in Nou Camp

MANCHESTER UNITED RE-WROTE THE HISTORY BOOKS ON May 26, 1999 after dramatically winning the European Cup. The Red Devils had already won the Premiership and FA Cup, and needed the ultimate in European silverware to complete an historic treble. With Roy Keane and Paul Scholes suspended, they certainly had a tough challenge, as German opponents Bayern Munich were chasing their own treble success. After falling behind after six minutes, there was no further score for the next 84 minutes and United's dream began to fade away. But substitute Teddy Sheringham equalised in injury-time and fellow sub Ole Gunnar Solskjaer prodded in from close range to seal a dramatic victory. On what would have been Sir Matt Busby's 90th birthday, Man. United were once again kings of Europe. In his last game for The Red Devils, captain Peter Schmeichel lifted the Cup on an incredible night in Barcelona that United fans will never forget.

European Cup all-time winners

Man. United lifted the European Cup for the second time in their history in 1999, but current holders Real Madrid have won it an amazing eight times.

CLUB	EUROPEAN CUPS	YEARS
REAL MADRID	8	1956, 1957, 1958, 1959, 1960, 1966, 1998, 2000
AC MILAN	5	1963, 1969, 1989, 1990, 1994
AJAX	4	1971, 1972, 1973, 1995
LIVERPOOL	4	1977, 1978, 1981, 1984
BAYERN MUNICH	3	1974, 1975, 1976
BENFICA	2	1961, 1962
INTER MILAN	2	1964, 1965
JUVENTUS	2	1985, 1996
MAN. UNITED	2	1968, 1999
NOTTINGHAM FOREST	2	1979, 1980

"MY FIRST CAP!"

PAUL SCHOLES

ENGLAND DEBUT: May 24, 1997
GAME: England 2 South Africa 1
ATTENDANCE: 52,676
MATCHFACTS RATING: 7/10

Man. United's goalscoring midfielder had a cracking season for his club in 1996-97 and deservedly collected his first international cap under Glenn Hoddle. Scholes came on in the 64th minute to replace Teddy Sheringham and he immediately set up Ian Wright to score England's winner. It wasn't a good performance by the home side, but Scholes looked lively and did enough to be considered for a call-up to Glenn Hoddle's World Cup qualifying squad.

MONDAY
28

○ FIRST DIVISION PLAY-OFF FINAL
○ BANK HOLIDAY IN UK

TUESDAY
29

Ⓑ **ROBERTO DI MATTEO** *born 1970, Schaffhausen, Switzerland*

WEDNESDAY
30

★ *MATCH on sale*

THURSDAY
31

FRIDAY
1

SATURDAY
2

○ REPUBLIC OF IRELAND v PORTUGAL
○ NORTHERN IRELAND v BULGARIA
○ WALES v POLAND

Ⓑ **MARLON BERESFORD** *born 1969, Lincoln, England*

SUNDAY
3

THE EYES HAVE IT
Who is this pint-sized Brazilian?

Last week's answer: CRAIG BURLEY

8 YEARS AGO

Swindon win the play-off final for a place in the Premiership

WEMBLEY WAS A BEAUTIFUL DAY FOR SWINDON TOWN ON May 31, 1993 when Glenn Hoddle's side beat Leicester City in the Division One play-off final to earn a place in the Premiership. There was a party atmosphere at Wembley with over 70,000 excited fans basking in the sunshine. Unfortunately, one set of supporters had to go home as losers, and it looked as though Swindon were running away with it as they cruised into a 3-0 lead through Hoddle, Maskell and Taylor. But Leicester didn't let their fans down by giving in to Swindon's early onslaught. Julian Joachim started the fightback and Walsh and Thompson made it 3-3. But football can be a cruel game and The Foxes' efforts were crushed when Swindon were awarded an 84th minute penalty which Bodin converted to win the match 4-3. Leicester fans were devastated, but they only had to wait one more season until they won promotion to the Premiership themselves!

The play-offs – a travesty or a triumph?

The play-offs are a controversial way of gaining promotion – many people don't like them, while some couldn't survive without them. So what makes them good or bad?

TRAVESTY:	You can finish third, but a team in fourth or fifth place can still go up instead of you!
TRIUMPH:	There's more to play for if you're near the top six towards the end of the season!
TRAVESTY:	The teams that are promoted from the play-offs often get relegated straight away!
TRIUMPH:	The play-offs give lots of teams and their supporters the chance to go to Wembley!
TRAVESTY:	Three teams will always end the season with heartbreak – just ask Ipswich fans!
TRIUMPH:	Play-off finals always produce exciting matches that are better than most Cup Finals!
TRAVESTY:	Fans have to pay to see more matches and fork out huge amounts for their tickets!
TRIUMPH:	The league turns into a cup competition, so you can still win a trophy at the end of it!
TRAVESTY:	It's a long season for players – they have to keep on going at the end of the season!
TRIUMPH:	There's more footy to watch, whether it's live at Wembley or in front of your telly!

THE FOOTBALL TIMES

28 MAY – 3 JUNE

2 YEARS AGO...
MAY 28, 1999: Rangers win a domestic treble by beating rivals Celtic 1-0 in the Scottish Cup Final. Rod Wallace scores his 29th goal of the season to clinch the win.

4 YEARS AGO...
MAY 28, 1997: Borussia Dortmund, despite all the odds, beat hot favourites Juventus 3-1 in the European Cup Final. Karl-Heinz Riedle, playing his last game for the German club, scores two of the goals.

9 YEARS AGO...
MAY 30, 1992: A new law is announced by FIFA which means goalkeepers will not be able to pick up a deliberate back-pass from their own player. The new rule is designed to encourage a flowing game.

11 YEARS AGO...
JUNE 2, 1990: England play Tunisia in a warm-up game ahead of the World Cup in Italy. Wolves striker Steve Bull spares England's blushes with a last-minute equaliser, but Bobby Robson's side create a number of chances in the 1-1 draw.

19 YEARS AGO...
MAY 28, 1982: Diego Maradona, the 21-year-old Argentinian wonderkid, signs for Barcelona for a world record fee of £4.2 million. 'Diego Mania' sweeps across Spain as the sensational youngster flies in.

"MY FIRST CAP!"
GARY NEVILLE

ENGLAND DEBUT: June 3, 1995
GAME: England 2 Japan 1
ATTENDANCE: 21,142
MATCHFACTS RATING: N/A

This game against Japan in the Umbro International Tournament should have been easier than the tricky matches against Sweden and Brazil, but England only scraped a win after David Platt's penalty in the dying minutes. Gary Neville was one of four debutants next to David Unsworth, Stan Collymore and John Scales. The assured young Man. United defender acquitted himself well in what was an under-strength, experimental side.

MONDAY 4

○ **PUBLIC HOLIDAY IN REPUBLIC OF IRELAND**

Ⓑ **ALEX MANNINGER** *born 1977, Salzburg, Austria*   Ⓑ **IAN TAYLOR** *born 1968, Birmingham, England*

TUESDAY 5

★ *MATCH on sale*

WEDNESDAY 6

○ **GREECE v ENGLAND**
○ **ESTONIA v REPUBLIC OF IRELAND**
○ **CZECH REPUBLIC v NORTHERN IRELAND**
○ **UKRAINE v WALES**

Ⓑ **ALBERT FERRER** *born 1970, Barcelona, Spain*

THURSDAY 7

FRIDAY 8

SATURDAY 9

SUNDAY 10

Ⓑ **STUART McCALL** *born 1964, Leeds, England*

CODE BREAKER
**Can you crack the secret code to name
this Premiership star?**

Last week's answer: JUNINHO

| 16 | 13 | 16 | 23 | | | R | |
| 2 | 3 | 10 | 25 | 14 | D | | | |

THIS WEEK IN 1993...

8 YEARS AGO

THE FOOTBALL TIMES

4 – 10 JUNE

2 YEARS AGO...

JUNE 10, 1999: Kenny Dalglish is named Director of Football Operations at Celtic, his first club, and John Barnes is named as the new head coach. The Celtic fans go wild as Kenny and John promise to give Rangers a serious challenge in the league.

3 YEARS AGO...

JUNE 10, 1998: The last World Cup of the millennium kicks off in Paris, France, with Scotland losing 2-1 to reigning champions Brazil. Scotland are unfortunate to lose out after Boyd's own goal seals Brazil's win.

4 YEARS AGO...

JUNE 4, 1997: England beat Italy for the first time in 20 years in Le Tournoi. A goal from Ian Wright and an exceptional strike from Paul Scholes, both without reply, help England to win the tournament.

9 YEARS AGO...

JUNE 5, 1992: The Football League holds its first meeting after the Premier League replaces the old Division One. The Second, Third and Fourth divisions become the First, Second and Third respectively.

10 YEARS AGO...

JUNE 7, 1991: Ron Atkinson is poached by Aston Villa, the team who abandoned him as a player. He leaves Sheffield Wednesday in the lurch and becomes known as Judas to the Yorkshire fans.

England are humiliated 2-0 by international minnows USA

THE TWO YEARS OF 1993 AND 1994 CERTAINLY WEREN'T the happiest of times for English football. Graham Taylor managed to turn the World Cup semi-finalists of 1990 into a laughing stock, with team selections that would have struggled in Division One. Names like Brian Deane, Tony Daley, Carlton Palmer and Keith Curle summed up the lack of quality in the England squad, particularly when players of the calibre of Peter Beardsley were available to Taylor. Not picking the little Geordie genius was the manager's most frustrating mistake. Graham Taylor was a good club manager but he managed to get it spectacularly wrong during his time with England. Not everything was his fault, of course – he had assistance from a terrible referee in the vital World Cup qualifier against Holland, when England's hopes of qualifying for the 1994 World Cup all but ended. But the performance on June 9, 1994 against America was the low point of his England reign. The USA hosted a competition that included England, Brazil and West Germany. After drawing 1-1 with Brazil, England should have stuffed a USA team that were minnows of international football. Instead, goals from Tom Dooley and weirdy beardie Alexei Lalas sent the team spinning to one of their most disastrous results ever.

England's worst international results!

It's great fun following your country and sharing all the highs, but it means you've got to face the lows as well. The faint-hearted should look away now!

1950	USA 1-0 ENGLAND	Embarrassing defeat in the second match of the World Cup.
1953	ENGLAND 3-6 HUNGARY	The first time England lost to a foreign side on home soil.
1973	ENGLAND 1-1 POLAND	Failed to make the 1974 World Cup after this bore draw.
1982	ENGLAND 0-0 SPAIN	Crashed out of the 1982 World Cup despite being unbeaten.
1990	ENGLAND 1-1 W. GERMANY	Tumbled out of the 1990 World Cup after dreadful penalties.
1992	SWEDEN 2-1 ENGLAND	This loss left England bottom of their group at Euro '92.
1993	HOLLAND 2-0 ENGLAND	Poor refereeing made World Cup qualification impossible.
1993	USA 2-0 ENGLAND	Another embarrassing defeat for manager Graham Taylor.
1996	ENGLAND 1-1 GERMANY	So close but yet so far as England lose again on penalties.
1998	ARGENTINA 2-2 ENGLAND	Hung on bravely with ten men, but another penalty disaster.

HAPPY BIRTHDAY...
IAN TAYLOR

BIRTHDATE: June 4, 1968
BIRTHPLACE: Birmingham, England
CLUB: Aston Villa
COUNTRY: England
PREVIOUS CLUBS: Moor Green, Port Vale, Sheffield Wednesday
HONOURS: League Cup winner (1996)

A true Villa fan, Taylor made his dream move to the club in 1994 after a brief spell at Sheffield Wednesday. The midfielder has been a consistent performer at the heart of Villa's team and he produced a magnificent display in the 1996 League Cup Final, scoring in their 3-0 demolition of Leeds United at Wembley.

MONDAY 11

TUESDAY 12

★ *MATCH on sale*

Ⓑ **THOMAS SORENSEN** *born 1976, Fredericia, Denmark*

WEDNESDAY 13

THURSDAY 14

FRIDAY 15

Ⓑ **TORE ANDRE FLO** *born 1973, Strin, Norway*

SATURDAY 16

Ⓑ **CHRIS BART-WILLIAMS** *born 1974, Freetown, Jamaica*

SUNDAY 17

✿ **FATHER'S DAY**

SHARP SHOOTER
Which team has won the European Cup a record eight times?

Last week's answer: RORY DELAP

THIS WEEK IN 1992...

9 YEARS AGO

Gary Lineker says farewell as England crash out of Euro '92

AFTER GOING SO CLOSE TO WORLD CUP GLORY IN 1990,
England crashed out of the European Championships in Sweden at
the first hurdle on June 17, 1992. The team drew 0-0 with Denmark
and France in their first two games and needed a win against hosts
Sweden to stand a chance of progressing to the next round. Having
failed to score in the first two matches, David Platt scored after just
three minutes to give England hope, but Sweden were the stronger
side and always seemed to find more space. The host nation fought
back and decisive strikes from Eriksson and Brolin put England on
the next plane home. To make matters worse, under-fire manager
Graham Taylor substituted Gary Lineker after 61 minutes of his last
ever appearance for England to bring on Arsenal forward Alan Smith.
The captain had been hanging tantalisingly on 48 international goals,
but Taylor's controversial substitution meant he wouldn't get another
chance to equal Bobby Charlton's record of 49 goals for England.

England's all-time **top ten goalscorers!**

Bobby Charlton and Gary Lineker are England's leading goalscorers, with Alan Shearer
in fifth place after scoring 30 goals. The likes of Michael Owen and co still have a way
to go before joining these striking legends.

		ENGLAND CAREER	GOALS	GAMES
1.	BOBBY CHARLTON	1958-1970	49	106
2.	GARY LINEKER	1984-1992	48	80
3.	JIMMY GREAVES	1959-1967	44	57
4.	NAT LOFTHOUSE	1950-1958	30	33
5.	ALAN SHEARER	1992-2000	30	63
6.	TOM FINNEY	1946-1958	30	76
7.	DAVID PLATT	1989-1996	27	62
8.	BRYAN ROBSON	1980-1991	26	90
9.	GEOFF HURST	1966-1972	24	49
10.	STAN MORTENSEN	1947-1953	23	25

THE FOOTBALL TIMES

3 YEARS AGO...
JUNE 15, 1998: England beat Tunisia 2-0
in the first game of the 1998 World Cup in
France. It's a fine start for Glenn Hoddle's
men, with goals from skipper Alan Shearer
and Man. United midfielder Paul Scholes.

4 YEARS AGO...
THIS WEEK IN 1997: Arsene Wenger
signs Dutch international Marc Overmars
from Ajax for £7 million, increasing The
Gunners' spending on foreign stars to an
impressive £14 million in only two weeks!

5 YEARS AGO...
JUNE 15, 1996: England take a step
closer to the quarter-finals of Euro '96 with
a 2-0 win over rivals Scotland at Wembley.
A header from Alan Shearer and a glorious
strike by Gazza sandwich a Gary McAllister
penalty miss for the heartbroken Scots.

6 YEARS AGO...
JUNE 17, 1995: Liverpool win the chase
to sign Stan Collymore. The Anfield club
pay a British transfer record of £8.5 million
for the Nottingham Forest striker, seeing
off competition from neighbours Everton.

19 YEARS AGO...
JUNE 17, 1982: At 17 years and 42 days
old, Northern Ireland's Norman Whiteside
becomes the youngest player to appear
in the World Cup. By playing in the game
against Yugoslavia, Whiteside beats the
previous tournament record, set by Pelé
at the 1958 World Cup, by 195 days.

"MY FIRST CAP!"
TIM FLOWERS

ENGLAND DEBUT:	June 13, 1993
GAME:	England 1 Brazil 1
ATTENDANCE:	54,118
MATCHFACTS RATING:	N/A

Flowers had a fine international
debut, holding Brazil at bay and
earning England a draw after
David Platt's strike. The result was
a glimmer of hope for England, who
were well short of confidence after
a shocking defeat against USA, awful
performances at Euro '92 and a poor
World Cup qualifying campaign. This
result against Brazil probably kept
Graham Taylor in a job, but he later
failed to take England to the 1994
World Cup and promptly resigned.

★ *MATCH on sale*

Ⓑ **CHRIS ARMSTRONG** *born 1971, Newcastle, England*

Ⓑ **NEIL REDFEARN** *born 1965, Dewsbury, England*

Ⓑ **PATRICK VIEIRA** *born 1976, Dakar, Senegal*

Ⓑ **DAVID MAY** *born 1970, Oldham, England*

FOOTY ANAGRAM
This goal assassin is loved by truckers.

Last week's answer: REAL MADRID

G	R	O	W	E	D		T	H	I	K	Y

THIS WEEK IN 1906...

95 YEARS AGO

THE FOOTBALL TIMES

2 YEARS AGO...
THIS WEEK IN 1999: After eight years at Man. United, Peter Schmeichel officially leaves Old Trafford. He leaves on a high note, though, having helped The Red Devils to a Premier League, FA Cup and European Cup treble in his final year with the club.

3 YEARS AGO...
JUNE 22, 1998: Michael Owen comes on as a substitute for Teddy Sheringham to score England's equalising goal against Romania in the 1998 World Cup. England lose the match 2-1, but Owen shines up front, hitting a post late on in the game.

5 YEARS AGO...
JUNE 18, 1996: England secure a thrilling 4-1 win over Holland in the group stages of Euro '96. The superb SAS partnership of Teddy Sheringham and Alan Shearer grab two goals each and it's the best England performance at Wembley for years.

8 YEARS AGO...
THIS WEEK IN 1993: Paul Gascoigne sports a Batman-style mask to protect his fractured cheekbone while he's playing for Lazio. Rumours are rife that Gazza will star in a film as the next Caped Crusader!

15 YEARS AGO...
JUNE 22, 1986: England lose to Argentina in the quarter-finals of the World Cup. After punching the ball past Peter Shilton for the first goal, Maradona then dribbles around half of England's team to secure a 2-1 win and send the unlucky Three Lions home.

Work begins on Liverpool's new Kop stand at Anfield

AFTER LIVERPOOL WON THEIR SECOND LEAGUE TITLE ON June 22, 1906, the club started to build a new stand to increase the capacity of Anfield. When it was finished, the 'Spion Kop' was the largest terrace ever built at an English football ground and held an incredible 30,000 fans. It became famous because of the people who stood on the terrace – cheering, singing their hearts out and creating an incredible atmoshpere and sportsmanship on matchdays. It soon became a feared part of Anfield and teams were often overawed at playing in front of the massive structure. In the '60s, the Kop sang songs by Gerry and the Pacemakers, The Searchers and The Beatles, and swung back and forth creating an amazing atmosphere around the ground. In Liverpool's successful '70s and '80s period, many people said playing in front of the famous stand was like starting the game one-nil behind. Before the Kop was demolished in May 1994 to make Anfield an all-seater stadium, Liverpool fans held a farewell concert to celebrate almost 90 years of unforgettable memories.

Brain bustin' facts about the Kop

The Spion Kop was named by a journalist from the Liverpol Echo who said the stand looked like a huge hill in South Africa called the 'Spion Kop'. The words literally mean 'look-out' in Africaans.

In 1928 the Kop was extended 80 feet in the air, so it measured a towering 425 feet x 131 feet. Liverpool's rebuilt stand was officially opened for the first home game of the 1928-29 season.

Some famous names stood on the Kop during their younger days, including Crystal Palace manager Steve Coppell, stalwarts Roy Evans and Ronnie Moran and present Reds manager Gerard Houllier.

Even when Liverpool lose at Anfield, the Kop often congratulate opposition players, teams and fans if they deserved to win. This spirit of sportsmanship is almost unrivalled in the world of football.

Liverpool sold the Kop when it was demolished in May 1994 to turn Anfield into an all-seater stadium. The Merseyside club gave all the proceeds to charity to build a new £4 million cancer unit in the city.

The new Kop only holds 12,000 fans now, but it's still the largest single-tier stand in English football.

"MY RED CARD DAY!"
ZINEDINE ZIDANE

DATE: June 18, 1998
GAME: France 4 Saudi Arabia 0
SENT-OFF: 70 mins
OFFENCE(S): Violent conduct
REFEREE: Brizio Carter (Mexico)

France were leading Saudi Arabia 2-0 in the World Cup and Mohammed Al-Khlaiwi had been sent-off for a foul on Bixente Lizarazu. They were cruising into the second round when Zidane needlessly stamped on Amin Fuad-Anwar with 20 minutes left. Fortunately, France still reached the final and Zidane was back to his brilliant best for 'Les Blues'.

MONDAY 25

Ⓑ **NEIL LENNON** *born 1971, Lurgan, Northern Ireland*   Ⓑ **JAMIE REDKNAPP** *born 1973, Barton on Sea, England*

TUESDAY 26

★ *MATCH on sale*   Ⓑ **PAOLO MALDINI** *born 1968, Milan, Italy*

WEDNESDAY 27

THURSDAY 28

Ⓑ **LORENZO AMORUSO** *born 1971, Palese, Italy*

FRIDAY 29

SATURDAY 30

Ⓑ **GARY PALLISTER** *born 1965, Ramsgate, England*

SUNDAY 1

Ⓑ **PATRICK KLUIVERT** *born 1976, Amsterdam, Holland*   Ⓑ **RUUD VAN NISTELROOY** *born 1976, Oss, Holland*

THE EYES HAVE IT
Who is this goal-starved striker?

Last week's answer: DWIGHT YORKE

3 YEARS AGO

THE FOOTBALL TIMES

4 YEARS AGO...

THIS WEEK IN 1997: Former Liverpool stopper Mark Lawrenson resigns as the defensive coach of Newcastle United and gets a new job as a TV and radio pundit. Give us a smile once in a while, Lawro!

5 YEARS AGO...

JUNE 26, 1996: England meet Germany in the semi-finals of Euro '96. In one of the tournament's best games, England lose on penalties after Gazza misses a chance and Anderton hits the post in golden goal time.

8 YEARS AGO...

THIS WEEK IN 1993: In an article on top signings, MATCH tips Middlesbrough's Jamie Pollock to be a star of the future. Southend's Stan Collymore, Blackpool's Trevor Sinclair and Leicester City's Julian Joachim were better predictions!

12 YEARS AGO...

THIS WEEK IN 1989: Despite being slated by the tabloid newspapers, MATCH says Bobby Robson *is* the man to lead England into the 1990 World Cup. After an excellent tournament, only a penalty shoot-out denies England a place in the final.

28 YEARS AGO...

JUNE 25, 1973: An international match between Chile and Uruguay is called off after the referee goes card-crazy and sends off 19 men! Ten Chile players and nine Uruguayans were dismissed and the ref thought it wasn't worth carrying on!

David Beckham is shown the red card at the '98 World Cup

DAVID BECKHAM WAS PLAYING IN ONE OF THE BIGGEST games of his life on June 30, 1998, when England were more than holding their own against Argentina in the 1998 World Cup. After Batistuta's early penalty, Shearer drew level from the spot before Michael Owen put England ahead after beating the entire opposition defence to score a memorable goal. Argentina then got an equaliser with a cleverly-worked free-kick, making it 2-2 at half-time. But two minutes after the break, Becks was grounded by a heavy challenge from Simeone and petulantly kicked out at the Argentine midfielder in front of the referee. He was sent-off for violent conduct and England's chances of winning the 1998 World Cup left with him. Argentina won the penalty shoot-out and the country blamed Beckham for the result. When the new season started, he was booed wherever he went, but this injected an extra determination into the midfielder's game. Within a year he had helped Man. United to win the treble and to his credit he proved his critics wrong. Just don't do it again Becks, please!

Heading for an early bath - the men who have been sent-off while playing for England!

PLAYER	OPPOSITION	DATE OF GAME
DAVID BATTY	**POLAND** (Euro 2000 qualifier)	Sep 8, 1999
PAUL SCHOLES	**SWEDEN** (Euro 2000 qualifier)	Jun 5, 1999
PAUL INCE	**SWEDEN** (Euro 2000 qualifier)	Sep 5, 1998
DAVID BECKHAM	**ARGENTINA** (1998 World Cup)	Jun 30, 1998
RAY WILKINS	**MOROCCO** (1986 World Cup)	Jun 6, 1986
TREVOR CHERRY	**ARGENTINA** (International friendly)	Jun 15, 1977
ALAN BALL	**POLAND** (World Cup qualifier)	Jun 6, 1973
ALAN MULLERY	**YUGOSLAVIA** (1968 European Championship)	Jun 5, 1968

HAPPY BIRTHDAY...
NEIL LENNON

BIRTHDAY: June 25, 1971
BIRTHPLACE: Lurgan, N. Ireland
CLUB: Leicester City
COUNTRY: Northern Ireland
PREVIOUS CLUBS: Manchester City, Crewe Alexandra.
HONOURS: League Cup (1997, 2000), 34 Northern Ireland caps.

Neil Lennon arrived at Leicester from Crewe Alexandra in 1996 and has established himself as one of the finest midfield playmakers in the country. He doesn't score many goals, but he's an excellent passer of the ball and has guided Leicester to three Cup Finals in four years. He may yet join old boss Martin O'Neill at Celtic.

25 JUNE - 1 JULY

**MONDAY
2**

**TUESDAY
3**

★ *MATCH on sale*

**WEDNESDAY
4**

B **TONY VIDMAR** *born 1970, Adelaide, Australia*

**THURSDAY
5**

B **GIANFRANCO ZOLA** *born 1966, Oliena, Italy*

**FRIDAY
6**

B **RORY DELAP** *born, 1976, Sutton Coldfield, England*

**SATURDAY
7**

JUNE 5, 1966

**SUNDAY
8**

CODE BREAKER
**Can you crack the secret code to
name this Premiership star?**

Last week's answer: CHRIS SUTTON

| 24 | 13 | 6 | 26 | 19 | | S | | | | |
| 12 | 20 | 6 | 25 | 10 | 23 | | | | | E | |

THE FOOTBALL TIMES

2 - 8 JULY

3 YEARS AGO...
JULY 5, 1998: With France '98 nearly over, it emerges that at least half the coaches who got their teams to the finals will lose their jobs when they get home.

4 YEARS AGO...
JULY 3, 1997: In a last-ditch attempt to prevent Rangers from beating their record nine league titles in a row, Celtic appoint former Dutch manager Wim Jansen.

8 YEARS AGO...
JULY 4, 1993: The Zambian international team beat Morocco 2-1 in a World Cup qualifier, less than ten weeks after the national tragedy in which all but three of their first team died in an air crash.

17 YEARS AGO...
JULY 6, 1984: Man. United's charismatic boss Ron Atkinson reveals to MATCH he's received a tempting offer from Aston Villa to become their new manager. However, Big Ron turns it down in order to stay in charge at Old Trafford for another season.

19 YEARS AGO...
JULY 7, 1982: After scoring a hat-trick against Brazil in the 1982 World Cup, Italian star Paolo Rossi is given the civic title of Commendatore, which is the equivalent of receiving a knighthood.

Bergkamp scores one of the greatest World Cup goals ever

ON JULY 4, 1998 DENNIS BERGKAMP SCORED ARGUABLY the best goal of his career in the last minute of Holland's World Cup quarter-final against Argentina. With the game at 1-1 and heading for extra-time, Frank de Boer hit a 50-yard pass to Bergkamp, who brought the high ball down with sublime skill. The striker took another touch to cut inside defender Roberto Ayala, then flicked the ball with the outside of his boot past the bewildered 'keeper. The Holland fans, dressed in their famous orange shirts, roared their approval, knowing Bergkamp had put them into the semi-final against Brazil. The rest of the game was packed with incident – Argentina star Ariel Ortega was sent-off for headbutting Edwin van der Sar and Arthur Numan saw red after clattering into midfielder Diego Simeone. But the final drama was Bergkamp's last-minute wonder goal, which finally avenged Holland's defeat by Argentina in the 1978 World Cup Final.

The best World Cup goals of all time!
Where were you when Owen scored in '98?

MICHAEL OWEN (ENGLAND)	1998	Beat the entire Argentina defence before hitting home.
JURGEN KLINSMANN (GERMANY)	1994	Flicked up and bicycle-kicked against South Korea.
SAEED OWAIRAN (SAUDI ARABIA)	1994	A stupendous long dribble and finish against Belgium.
LOTHAR MATTHAUS (GERMANY)	1990	Thunderous low drive from 40 yards against Yugoslavia.
DIEGO MARADONA (ARGENTINA)	1986	Waltzed through England's defence for a wonder goal.
MICHAEL LAUDRUP (DENMARK)	1986	Glided past everybody against Uruguay in a 6-1 win.
VASILY RATS (USSR)	1986	Thunderbolt from nearly 40 yards out against France.
JOSIMAR (BRAZIL)	1986	Hammered into the top corner against Northern Ireland.
ARCHIE GEMMILL (SCOTLAND)	1978	Superb curling finish against much-fancied Holland.
GEOFF HURST (ENGLAND)	1966	The classic hat-trick strike. They think it's all over...

▶ HAPPY BIRTHDAY...
GEORGI KINKLADZE

BIRTHDATE: July 6, 1973
BIRTHPLACE: Tblisi, Georgia
CLUB: Derby County
COUNTRY: Georgia
PREVIOUS CLUBS: Dynamo Tblisi, Saarbrucken (loan), Man. City, Ajax.
HONOURS: 34 Georgian caps

Kinkladze has been a joy to watch wherever he's played. His incredible skill and ball control have produced some memorable and truly stunning goals. He showed remarkable loyalty to Man. City until they were relegated to the Second Division, when he then moved to Ajax. But he's now back in English football, lighting up the play at Derby County. A real tricky genius!

B **GARY KELLY** *born 1974, Drogheda, Republic of Ireland*

★ *MATCH on sale*

B **TONY COTTEE** *born 1965, West Ham, England*

O **BANK HOLIDAY IN NORTHERN IRELAND**

JUNE 9, 1988

B **JASON WILCOX** *born 1971, Bolton, England*

SHARP SHOOTER
Who has scored the most international goals for England?

Last week's answer: SHAUN GOATER

THIS WEEK IN 1998...

3 YEARS AGO

France win the World Cup for the first time in their history

BEFORE THE WORLD CUP HAD EVEN STARTED, CRITICS said France, the host nation, had no hope of winning the trophy in 1998 because they lacked truly world-class strikers. But they cruised through the early rounds of the tournament, and in the final Aime Jacquet's team proved everyone wrong by beating Brazil 3-0, with all the goals coming from France's talented midfield. Zinedine Zidane scored with two headed goals and Emmanuel Petit added to Brazil's misery with a 90th minute strike. France lifted the trophy for the first time in their history on July 12, 1998, having devised the idea of the World Cup in 1904. There was some controversy though – French defender Marcel Desailly was sent-off after 64 minutes and Ronaldo played despite a career-threatening injury. But nothing could take the shine off this victory and celebrations in France went on all night.

World Cup Final Results 1930-1998

YEAR	VENUE	RESULT
1998	Paris, France	France 3 Brazil 0
1994	Los Angeles, USA	Brazil 0 Italy 0 (Brazil won 3-2 on penalties)
1990	Rome, Italy	West Germany 1 Argentina 0
1986	Mexico City, Mexico	Argentina 3 West Germany 2
1982	Madrid, Spain	Italy 3 West Germany 1
1978	Buenos Aires, Argentina	Argentina 3 Holland 1
1974	Munich, West Germany	West Germany 2 Holland 1
1970	Mexico City, Mexico	Brazil 4 Italy 1
1966	London, England	England 4 West Germany 2
1962	Santiago, Chile	Brazil 3 Czechoslovakia 1
1958	Stockholm, Sweden	Brazil 5 Sweden 2
1954	Berne, Switzerland	West Germany 3 Hungary 2
1950	Rio de Janeiro, Brazil	Uruguay 2 Brazil 1
1938	Paris, France	Italy 4 Hungary 2
1934	Rome, Italy	Italy 2 Czechoslovakia 1
1930	Montevideo, Uruguay	Uruguay 4 Argentina 2

THE FOOTBALL TIMES

9 - 15 JULY

4 YEARS AGO...
JULY 15, 1997: Winger David Ginola joins Tottenham Hotspur from Newcastle for £2 million, after allegedly refusing to take part in pre-season training. Spurs manager Gerry Francis hopes he will help transform the fortunes of the North London club.

13 YEARS AGO...
JULY 10, 1988: A bidding war begins for the right to screen live football on English television. BBC, ITV and BSB submit offers of up to £50 million each, but it threatens to split up the league as only ten select clubs are named to receive the money.

19 YEARS AGO...
JULY 11, 1982: Italy beat West Germany 3-1 in the World Cup Final. Paolo Rossi scores his sixth goal of the tournament in the final, which Italy win 3-1 to lift the famous golden trophy for the third time.

27 YEARS AGO...
THIS WEEK IN 1974: Boss Bill Shankly announces his retirement from Liverpool Football Club. It's a sad day at Anfield, but the manager transformed The Reds from a struggling team into a footballing giant that ruled Europe for years to come.

71 YEARS AGO...
JULY 13, 1930: France and Mexico contest the first game of the first ever World Cup in Uruguay. The first goal in the competition is scored by the French striker Lucien Laurent, but hosts Uruguay make history by winning the tournament.

HAPPY BIRTHDAY...
PAOLO DI CANIO

BIRTHDATE: July 9, 1968
BIRTHPLACE: Rome, Italy
CLUB: West Ham
COUNTRY: Italy
PREVIOUS CLUBS: Lazio, Ternana, Lazio, Juventus, Napoli, AC Milan, Celtic, Sheffield Wednesday.
HONOURS: Italian Cup (1990), UEFA Cup (1990, 1993), European Super Cup (1995), Italian League (1996).
Di Canio is enjoying his football again after troubled seasons at Celtic and Sheffield Wednesday. Despite being branded a troublemaker, he's been a bargain buy for West Ham and his wonder goal against Wimbledon last year was voted Goal Of The Season.

MONDAY 16

TUESDAY 17

★ *MATCH on sale*   Ⓑ **CLAUDIO LOPEZ** *born 1974, Riotercero, Argentina*   Ⓑ **JAAP STAM** *born 1972, Kampen, Holland*

WEDNESDAY 18

THURSDAY 19

FRIDAY 20

Ⓑ **CLAUDIO REYNA** *born 1973, New Jersey, USA*

SATURDAY 21

JULY 18, 1992

SUNDAY 22

FOOTY ANAGRAM
This midfielder, 'he scores goals'.

Last week's answer: BOBBY CHARLTON

A P O U C H S E L L S

THIS WEEK IN 1965...

36 YEARS AGO

Tottenham's John White is tragically killed by lightning

WHATEVER SOME PEOPLE SAY, BEING A PROFESSIONAL footballer isn't always easy, so with all the pressures associated with the game it's good to be able to get away from it all. Many of the top footy stars spend their spare time playing golf – it's a relaxing hobby that seems like the perfect way to unwind after the rigours of playing top-flight football. But this certainly wasn't the case for Tottenham's John White on July 21, 1965. He was waiting under a tree for the rain to stop so he could continue his round when he was tragically struck by lightning and died instantly from his injuries. It showed not only how dangerous it is to stand under trees during lightning spells, but also proved that no-one, not even footballers, are immune to tragedy.

Footballing fatalities – shocking accidents from the 'beautiful game'

1998	Two South African club players were hospitalised after a bolt of lightning struck the pitch in the game between Moroka Swallows and Jomo Cosmos. The accident was captured by television cameras where seven players and the referee had been knocked to the ground.
1993	Hungary goalkeeper Gabor Zsiboras died from a blood clot on the brain while he was training with the national side in 1993. His sudden death was met with extreme sadness in Hungary.
1990	York City striker Dave Longhurst, who was only 25 years old, suddenly collapsed and died shortly before half-time during York's home game against Lincoln at Bootham Crescent.
1973	Pedro Berruezo collapsed and died on the pitch due to heart failure while playing for Seville.
1969	Referee Roy Harper died while he was in charge of the fixture between York and Halifax.
1934	Gillingham striker Sam Raleigh tragically died after suffering a brain haemorrhage following an accidental clash of heads with Paul Mooney in the game against Brighton & Hove Albion.
1931	Celtic and Scotland 'keeper John Thomson died following a collision with Rangers striker Sam English in an Old Firm clash after diving bravely at the striker's feet to prevent a goal.
1927	Bury's Sam Wynne became the first recorded player to die in a football match when he collapsed with pneumonia while playing in the match against Sheffield United.
1923	Port Vale's Tom Butler died from tetanus eight days after breaking an arm in a match against Clapton Orient. Hospitals were not as advanced as they are now and tetanus was fatal.
1916	Ex-England international Bobby Benson died playing for his old club Arsenal against Reading after being out of the game for a year. He was asked to play for The Gunners because they were short of players after an injury crisis. Tragically, the exertion of the match killed him.
1909	Hibernian right-back James Main suffered internal injuries from an accidental kick to the stomach. The Scottish international defender was taken to hospital but died four days later.
1892	St. Mirren's James Dunlop lost his life after contracting tetanus from a large gash to his leg.

THE FOOTBALL TIMES

4 YEARS AGO...
JULY 18, 1997: Liverpool complete the signing of England midfielder Paul Ince from Inter Milan for £4.2 million. In doing so, the former Man. United star ensures himself a warm reception when he returns to Old Trafford with his new team-mates!

5 YEARS AGO...
JULY 17, 1996: Chelsea sign the Italian international Roberto Di Matteo from Lazio for £4.9 million. On the same day, in order to recoup some of their expensive outlay, striker Paul Furlong leaves The Blues to join Birmingham City in a £1.5 million deal.

6 YEARS AGO...
JULY 22, 1995: Tottenham, eager to gain a place in European competition after missing out through their final league placing, slump to an embarrassing 8-0 defeat at the hands of FC Cologne in the InterToto Cup. Was it worth it then, lads?

10 YEARS AGO...
JULY 22, 1991: Aston Villa and England midfielder David Platt is transferred from the Midlands to the sunnier climes of Bari in Italy for £5.5 million, a record transfer fee involving a British player.

20 YEARS AGO...
JULY 19, 1981: Newcastle announce that they've beaten off stiff competition from Sunderland to sign sausage factory worker Chris Waddle from Tow Law Town.

HAPPY BIRTHDAY...
JAAP STAM

BIRTHDATE: July 17, 1972
BIRTHPLACE: Kampen, Holland
CLUB: Man. United
COUNTRY: Holland
PREVIOUS CLUBS: Zwolle, Cambuur, Willem II, PSV Eindhoven.
HONOURS: Premiership (1999, 2000), FA Cup (1999), European Cup (1999), World Club Cup (1999), 36 Holland caps.

Eyebrows were raised when United paid £10.5 million for the Dutchman who looked average at World Cup '98. But Stam is a respected international now and was one of the defenders of the tournament in Euro 2000.

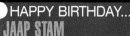

MONDAY
23

TUESDAY
24

★ *MATCH on sale*

B **MARTIN KEOWN** *born 1966, Oxford, England*

WEDNESDAY
25

B **KEVIN PHILLIPS** *born 1973, Hitchin, England*

THURSDAY
26

FRIDAY
27

B **ALESSANDRO PISTONE** *born 1975, Milan, Italy*   B **DEAN STURRIDGE** *born 1973, Birmingham, England*

SATURDAY
28

SUNDAY
29

THE EYES HAVE IT
Who is this hair-raising midfielder?

Last week's answer: PAUL SCHOLES

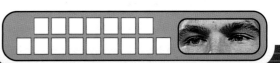

5 YEARS AGO

Shearer joins Newcastle in record £15 million transfer

BLACKBURN FANS WERE SHOCKED WHEN ALAN SHEARER joined Newcastle United for a world-record fee of £15 million in July 1996 – after all, he'd won the Premiership title with Rovers in 1995. But the England captain jumped at the chance to work with boyhood hero Kevin Keegan, who he met at Newcastle's training ground when he was a star-struck 13-year-old. Blackburn chairman Jack Walker tried everything to get the prolific striker to stay, but a transfer fee that shattered the world record eventually managed to prise him away from Ewood Park. By splashing out £15 million, Kevin Keegan beat Man. United, Liverpool and several top European clubs to Shearer's signature and handed the local boy Newcastle's famous No. 9 shirt.

Ten historic football transfers

Fans are constantly staggered at how much football clubs will pay for new players. Alf Common's £1,000 transfer to Middlesbrough was considered unbelievable nearly 100 years ago, while people thought football had gone mad when Nottingham Forest paid over £1 million for Trevor Francis in 1979.

ALF COMMON	Sunderland to Middlesbrough	1905	£1,000
SYD PUDDEFOOT	West Ham to Falkirk	1922	£5,000
DAVID JACK	Bolton Wanderers to Arsenal	1928	£10,000
DENIS LAW	Huddersfield Town to Manchester City	1960	£50,000
ALAN BALL	Blackpool to Everton	1966	£110,000
TREVOR FRANCIS	Birmingham City to Nottingham Forest	1979	£1.15 million
GIANLUIGI LENTINI	Torino to AC Milan	1992	£13 million
ALAN SHEARER	Blackburn Rovers to Newcastle United	1996	£15 million
DENILSON	Sao Paulo to Real Betis	1998	£21.5 million
CHRISTIAN VIERI	Lazio to Inter Milan	1999	£31 million

THE FOOTBALL TIMES

23 - 29 JULY

6 YEARS AGO...
JULY 29, 1995: After joining Rangers from Lazio for £4.3 million, Paul Gascoigne makes a goalscoring home debut at Ibrox. The England midfielder inspires his new team to a 4-0 win over Steaua Bucharest in the International Challenge Trophy.

7 YEARS AGO...
JULY 27, 1994: Newcastle United lose a friendly match 2-1 to Mypa in Finland. A tall, lanky defender called Sami Hyypia wins the game for the home side and is invited to St James' Park for a trial, but he fails to impress and is not offered a deal.

14 YEARS AGO...
THIS WEEK IN 1987: John McGrath, the Preston manager, says his players will be made to clean the club's toilets if they get booked for arguing with match officials!

32 YEARS AGO...
JULY 28, 1969: Bobby Charlton and George Best are among the stars to play in a Wales v Rest Of The United Kingdom game to mark Prince Charles becoming the Prince of Wales. The United Kingdom side won 1-0. Ears to you, Charles!

44 YEARS AGO...
JULY 26, 1957: Michael Jackson decides against signing for Man. United and joins his hometown club Celtic instead – true. He has plastic surgery, learns to dance the moonwalk and leads a bizarre double life as the undisputed 'King of Pop' – false.

HAPPY BIRTHDAY...
KEVIN PHILLIPS

BIRTHDATE: July 25, 1973
BIRTHPLACE: Hitchin, England
CLUB: Sunderland
COUNTRY: England
PREVIOUS CLUBS: Southampton, Baldock Town, Watford.
HONOURS: Division One winner (1999), Five England caps.

After being dumped out of football by Southampton, Phillips made his league comeback with Watford. He was then snapped up by Sunderland, where he blasted Peter Reid's team into the Premiership and scored an incredible 30 goals last season.

MONDAY 30

TUESDAY 31

★ *MATCH on sale*

B **PAULO WANCHOPE** *born 1976, Heredia, Costa Rica*

WEDNESDAY 1

B **NWANKWO KANU** *born 1976, Owerri, Nigeria*

THURSDAY 2

FRIDAY 3

B **NIKOS DABIZAS** *born 1973, Amypeo, Greece*

JULY 30, 1994

SATURDAY 4

SUNDAY 5

CODE BREAKER
Can you crack the secret code to
name this Premiership star?

Last week's answer: FREDDIE LJUNGBERG

| 2 | 16 | 7 | 24 | 16 | 3 | | | | I | | |
| 5 | 16 | 23 | 16 | 7 | 8 | P | | | | | |

THIS WEEK IN 1966...

35 YEARS AGO

England beat West Germany to clinch the 1966 World Cup!

WHERE WERE YOU WHEN ENGLAND WON THE WORLD CUP on July 30, 1966? Well not born yet, but that's always the question people ask when talking about the nation's finest footballing moment. In their first ever World Cup Final, England faced West Germany at Wembley with the famous Jules Rimet trophy at stake. Both teams started nervously, but West Germany got into their stride the quickest and took the lead after 13 minutes. But England weren't down for long and Geoff Hurst equalised after 19 minutes. When Peters scored to make it 2-1 with only 12 minutes left, Wembley sensed history in the making. But Weber equalised for West Germany at the death to force extra-time and prolong the agony for the 90,000 fans packed inside Wembley. England took the advantage when Geoff Hurst's shot rebounded off the underside of the crossbar and was controversially adjudged to have crossed the line. With the clock ticking down, Hurst cracked home his hat-trick, the first ever in a World Cup Final, and England's fourth. England were champions of the world at long last and had beaten a highly-rated German team into the bargain!

England's 1966 heroes! The team that led their country to World Cup glory

1.	GORDON BANKS	Widely regarded as England's finest-ever 'keeper and solid on the day.
2.	GEORGE COHEN	A tidy defender who kept Liverpool's Jimmy Armfield out of the side.
3.	RAY WILSON	The full-back was an experienced international at the World Cup.
4.	NOBBY STILES	Tremendous tenacity and work-rate from the pint-sized midfielder.
5.	JACK CHARLTON	A collossus at the back and the older of the two Charlton brothers.
6.	BOBBY MOORE	Cool, calm, collected under pressure – and captain. A true legend.
7.	ALAN BALL	Young Ball was tremendous, making probing runs down the right flank.
8.	GEOFF HURST	The first-ever player to score a World Cup Final hat-trick. Fantastic!
9.	ROGER HUNT	Missed a golden first-half chance but all turned out well in the end.
10.	BOBBY CHARLTON	England's playmaker kept pushing and probing the team forward.
11.	MARTIN PETERS	Started the World Cup on the bench but ended it scoring in the final!

THE FOOTBALL TIMES

3 YEARS AGO...
JULY 30, 1998: Defender David Unsworth makes an amazing U-turn as he demands a move away from Aston Villa just a week after joining the Midlands club. Unsworth says he wants a transfer to Everton.

4 YEARS AGO...
AUGUST 1, 1997: Man. United manager Alex Ferguson decides to rest his young England star David Beckham for the first three weeks of the 1997-98 season.

5 YEARS AGO...
AUGUST 1, 1996: Czech Republic winger Patrik Berger, one of the brightest stars of Euro '96, is signed by Liverpool for £3.25 million from Borussia Dortmund.

8 YEARS AGO...
AUGUST 3, 1993: AC Milan's £13 million world-record signing, Gianluigi Lentini, crashes his car and fractures his skull in Italy. The club says the injury is serious but does not appear to be career-threatening.

10 YEARS AGO...
AUGUST 1, 1991: Everton manage to pull off a transfer sensation by signing Peter Beardsley from Liverpool. The player, who was never really guaranteed a place under Kenny Dalglish, is a snip at just £1 million.

"MY CLUB DEBUT!"
TEDDY SHERINGHAM

UNITED DEBUT:	August 3, 1997
GAME:	Chelsea 1 Man. United 1
ATTENDANCE:	73, 636
MATCHFACTS RATING:	7/10

Sheringham made his debut for the Premiership champions in this bad-tempered Charity Shield match against FA Cup winners Chelsea, but he was substituted to make way for Ole Gunnar Solskjaer. It was a tight match that had to be decided on penalties and United won 4-2 thanks to Peter Schmeichel. Sheringham went on to prove what a good signing Alex Ferguson had made by scoring United's last-minute goal in the 1999 European Cup Final.

6 MONDAY

○ BANK HOLIDAY IN SCOTLAND & REPUBLIC OF IRELAND

7 TUESDAY

★ MATCH on sale

8 WEDNESDAY

9 THURSDAY

Ⓑ **FILIPPO INZAGHI** born 1973, Piacenza, Italy

10 FRIDAY

Ⓑ **ROY KEANE** born 1971, Cork, Republic of Ireland

11 SATURDAY

Ⓑ **NIGEL MARTYN** born 1966, St Austell, England   Ⓑ **NEIL McCANN** born 1974, Greenock, Scotland

12 SUNDAY

SHARP SHOOTER
Which team won the World Cup in 1994?

Last week's answer: MARIAN PAHARS

THIS WEEK IN 1995...

6 YEARS AGO

Debut nightmare for 'keeper beaten by opponent's No.1

BEING HANDED A FIRST-TEAM DEBUT IS BOUND TO BE a daunting time for any player, whether it's a Premiership game or in the Third Division with Barnet. But goalkeeper Maik Taylor had one he'd certainly rather forget on August 12, 1995. Taylor was making his first-team debut for The Bees against Hereford on the opening day of the 1995-96 season. Already 2-0 down just before half-time, he was looking forward to the solace of the dressing room and a cup of tea. But Taylor was left red-faced and embarrassed when Chris McKenzie, the Hereford 'keeper, spotted him off his line and sent a massive clearance over his head and into the net. Barnet lost the game 4-1 and the fed-up 'keeper wouldn't have been pleased with his five out of ten rating in MATCHfacts. But he came back with a bang and he's now a regular between the posts for Fulham and Northern Ireland!

Goalscoring 'keepers! Ten stoppers who've shown their strikers how it's done!

PETER SCHMEICHEL MAN. UNITED: With United 2-1 down in the last minute of this UEFA Cup First Round tie on September 26, 1995, the Great Dane strode forward for a corner and headed an unlikely equaliser. But it was all in vain as The Red Devils went out of the competition on the away goals rule.

JIMMY GLASS CARLISLE: In injury-time, the on-loan 'keeper raced upfield for a corner and bundled the ball in the back of the net to rescue Carlisle United from dropping out of the Nationwide League.

ANDY GORAM HIBERNIAN: Former international stopper Andy Goram scored in the Scottish Premier League in May 1988, looping the ball over the head of Morton's unlucky goalkeeper David Wylie.

PETER SHILTON LEICESTER CITY: Shilts only managed one goal in 1,000 league games, but he probably won't forget it. In 1967 he scored for Leicester against Southampton's Campbell Forsyth.

PAT JENNINGS TOTTENHAM HOTSPUR: Jennings scored for Tottenham during the 3-3 draw in the 1967 Charity Shield against Man. United when his clearance beat Alex Stepney in the opposing goal.

STEVE OGRIZOVIC COVENTRY: Stalwart Oggy grabbed his only goal for The Sky Blues against Sheffield Wednesday in October 1986. His huge boot upfield beat Martin Hodge in the home goal.

STEVE SHERWOOD WATFORD: Steve Sherwood got his name on the scoresheet in a First Division game in 1984, beating Coventry's Roddy Avramovic. Surely Oggy wouldn't have let that one go in?

RAY CASHLEY BRISTOL CITY: Bristol 'keeper Ray Cashley scored his first ever goal when he sent a lofted goal-kick over Hull City's Jeff Wealands and into the net in September 1993.

IAIN HESFORD MAIDSTONE: Scored Maidstone's winner against Hereford in a Fourth Division match in November 1991. His clearance beat Hereford's stranded goalkeeper Tony Elliot with one bounce.

ALAN PATERSON GLENTORAN: The 1989 Roadferry Cup Final came to life when Glentoran's No.1 Alan Paterson embarrassed Linfield's 'keeper George Dunlop with a towering clearance.

THE FOOTBALL TIMES

6 - 12 AUGUST

2 YEARS AGO...
AUGUST 7, 1999: Bradford, back in the top flight for the first time in 78 years, make a winning return with a 1-0 victory over Middlesbrough at The Riverside.

3 YEARS AGO...
AUGUST 12, 1998: Former Swedish hero Tomas Brolin, who graced the English football stadia of Crystal Palace and Leeds, announces his retirement at the age of 28. Reports suggesting he was turning into a professional pie-eater were unfounded!

6 YEARS AGO...
THIS WEEK IN 1995: Man. United boss Alex Ferguson watches Marc Overmars destroy Liverpool. The £10 million-rated winger scores one goal and sets up three more as Ajax trounce The Reds 5-0.

9 YEARS AGO...
AUGUST 7, 1992: Cambridge United striker Dion Dublin joins Man. United for £1 million, plus a further £300,000 if he plays for England. Dublin did play for his country, but four years later against the Czech Republic after moving to Coventry.

24 YEARS AGO...
AUGUST 10, 1977: Kenny Dalglish leaves Celtic for Liverpool in a British transfer record of £440,000. In 328 appearances for The Bhoys, Dalglish scored 199 goals and won five League Championships, four Scottish Cups and one League Cup.

"MY CLUB DEBUT!"
JAAP STAM

UNITED DEBUT: August 9, 1998
GAME: Arsenal 3 Man. United 0
ATTENDANCE: 67,000
MATCHFACTS RATING: 7/10

If Jaap Stam was looking for an easy introduction to English football after his £10.6 million transfer from PSV Eindhoven, he wasn't going to get it in the Charity Shield. Arsenal took a 2-0 lead at Wembley through Overmars and Wreh, before Anelka held off the attentions of Stam to make it 3-0. It wasn't the best start for the big Dutchman, but he soon showed his class to become one of the best defenders in the world.

MONDAY 13

Ⓑ **ALAN SHEARER** *born 1970, Newcastle, England*

TUESDAY 14

★ *MATCH on sale*

Ⓑ **BENITO CARBONE** *born 1971, Begnara, Italy*

WEDNESDAY 15

THURSDAY 16

Ⓑ **STEFAN KLOS** *born 1971, Dortmund, Germany*

FRIDAY 17

Ⓑ **OYVIND LEONHARDSEN** *born 1970, Kristiansund, Norway*

SATURDAY 18

SUNDAY 19

FOOTY ANAGRAM
This former Leeds man is a Boro boy.

Last week's answer: BRAZIL

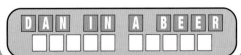

D A N   I N   A   B E E R

THIS WEEK IN 1992...

9 YEARS AGO

Arsenal unveil a mural to hide building work at Highbury

AFTER THE HILLSBOROUGH DISASTER WHEN FANS WERE tragically crushed against fences separating the crowd and the pitch, the Government said that every top-flight stadium in England had to be converted to an all-seater ground. Standing terraces across the country were torn down and replaced by modern seating, providing a more sophisticated way of watching football. Arsenal were keen to start work on their North Bank stand but the club knew it was going to take some time to complete. To protect the workforce from booted clearances or missed shots, and to disguise the ugly-looking building site, Arsenal covered the entire area with an unusual screen. A team of artists was commissioned to produce a huge mural of cheering fans to make up for the reduced atmosphere around Highbury. On August 15, 1992 – the opening day of the season – the brand new North Bank mural made its debut. It seemed like the piece of art was a good luck charm as The Gunners stormed into a 2-0 lead against Norwich City. Unfortunately, the luck didn't last too long and Norwich bagged four goals to win 4-2 by the final whistle. And what did the crowd think of it all? Not very much, judging by their response!

Ten brain-bustin' facts about Arsenal!

1. During the 1912-13 season, Arsenal only managed to win three games in the entire season!
2. In the same season, the North London club registered a measly 18 points and were relegated!
3. In 1934, lethal striker Ted Drake bagged a staggering 42 goals – and that was just in the league!
4. In 1935 Drake scored all of Arsenal's goals in their 7-1 win over Aston Villa – and he was injured!
5. Leeds boss David O'Leary made a staggering 722 appearances for The Gunners – a club record!
6. Arsenal's biggest league defeat was 8-0 at the hands of the mighty, er, Loughborough Town!
7. Arsenal took revenge four years later by beating Loughborough 12-0 – their biggest-ever victory!
8. The largest ever Highbury attendance is 73,295, when The Gunners played Sunderland in 1935!
9. In Arsenal's first recorded game, The Gunners lost 2-1 to arch London rivals Tottenham Hotspur!
10. The club's first name was Dial Square FC. Catchy, eh? It became Arsenal Football Club in 1914!

THE FOOTBALL TIMES

13-19 AUGUST

3 YEARS AGO...

AUGUST 13, 1998: The FA drops its bung enquiries into former Nottingham Forest manager Brian Clough due to his ill health. The investigation into his transfer dealings had been running for three years.

4 YEARS AGO...

AUGUST 13, 1997: Derby County's first home match at Pride Park is abandoned after the floodlights fail. Referee Uriah Rennie has to abandon the game with the home side 2-1 ahead against Wimbledon.

5 YEARS AGO...

AUGUST 17, 1996: Just a few months after lifting the European Cup for Juventus, Fabrizio Ravanelli makes his debut for Middlesbrough against Liverpool, hitting a remarkable hat-trick in a 3-3 draw.

8 YEARS AGO...

AUGUST 14, 1993: A police report is sent to the FA after Wimbledon's unconventional owner Sam Hammam admits to scribbling obscenities on the dressing room wall after the game against West Ham at Upton Park.

20 YEARS AGO...

AUGUST 17, 1981: Aston Villa, fresh from being crowned league champions and playing some of the best football of the club's history, demolish East Germany's World Cup team 4-2 at Villa Park.

HAPPY BIRTHDAY...
STEFAN KLOS

BIRTHDATE: August 16, 1971
BIRTHPLACE: Dortmund, Germany
CLUB: Rangers
COUNTRY: Germany
PREVIOUS CLUBS: Borussia Dortmund
HONOURS: German League (1995, 1996), World Club Cup (1995) European Cup (1997), Scottish Premier League (1999, 2000), Scottish Cup (1999, 2000), Scottish League Cup (1999)
Klos has added five major honours to his impressive CV since joining Rangers on Christmas Eve 1998.

MONDAY 20

Ⓑ **STEVE STONE** born 1971, Gateshead, England

TUESDAY 21

★ *MATCH on sale*   Ⓑ **DAVID HOPKIN** born 1970, Greenock, Scotland   Ⓑ **PAUL RITCHIE** born 1975, Kirkcaldy, Scotland

WEDNESDAY 22

THURSDAY 23

FRIDAY 24

SATURDAY 25

SUNDAY 26

Ⓑ **NICKY SUMMERBEE** born 1971, Altrincham, England

THE EYES HAVE IT
Who is this fishy-sounding winger?

Last week's answer: BRIAN DEANE

THIS WEEK IN 1964...

37 YEARS AGO

BBC launches new show on TV called 'Match Of The Day'

ON AUGUST 22, 1964 LIVERPOOL ENTERTAINED ARSENAL at Anfield and ended the game with a 2-0 win, so Arsenal travelled back to London with nothing to show for their trouble. But this was no ordinary match, it was the first game to be shown on the BBC's new football programme 'Match Of The Day'. The television audience that night was a mere 75,000, so the BBC worried about how well it would be received, but it soon became one of the most important programmes of the week. People used to come home early from the pub, interrupt parties and even stay in to make sure they saw the highlights of the day's action. In June 2000, the FA announced that the BBC would lose the right to show Premiership highlights after the 2000-2001 season. It ended the channel's 37-year flagship football programme as we know it, with ITV winning the rights instead.

The 'Match Of The Day' timeline

YEAR	LANDMARK EVENTS IN THE SHOW'S DISTINGUISHED HISTORY
1964	The first ever 'Match of The Day' is screened on August 22. Liverpool beat Arsenal 2-0.
1966	The show moves from BBC2 to BBC1 after the excitement of the 1966 World Cup.
1968	ITV creates a new show called 'The Big Match' to compete with 'Match Of The Day'.
1969	The BBC shows the first football match in colour, with Liverpool beating West Ham 2-0.
1971	BBC lead the ratings battle, with 12 million viewers compared to ITV's eight million.
1973	Jimmy Hill and Bob Wilson sign up as pundits – Jimmy's now at Sky and Bob's with ITV!
1978	Snatch of the Day! ITV grab the right to share coverage of Saturday's top-flight footy.
1988	With only the FA Cup to show, it's renamed 'Match of the Day – The Road to Wembley'.
1992	The show returns to its regular Saturday night slot with Premiership highlights.
2000	On June 14 the FA announce that the BBC has lost the rights to screen Premiership highlights. ITV's £61 million deal will come into effect after the 2000-2001 season.

THE FOOTBALL TIMES

20 - 26 AUGUST

2 YEARS AGO...
AUGUST 22, 1999: In a bad-tempered game at Highbury, Arsenal face champions Man. United at Highbury in a clash that's billed as a title showdown even at this early stage of the season. United win 2-1.

3 YEARS AGO...
AUGUST 20, 1998: Dwight Yorke joins Man. United for £12.6 million, then a club record fee. It takes United's spending to £23.2 million on two players after signing defender Jaap Stam from PSV Eindhoven.

5 YEARS AGO...
THIS WEEK IN 1996: Bruce Rioch plans a £14 million swoop for Everton's Andrei Kanchelskis and Bolton duo Jason McAteer and Alan Stubbs, reports MATCH. The trio do move clubs, but not to Highbury!

6 YEARS AGO...
THIS WEEK IN 1995: Middlesbrough boss Bryan Robson hits out at soaring transfer fees. "It's getting silly," he tells MATCH. "You expect to pay for quality, but you don't expect to pay similar prices for players who aren't in the same street."

36 YEARS AGO...
AUGUST 21, 1965: Keith Peacock is the first substitute to be used in the league when he comes on for Charlton against Bolton. Before this, a player had to be injured in order to be substituted, but the FA changed this rule because players began to feign injury to help with tactics.

"MY CLUB DEBUT!"
OLE GUNNAR SOLSKJAER

UNITED DEBUT: August 25, 1996
GAME: Man. United 2 Blackburn 2
ATTENDANCE: 54,178
MATCHFACTS RATING: 8/10

Despite only coming on at Old Trafford as a substitute after an hour, Solskjaer still managed a memorable Man. United debut. The Red Devils were 2-1 down at that point, but Solskjaer wasted no time in getting off the mark. Within ten minutes of coming on, the Norwegian striker had scored the equaliser for his new side, and despite his all-too brief introduction, he managed to earn the star rating for his team in the process. Not bad for an afternoon's work!

○ BANK HOLIDAY IN UK

Ⓑ **DIETMAR HAMANN** *born 1973, Munich, Germany*

★ *MATCH on sale*

Ⓑ **CELESTINE BABAYARO** *born 1978, Kaduna, Nigeria*

Ⓑ **IAN HARTE** *born 1977, Drogheda, Republic of Ireland*

○ **GERMANY v ENGLAND**
○ **SCOTLAND v CROATIA**
○ **REPUBLIC OF IRELAND v HOLLAND**
○ **DENMARK v NORTHERN IRELAND**
○ **WALES v ARMENIA**

CODE BREAKER

Can you crack the secret code to
name this Premiership star?

Last week's answer: STEVE GUPPY

8	19	13	4	P		
1	6	21	23			E

4 YEARS AGO

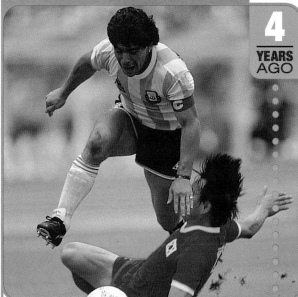

THE FOOTBALL TIMES

27 AUGUST - 2 SEPTEMBER

8 YEARS AGO...

AUGUST 29, 1993: England international David Platt marks his Sampdoria debut following his transfer from Aston Villa by getting his name on the scoresheet during their 2-1 win over Serie A rivals Napoli.

20 YEARS AGO...

AUGUST 27, 1981: Ron Greenwood is forced to name his England squad for the World Cup qualifier against Norway before the English season has started!

23 YEARS AGO...

SEPTEMBER 1, 1978: Bob Paisley's rampant Liverpool side thrash Tottenham 7-0 at Anfield. Paisley describes the win as 'one of the best in the club's history' with goals from Dalglish (2), Johnston (2), Kennedy, Neal (penalty) and McDermott.

29 YEARS AGO...

SEPTEMBER 2, 1972: The Borough of Newham in London names several streets after West Ham and England internationals Bobby Moore and Trevor Brooking.

65 YEARS AGO...

AUGUST 29, 1936: The First Division game at Highbury between Arsenal and Everton is the first match to be shown on television. In an exciting game, Arsenal hang on to beat The Toffees 3-2.

Diego Maradona fails a third drugs test at the age of 36

ON AUGUST 29, 1997 IT WAS ANNOUNCED THAT DIEGO Maradona, once proclaimed as the best footballer in the world, had failed a drugs test for the third time. It signalled a sad end to a career that should have been remembered for breathtaking skill and ability. He was at his best in the 1986 World Cup when he single-handedly led Argentina to the trophy. He was surrounded by controversy after punching the ball into the net to beat England in the quarter-finals, but he was undoubtedly the star of the tournament. The world first knew there was something wrong when Maradona ran to a television camera in the 1994 USA World Cup and screamed like a hysterical schoolkid. His actions prompted pundit Bob Wilson to say: "If he'd done that to me he'd have had the hand of Bob in his face." He was later found to have been taking illegal drugs and was promptly sent home. Diego that is, not Bob! The most recent pictures of Maradona show a bloated and wasted man who looks far older than 41.

Ten things you never knew about **Maradona!**

1. He once played for a team called 'The Little Onions' – they always cried on the team bus!
2. Maradona and his friends started a team that became the Argentinos Juniors youth side.
3. He made his league debut in Argentina aged 15 – and immediately stopped growing in size!
4. His international debut was only one year later, an incredible feat for any player in the world.
5. Maradona won the 1979 Youth World Cup in Japan – his first taste of World Cup success.
6. Boca Juniors bought him and sold him for a record fee, so at least he balanced the books!
7. Napoli paid another world record for him – £5million – which was unheard of at the time.
8. While playing for Napoli, Maradona scored the penalty that knocked Italy out of the World Cup!
9. Napoli sold 70,000 season tickets in just a few weeks after Maradona signed from Barcelona.
10. He had five attempts at a comeback, but they all failed because of weight or drug problems.

HAPPY BIRTHDAY...
IAN HARTE

BIRTHDATE: August 31, 1977
BIRTHPLACE: Drogheda, Republic of Ireland
CLUB: Leeds United
COUNTRY: Republic of Ireland
PREVIOUS CLUBS: None
HONOURS: 20 Republic of Ireland caps

Harte took his opportunity of first-team football with Leeds when John Robertson picked up a cartilage injury in 1997-98. He fought off Danny Granville's claims to the position in 1998-99 and has become a virtual ever-present under manager David O'Leary.

MONDAY
3

Ⓑ **GARETH SOUTHGATE** *born 1970, Watford, England*

TUESDAY
4

★ *MATCH on sale*

WEDNESDAY
5

○ **ENGLAND v ALBANIA**
○ **BELGIUM v SCOTLAND**
○ **NORTHERN IRELAND v ICELAND**
○ **NORWAY v WALES**

THURSDAY
6

Ⓑ **STEFAN OAKES** *born 1978, Leicester, England*   Ⓑ **IGOR STIMAC** *born 1967, Metkovic, Croatia*

FRIDAY
7

SATURDAY
8

Ⓑ **MARKUS BABBEL** *born 1972, Munich, Germany*   Ⓑ **GARY SPEED** *born 1969, Mancot, Wales*

SUNDAY
9

SHARP SHOOTER
In what year did 'Match Of The Day' start broadcasting?

Last week's answer: PAUL INCE

THIS WEEK IN 1980...

21 YEARS AGO

Eamonn Collins becomes youngest ever pro footballer

MANY FANS MARVELLED AT YOUNGSTERS LIKE JOE COLE, Jon Harley and Michael Owen when they made their debuts – some players had to ask permission from their school before playing for their club. But no-one compares with Blackpool's Eamonn Collins, who became the youngest professional footballer ever when he made his debut aged 14 years and 323 days old! The match, played on September 9, 1980, was an Anglo-Scottish Cup quarter-final against Kilmarnock, but Collins wasn't afraid of displaying his skills – even though Blackpool fans thought he was the club mascot! The young star had a good game, inspiring The Seasiders to a 2-1 win, despite the fact that it was a midweek match and he was due at school the next day, so he wasn't allowed any of the celebratory champagne!

Shouldn't you be at school, son?
The youngest players to represent their clubs!

CLUB	PLAYER	DEBUT	AGE
ARSENAL	GERRY WARD	v Huddersfield (Aug 22, 1953)	16 years, 321 days
ASTON VILLA	JIMMY BROWN	v Bolton (Sep 17, 1969)	15 years, 349 days
BRADFORD	ROBERT CULLINGFORD	v Mansfield (Apr 22, 1970)	16 years, 141 days
CHARLTON	PAUL KONCHESKY	v Oxford (Aug 16, 1997)	16 years, 93 days
CHELSEA	IAN HAMILTON	v Tottenham (Mar 18, 1967)	16 years, 138 days
COVENTRY	GARY MCSHEFFREY	v Aston Villa (Feb 27, 1999)	16 years, 198 days
DERBY	STEVE POWELL	v Arsenal (Oct 23, 1971)	16 years, 33 days
EVERTON	JOE ROYLE	v Blackpool (Jan 15, 1966)	16 years, 282 days
IPSWICH	JASON DOZZELL	v Coventry (Feb 4, 1984)	16 years, 56 days
LEEDS	PETER LORIMER	v Southampton (Sep 29, 1962)	15 years, 289 days
LEICESTER	DAVE BUCHANAN	v Oldham (Jan 1, 1979)	16 years, 192 days
LIVERPOOL	MICHAEL OWEN	v Wimbledon (May 6, 1997)	17 years, 144 days
MAN. CITY	GLYN PARDOE	v Birmingham (Apr 11, 1961)	15 years, 314 days
MAN. UNITED	JEFF WHITEFOOT	v Portsmouth (Apr 15, 1950)	16 years, 105 days
MIDDLESBROUGH	STEPHEN BELL	v Southampton (Jan 30, 1982)	16 years, 323 days
	SAM LAWRIE	v Arsenal (Nov 3, 1951)	16 years, 323 days
NEWCASTLE	STEVE WATSON	v Wolves (Nov 10, 1990)	16 years, 223 days
SOUTHAMPTON	DANNY WALLACE	v Man. United (Nov 29, 1980)	16 years, 313 days
SUNDERLAND	DEREK FORSTER	v Leicester (Aug 22, 1964)	15 years, 184 days
TOTTENHAM	ALLY DICK	v Man. City (Feb 20, 1982)	16 years, 301 days
WEST HAM	NEIL FINN	v Man. City (Jan 1, 1996)	17 years, 3 days

THE FOOTBALL TIMES

3-9 SEPTEMBER

3 YEARS AGO...
SEPTEMBER 5, 1998: Despite taking a second-minute lead from Alan Shearer's free-kick, England have Paul Ince sent-off and crash to a 2-1 defeat against Sweden in their first qualifying game of Euro 2000.

6 YEARS AGO...
SEPTEMBER 9, 1995: Wimbledon beat Liverpool 1-0 despite having Vinnie Jones sent-off for the tenth time in his career. Andy Thorn leaves the field thinking he's also been shown the red card and has to be called back from the dressing room!

40 YEARS AGO...
SEPTEMBER 9, 1961: Sunderland striker Brian Clough nets his 200th league goal against Leeds United. Incredibly, Cloughie reaches this scoring milestone after only 219 games! The former Nottingham Forest manager was also a formidable striker!

103 YEARS AGO...
SEPTEMBER 3, 1898: After playing in blue and white quartered shirts for five years, Liverpool decide to change to their now famous all-red strip for the first time at home to Sheffield Wednesday. They win 4-0 and have worn red ever since!

105 YEARS AGO...
SEPTEMBER 3, 1896: The referee in the First Division match between Blackburn and Liverpool disallows a record six goals! He only lets one goal, a Blackburn effort, stand and Rovers win the game 1-0.

HAPPY BIRTHDAY...
GARETH SOUTHGATE

BIRTHDATE: September 3, 1970
BIRTHPLACE: Watford, England
CLUB: Aston Villa
COUNTRY: England
PREVIOUS CLUBS: Crystal Palace
HONOURS: League Cup winner (1996), 37 England caps.

After starting out as a midfielder at Crystal Palace, Gareth Southgate has established himself as an assured centre-back. He moved to Aston Villa in 1995 for £2.5 million and soon became captain of the side. A regular member of the England squad, he will unfortunately be remembered as the man who missed the deciding penalty against Germany in the semi-finals of Euro '96.

MONDAY 10

B **PETER KENNEDY** *born 1973, Lisburn, Northern Ireland*

TUESDAY 11

★ *MATCH on sale*

B **ALESSANDRO DEL PIERO** *born 1974, Conegliano, Italy*

WEDNESDAY 12

B **DAVID THOMPSON** *born 1977, Birkenhead, England*

THURSDAY 13

B **ANDREW IMPEY** *born 1971, Hammersmith, England*

FRIDAY 14

SATURDAY 15

SUNDAY 16

FOOTY ANAGRAM
This 'keeper likes making baskets.

Last week's answer: 1964

DID YOU KNOW?
Lee Hendrie was too nervous to even talk to his
England team-mates when he got his senior call-up!

THIS WEEK IN 1997...

4 YEARS AGO

Ian Wright breaks Arsenal's all-time goalscoring record

WHEN IAN WRIGHT SCORED A HAT-TRICK FOR ARSENAL
against Bolton Wanderers on September 13, 1997, it sent him past
Cliff Bastin's club record of 178 goals. Wright was desperate to break
Bastin's 52-year-old record and the former Crystal Palace striker only
took seven years, between 1991 and 1998, to do it. His best season
was in 1997-98, when he scored 28 goals in 39 games. To become
a leading goalscorer, strikers have to stay loyal to their club for a long
period of time and bang the goals in left, right and centre! Dixie Dean
scored an incredible 377 goals for Everton in a 12-year career with
the club, while Tottenham Hotspur legend Jimmy Greaves notched
up an amazing 266 goals in just nine years. Now that's a top striker!

Record goalscorers – the best ever!
How many goals do your current strikers need to break the long-standing records?

CLUB	PLAYER	GOALS	CLUB CAREER
Arsenal	Ian Wright	185	1991-1998
Aston Villa	Billy Walker	244	1919-1934
Bradford City	Bobby Campbell	143	1979-1986
Charlton Athletic	Stuart Leary	153	1953-1962
Chelsea	Bobby Tambling	202	1959-1970
Coventry City	Clarrie Bourton	181	1931-1937
Derby County	Steve Bloomer	331	1892-1914
Everton	Dixie Dean	377	1925-1937
Ipswich Town	Ray Crawford	227	1958-1969
Leeds United	Peter Lorimer	238	1965-1986
Leicester City	Arthur Chandler	273	1923-1934
Liverpool	Ian Rush	344	1980-1997
Manchester City	Eric Brook	178	1928-1939
Man. United	Bobby Charlton	198	1956-1973
Middlesbrough	George Camsell	325	1925-1939
Newcastle United	Jackie Milburn	200	1946-1957
Southampton	Mike Channon	185	1966-1982
Sunderland	Bob Gurney	228	1926-1939
Tottenham Hotspur	Jimmy Greaves	266	1961-1970
West Ham United	Vic Watson	298	1920-1935

THE FOOTBALL TIMES

2 YEARS AGO...
THIS WEEK IN 1999: Kieron Dyer offers
Rob Lee his No. 7 shirt on Lee's return to
the Newcastle squad after the departure of
Ruud Gullit. MATCH reports that new boss
Bobby Robson wants to sign another Ruud,
PSV Eindhoven's Ruud Van Nistelrooy.

5 YEARS AGO...
THIS WEEK IN 1996: Leicester City's new
signing, Spencer Prior, raves to MATCH
about an exciting 18-year-old prospect
called Emile Heskey. "Emile is very strong,
with real pace," says Prior, after the young
Foxes striker blasts two goals against
Southampton. How right Mr Prior was!

7 YEARS AGO...
SEPTEMBER 13, 1994: In Newcastle's
first European game for 17 years, The
Magpies thrash Royal Antwerp 5-0 in the
UEFA Cup. Kevin Keegan is delighted as
Rob Lee grabs a hat-trick in 51 minutes.

10 YEARS AGO...
SEPTEMBER 11, 1991: England lose 1-0
against Germany in a friendly international
at Wembley. It's an exciting game, though,
with David Platt hitting the bar and Gary
Lineker having a shot cleared off the line.

45 YEARS AGO...
SEPTEMBER 14, 1956: Ray Wilkins is
born. The Chelsea coach and TV pundit
had a glorious career, playing for European
giants AC Milan and Paris St Germain,
captaining Chelsea and Man. United, and
winning 84 senior caps for England.

"MY RED CARD DAY!"
ANDY COLE

DATE: September 11, 1999
GAME: Liverpool 2 Man. United 3
SENT-OFF: 72 mins
OFFENCE(S): Dissent, retaliation
REFEREE: Graham Barber (Tring)

After Carragher's early own goal,
Cole headed Man. United 2-0 in
front, then missed an open goal
and was booked for dissent after
24 minutes. With Man. United
3-2 ahead, the striker was
sent-off for reacting violently
to a thunderous challenge
from Song. England team-mates
Redknapp and Beckham were both
cautioned towards the end and were
lucky to stay on the pitch.

10 – 16 SEPTEMBER

MONDAY 17

Ⓑ **MARCEL DESAILLY** *born 1968, Accra, Ghana*

TUESDAY 18

★ *MATCH on sale*   Ⓑ **SOL CAMPBELL** *born 1974, Newham, England*   Ⓑ **STEPHEN HUGHES** *born 1976, Wokingham, England*

WEDNESDAY 19

Ⓑ **DAVID SEAMAN** *born 1963, Rotherham, England*

THURSDAY 20

FRIDAY 21

SATURDAY 22

Ⓑ **HARRY KEWELL** *born 1978, Sydney, Australia*   Ⓑ **EMMANUEL PETIT** *born 1970, Dieppe, France*

SUNDAY 23

THE EYES HAVE IT
Who is this mad-sounding terrier?

Last week's answer: NICKY WEAVER

THIS WEEK IN 1993...

8 YEARS AGO

Robbie Fowler scores in his first ever game for Liverpool

ROBBIE FOWLER SCORED ON HIS DEBUT FOR LIVERPOOL on September 22, 1993 in the League Cup Second Round at Fulham. Ian Rush also scored for Liverpool in the 3-1 win at Craven Cottage, but it was the youngster who impressed with his enthusiasm up front. In the second leg at Anfield, Fowler scored all five of Liverpool goals in a 5-0 demolition of The Cottagers and was nicknamed 'God' by the ecstatic Kop. The exciting youngster was immediately hailed as the successor to Ian Rush and went on to score 18 goals for The Reds during the 1993-94 season. In the following year, Fowler became the first Liverpool striker for 30 years to score over 30 goals in a season, matching the feat of Anfield legend Roger Hunt. The talented forward has struggled with injuries in recent seasons, but he's already gone down in history as one of the greatest strikers Anfield has ever seen.

Liverpool's all-time **top goalscorers**

Robbie Fowler is part of an Anfield dynasty of great goalscorers stretching back to Billy Liddell in the 1950s. The Reds have always had players with a golden touch in front of goal and Fowler's one of the finest natural goalscorers of his generation.

PLAYER	GAMES	LIVERPOOL CAREER	GOALS
1. IAN RUSH*	616	1980-1997	344
2. ROGER HUNT	484	1959-1969	285
3. BILLY LIDDELL	537	1945-1960	229
4. KENNY DALGLISH	481	1977-1989	168
5. ROBBIE FOWLER	258	1993-present	149
6. IAN ST JOHN	418	1961-1970	118
7. JOHN BARNES	401	1987-1997	106
8. KEVIN KEEGAN	321	1971-1976	100
9. JOHN TOSHACK	236	1970-1977	95
10 = DAVID JOHNSON	174	1976-1981	78
= JIMMY MELIA	287	1955-1963	78

* During two periods: 1980-1986, 1988-1995

THE FOOTBALL TIMES

2 YEARS AGO...

SEPTEMBER 19, 1999: Bobby Robson takes charge of his first game in front of the Newcastle fans and sees his team thrash Sheffield Wednesday 8-0. After sitting on the bench during Ruud Gullit's reign, Alan Shearer bangs in five goals.

5 YEARS AGO...

SEPTEMBER 22, 1996: Arsene Wenger arrives at Highbury from Japanese side Grampus Eight following the sacking of former boss Bruce Rioch. Wenger, once manager of French side Monaco, uses his club contacts to sign Emmanuel Petit and Gilles Grimandi from his former club.

8 YEARS AGO...

SEPTEMBER 22, 1993: In France, the Football Federation strip Marseille of their 1993 league title and indefinitely suspend all of the club's players and officials that are facing charges of unlawful corruption.

9 YEARS AGO...

SEPTEMBER 17, 1992: Man. United boss Alex Ferguson is furious to learn that he needlessly left out Wales international Ryan Giggs from a UEFA Cup tie because of the competition's foreign player rule.

11 YEARS AGO...

SEPTEMBER 19, 1990: English clubs return to Europe after their five-year ban following the Heysel Stadium disaster. Man. United beat Pecsi Munkas 2-0 and Aston Villa defeat Banik Ostrava 3-1.

FIRST ARSENAL GOAL!
THIERRY HENRY

DATE: September 18, 1999
GAME: Southampton 0 Arsenal 1
ATTENDANCE: 15,242
MATCHFACTS RATING: N/A

Henry had gone eight games without a goal after arriving at Arsenal, so he was an odd choice to replace Kanu after 71 minutes, with Arsenal fans chanting for fellow sub Davor Suker. But it didn't take Henry long to make an impact. He collected a pass from Adams, spun away from his marker and curled a low shot past the 'keeper. His celebration was full of relief and he never stopped scoring after that!

MONDAY 24

🅑 **CRAIG BURLEY** *born 1971, Ayr, Scotland*   🅑 **ALLY McCOIST** *born 1962, Belshill, Scotland*

TUESDAY 25

★ *MATCH on sale*   🅑 **OLIVIER DACOURT** *born 1974, Montreuil, France*

WEDNESDAY 26

THURSDAY 27

🅑 **STEVE CHETTLE** *born 1968, Nottingham, England*

FRIDAY 28

SATURDAY 29

🅑 **ANDRIY SHEVCHENKO** *born 1976, Dvirklvshchyna, Ukraine*

SUNDAY 30

CODE BREAKER

Can you crack the secret code to name this Premiership star?

Last week's answer: DAVID BATTY

12	6	23	10	15

	E			

9	16	19	13	16	4	12

H						

THIS WEEK IN 1981...

20 YEARS AGO

THE FOOTBALL TIMES

4 YEARS AGO...
THIS WEEK IN 1997: Sir John Hall steps down as Newcastle's chairman to make way for Freddie Shepherd and Douglas Hall. It's the end of a golden era at the club and Magpies fans are sad to see him go.

7 YEARS AGO...
THIS WEEK IN 1994: Arsenal's Ian Wright faces FA disciplinary action after saying the referee for the game against Norwich was 'straight out of the Muppet Show'. Now everyone knows the favourite show of the football player turned TV celebrity!

11 YEARS AGO...
THIS WEEK IN 1990: Italian side Juventus try to sign Nottingham Forest and England defender Des Walker for £6.5 million. MATCH reports that the deal falls through after Brian Clough accuses their manager of being a glorified car salesman. Tactful!

16 YEARS AGO...
THIS WEEK IN 1985: A young striker called Gary Lineker is heralded in MATCH as an exciting new talent. The feature says: "His pace and appetite for scoring mean he will always get plenty of goals for club and country." As usual, spot on!

49 YEARS AGO...
SEPTEMBER 24, 1952: The first of Matt Busby's great Man. United sides records a 4-2 victory in the Charity Shield against Newcastle United. Those were the days when fans of The Red Devils came from Manchester, not all over the country!

Liverpool's legendary manager Bill Shankly dies

LIVERPOOL FANS MAY BE HAPPY WITH GERARD HOULLIER after his promising start at Anfield, but ask them to name the club's greatest ever manager and they'll say Bill Shankly without needing to think about it. On September 29, 1981 Liverpool went into mourning at the news that 'Shanks' had died. The determined Scotsman was the first person to point out what football meant to people when he declared: "Football is not just a matter of life and death. It's much more important than that." It was this kind of attitude that helped to give Liverpool fans their 100 per cent commitment to the club. After moving to Merseyside from Huddersfield Town in 1959, Bill Shankly transformed Liverpool into the most powerful side in Britain. During the '70s, when unemployment was high in the area, he gave the red half of the city at least one reason to be happy by creating sides that played attractive and exciting football. He brought trophy after trophy back to Anfield and laid the foundations of the team that dominated English football from the '70s until the early '90s. As a tribute to the club's greatest ever manager, Liverpool built the Shankly Gates (see picture below) outside Anfield a year after his death in August 1982.

The glorious Shankly years at Anfield

It doesn't matter how well the team plays if the trophy cabinet is bare at the end of the season, so how successful was Bill Shankly in terms of silverware at Liverpool?

1961-62	Division Two Champions
1963-64	Division One Champions
1964-65	FA Cup Winners
1965-66	Division One Champions & Cup-Winners' Cup Runners-Up
1968-69	Division One Runners-up
1970-71	FA Cup Runners-up
1972-73	Division One Champions & UEFA Cup Winners
1973-74	FA Cup Winners & Division One Runners-up

"MY RED CARD DAY!"
JOHN HARTSON

DATE: September 26, 1999
GAME: Wimbledon 1 Tottenham 1
SENT-OFF: 76 mins
OFFENCE(S): Foul, violent conduct
REFEREE: Graham Poll (Tring)

John Hartson showed both sides of his character in this game. He was cautioned for an over-zealous tackle before the break, then powered Wimbledon in front after 57 minutes. He received his second yellow for elbowing Luke Young in the face after 76 minutes. Wimbledon defended well, but Spurs eventually got the breakthrough to grab a point.

MONDAY 1

TUESDAY 2

★ *MATCH on sale* Ⓑ **ROD WALLACE** *born 1969, Lewisham, England* Ⓑ **MICHAEL BALL** *born 1979, Liverpool, England*

WEDNESDAY 3

THURSDAY 4

FRIDAY 5

SATURDAY 6

OCTOBER 2, 1993

◌ **ENGLAND v GREECE**
◌ **SCOTLAND v LATVIA**
◌ **REPUBLIC OF IRELAND v CYPRUS**
◌ **MALTA v NORTHERN IRELAND**
◌ **WALES v BELARUS**

Ⓑ **NIALL QUINN** *born 1966, Dublin, Republic of Ireland*

SUNDAY 7

SHARP SHOOTER
Who is Tottenham's record goalscorer?

Last week's answer: KEVIN HORLOCK

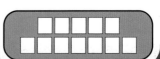

THIS WEEK IN 1976...

Red cards are used for the first time in English football

RED AND YELLOW CARDS WERE INTRODUCED INTO THE English Football League on October 2, 1976. Disciplinary cards had been used at international level before this date, but England took a long time to adopt them. The first recipient of the red card didn't have to wait long – Blackburn's David Wagstaffe was dismissed on the first day of the new cards against Leyton Orient. A new record was set in 1980-81 when 157 players were sent-off in the English football league, leading to a clampdown on deliberate fouls for the beginning of the 1982-83 season. Leicester City's Eddie Kelly was the first victim, receiving his marching orders for an intentional handball.

Famous red-card incidents

APRIL 1, 2000: Arsene Wenger sees his 29th player dismissed since taking charge at Arsenal when defender Oleg Luzhny is sent off against Wimbledon for a professional foul just before half-time.

JUNE 30, 1998: David Beckham is sent-off for England in the World Cup Second Round meeting with Argentina for a petulant kick at midfielder Diego Simeone and ten-man England lose on penalties.

DECEMBER 3, 1994: Stranraer set a new Scottish record when they have four players sent-off in their clash with Airdrie on their way to an 8-1 defeat. Eleven players versus seven isn't fair!

SEPTEMBER 6, 1992: The same feat is achieved two years earlier in England, when Hereford United have four players sent-off in their bruising 1-1 draw away to Northampton Town in the Third Division!

DECEMBER 9, 1990: Giuseppe Lorenzo of Italian side Bologna sets a new world record when he is sent-off after only ten seconds of a league match with Parma – he was like a man possessed!

AUGUST 10, 1974: In the Charity Shield, Liverpool's Kevin Keegan and Leeds United's Billy Bremner become the first British players to be sent-off at Wembley when they start fighting and leave topless!

THE FOOTBALL TIMES

2 YEARS AGO...
OCTOBER 3, 1999: Chelsea hammer Man. United 5-0. Massimo Taibi suffers a torrid time in goal and even Chris Sutton gets on the scoresheet with his first and only Premiership goal of the season.

3 YEARS AGO...
OCTOBER 7, 1998: The Daily Mirror prints a picture showing John Hartson booting Eyal Berkovic in the face at West Ham's training ground. The pair say there is no ill feeling, but Berkovic leaves the club soon after and Hartson's not far behind him!

6 YEARS AGO...
OCTOBER 1, 1995: After being suspended for eight months following his 'kung-fu' kick on a Crystal Palace fan, Eric Cantona marks his comeback for Man. United by equalising from the spot as The Red Devils draw 2-2 with Liverpool at Old Trafford.

45 YEARS AGO...
OCTOBER 6, 1956: Stanley Matthews becomes England's oldest ever goalscorer when, aged 41 years and 248 days old, he notches against Northern Ireland in a 1-1 draw. And to think Alan Shearer retired from international football aged 29!

73 YEARS AGO...
OCTOBER 6, 1928: Newcastle's team that plays Leeds is made up of ten Scottish players and one Welshman! This was 73 years ago, so who said Chelsea were the first English team to field 11 foreigners?

"MY FIRST CAP!"
MARK BURCHILL

SCOTLAND DEBUT: October 5, 1999
GAME: Scotland 1 Bosnia 0
ATTENDANCE: 30,574
MATCHFACTS RATING: N/A

Burchill was rewarded for his fine form in the Scottish Premier League with Celtic (scoring 9 goals in 21 games in the 1998-99 season) by making his Scotland debut after 79 minutes of this vital Euro 2000 qualifying game against Bosnia. Burchill had to work tirelessly to chase the ball as Bosnia had most of the play in this match, but Craig Brown's side made sure of second spot in Group Nine behind the Czech Republic thanks to a John Collins penalty winner.

MONDAY 8

TUESDAY 9

★ *MATCH on sale*

WEDNESDAY 10

B **TONY ADAMS** *born 1966, London, England*

THURSDAY 11

FRIDAY 12

B **DANNY CADAMARTERI** *born 1979, Bradford, England*

SATURDAY 13

OCTOBER 11, 1986

SUNDAY 14

B **MICHAEL DUBERRY** *born 1975, Enfield, England*

FOOTY ANAGRAM
This South African could be found in a pond.

Last week's answer: JIMMY GREAVES

THIS WEEK IN 1935...

66 YEARS AGO

Stamford Bridge holds the largest ever league crowd

OLD TRAFFORD CAN HOLD NEARLY 70,000 SPECTATORS after its latest expansion – an impressive capacity compared to most football grounds, but it doesn't beat the crowd of 82,905 people that squeezed into Stamford Bridge on October 12, 1935. This attendance was a record for an English league ground as fans poured into the stadium to watch Chelsea take on London rivals Arsenal. These huge numbers weren't unusual as thousands of football fanatics packed onto the terraces. Wembley regularly housed over 100,000 spectators for internationals and cup finals, creating some amazing atmospheres on the big occasions. It did have its downsides though, because the huge crowds meant it was difficult to see the game. It also got smelly with lots of people crammed in next to each other and it was difficult to get to the toilets, which often led to disastrous results. We don't know how lucky we are these days in our all-seater modern stadia!

So you want to see a massive stadium?

STADIUM	TEAM	COUNTRY	CAPACITY
Maracana	Brazil	Brazil	199,500
Santiago Bernabeu	Real Madrid	Spain	106,500
Nou Camp	Barcelona	Spain	98,000
Crvena Zvezda	Red Star Belgrade	Yugoslavia	97,422
Giuseppe Meazza	Inter & AC Milan	Italy	85,443
Komplex Olimpiyskyi	Dynamo Kiev	Ukraine	83,160
Stadio Olimpico	Lazio & Roma	Italy	83,000
NEP Stadium	Hungary	Hungary	80,000
Stade de France	St. Denis	France	80,000
Stadium of Light	Benfica	Portugal	77,844

THE FOOTBALL TIMES

8 - 14 OCTOBER

2 YEARS AGO...
OCTOBER 10, 1999: In a friendly against Belgium at The Stadium Of Light, Jamie Redknapp scores his first ever goal for his country in a 2-1 win. Skipper Alan Shearer puts England 1-0 ahead and Redknapp's stunning 30-yard strike wins the match.

3 YEARS AGO...
THIS WEEK IN 1998: Nottingham Forest ask for a £4 million loan from the Premier League to replace Pierre van Hooijdonk, who is on strike. Manager Dave Bassett says he's even hopeful of getting it, reports MATCH. Yeah, sure Dave – dream on!

5 YEARS AGO...
THIS WEEK IN 1996: Newcastle United manager Kevin Keegan joins Man. United boss Alex Ferguson in the race to sign top defender Miguel Nadal from Barcelona. They fight so hard that neither gets him!

53 YEARS AGO...
OCTOBER 9, 1948: Jackie Milburn makes his debut for England in a 6-2 victory over Northern Ireland. In a cruel twist of fate, the Newcastle United forward died on the same date 40 years later in 1988.

115 YEARS AGO...
OCTOBER 13, 1886: Aston Villa record their biggest ever win – 13-0 – against the mighty Wednesbury Old Athletic. But Villa fans shouldn't shout about this victory too loudly – it sounds like they had a field day beating a team made up of old men!

HAPPY BIRTHDAY...
WES BROWN

BIRTHDATE: October 13, 1979
BIRTHPLACE: Manchester, England
CLUB: Man. United
COUNTRY: England
PREVIOUS CLUBS: None
HONOURS: Premier League (1999), FA Cup (1999), European Cup (1999), one England cap.

After making his debut in 1998, Brown made rapid progress and won praise for his assured performances in the right-back role. He made his international debut against Hungary in April 1999, but serious injury has so far hindered his development.

MONDAY 15

Ⓑ **ANDY COLE** *born 1971, Nottingham, England*   Ⓑ **DIDIER DESCHAMPS** *born 1968, Bayonne, France*

TUESDAY 16

★ *MATCH on sale*   Ⓑ **THOMAS MYHRE** *born 1973, Sarpsborg, Norway*   Ⓑ **DAVID UNSWORTH** *born 1973, Chorley, England*

WEDNESDAY 17

THURSDAY 18

Ⓑ **ROBBIE SAVAGE** *born 1974, Wrexham, Wales*

FRIDAY 19

IN COLOUR...
Sheffield United
Simon Stainrod
John Chiedozie
Mark Lillis

Hammers'
hit man!
Just how
good is
McAvennie?

FAMOUS
FOOTBALL
GROUNDS
— MORE
CUT-OUTS

SATURDAY 20

OCTOBER 19, 1985

SUNDAY 21

THE EYES HAVE IT
Who is this stylish Italian supremo?

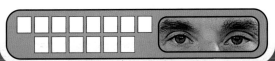

Last week's answer: MARK FISH

THIS WEEK IN 1996...

5 YEARS AGO

Newcastle thrash Man. United 5-0 at jubilant St James' Park

AFTER MAN. UNITED JUST PIPPED NEWCASTLE TO THE Premier league title in 1996 and beat them 4-0 in the Charity Shield, The Magpies were out for revenge when the two teams met in the league on October 20, 1996. Newcastle hadn't even scored against The Red Devils in their last three meetings, but this was set to change dramatically. Peacock scrambled the ball in from Ginola's corner to put The Magpies ahead after 12 minutes. Ginola scored the second himself before the break, lashing a 25-yard shot past the stranded Schmeichel. The new partnership of Les Ferdinand and Alan Shearer was terrorising the Man. United defence and both strikers scored in the second half to make it 4-0. St James' Park was jubilant and United were humiliated. Phillipe Albert calmly chipped the fifth goal from 25 yards to round off a magical day for the Newcastle faithful.

The heaviest post-war league defeats suffered by Man. United

1.	Leicester 6 Man. United 0	January 21, 1961
2.	Ipswich 6 Man. United 0	March 1, 1980
3.	Burnley 6 Man. United 1	December 26, 1963
4.	Middlesbrough 5 Man. United 0	April 25, 1953
5.	Man. United 0 Man City 5	February 12, 1955
6.	Crystal Palace 5 Man. United 0	December 16, 1972
7.	Everton 5 Man. United 0	October 27, 1984
8.	Newcastle 5 Man. United 0	October 20, 1996
9.	Chelsea 5 Man. United 0	October 3, 1999
10.	Newcastle 7 Man. United 3	January 2, 1960

THE FOOTBALL TIMES

2 YEARS AGO...

OCTOBER 20, 1999: Glasgow Rangers put in a thrilling display to beat PSV Eindhoven 4-1 in the group stages of the Champions League. Goals from Amoruso and McCann, and a brace from Dutchman Michael Mols, give The Gers a memorable win at Ibrox.

6 YEARS AGO...

OCTOBER 16, 1995: Falkirk's Steve Kirk is fined £250 in court after being found guilty of recklessly kicking the ball into the crowd and injuring a 12-year-old girl in Falkirk's game at Hearts in April 1995.

9 YEARS AGO...

OCTOBER 18, 1992: Ian Rush breaks Roger Hunt's Liverpool scoring record with his 287th goal for The Reds in a 2-2 draw with Man. United. In the same week five years later, Rushie equals Geoff Hurst's League Cup scoring record of 46 goals.

11 YEARS AGO...

OCTOBER 15, 1990: Welsh club Wrexham are forced to leave home 24 hours before their European Cup Winners' Cup fixture against Man. United, even though it's only a 40-mile trip! UEFA states that opposing teams must arrive the day before a game!

76 YEARS AGO...

OCTOBER 17, 1925: Aston Villa lead Birmingham City 3-0 with ten minutes to play when Joe Bradford scores two goals in quick succession. The Villa goalkeeper then throws the ball into his own net while he's trying to clear to end the game 3-3!

FIRST LEEDS GOAL!
HARRY KEWELL

DATE: October 15, 1997
GAME: Stoke 1 Leeds United 3
ATTENDANCE: 18,671
MATCHFACTS RATING: 7/10

Stoke thought they were heading for a giantkilling in the third round of the League Cup after converting a 66th minute penalty. But they weren't ahead for long. Leeds found their inspiration from the young Wizard of Oz Harry Kewell. His first goal for Leeds was a crucial one, sending a screaming left-footed drive past 'keeper Muggleton to force extra-time. Rod Wallace scored two goals to win the tie and end the hopes of his brother Ray, who was playing for Stoke!

MATCH 22-28 OCTOBER

MONDAY
22

TUESDAY
23

★ *MATCH on sale*

Ⓑ **CHRISTIAN DAILLY** *born 1973, Dundee, Scotland*

WEDNESDAY
24

Ⓑ **JACKIE McNAMARA** *born 1973, Glasgow, Scotland*

THURSDAY
25

FRIDAY
26

Ⓑ **STEVE HOWEY** *born 1971, Sunderland, England*

SATURDAY
27

OCTOBER 24, 1987

Ⓑ **LEE CLARK** *born 1972, Wallsend, England*

SUNDAY
28

Ⓑ **ALAN SMITH** *born 1980, Leeds, England*

CODE BREAKER
**Can you crack the secret code to
name this Premiership star?**

Last week's answer: GIANLUCA VIALLI

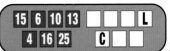

THIS WEEK IN 1988...

13 YEARS AGO

Three brothers play on same side for first time in 68 years!

THE CLOSEST MOST PEOPLE GET TO PLAYING FOOTBALL with their brothers is on the park after school, but that's not always the case. Some even make it to professional level and end up in the same team, like the Nevilles, who have played for Man. United and England together. But this doesn't happen very often, so that's why October 22, 1988 was such a landmark occasion for the Wallace brothers of Southampton. There weren't just two brothers playing in the same team, there were three of them! Danny, along with younger twins Rod and Ray, became the first trio of brothers to play on the same Football League side since 1920, when the three Carr brothers turned out for Middlesbrough. Unfortunately, the three amigos didn't have the happiest of afternoons together as The Saints went down 2-1 to Sheffield Wednesday at The Dell. But all three of the Wallace brothers went on to have long careers, with Rod – who is still banging the goals in for Glasgow Rangers – the best known of the three.

We are family! The most famous family connections in world football!

PLAYERS	RELATIONSHIP	TEAM(S)
Gary & Phil Neville	Brothers	Man. United
Gary Kelly & Ian Harte	Uncle & nephew	Leeds
Rio & Les Ferdinand	Cousins	West Ham & Tottenham
Alex & Darren Ferguson	Father & son	Man. United & Wrexham
Harry & Jamie Redknapp	Father & son	West Ham & Liverpool
Frank Lampard Snr & Jnr	Father & son	West Ham
Ian Wright & Shaun Wright-Phillips	Father & son	Retired & Manchester City
Ronald & Frank de Boer	Brothers	Barcelona & Holland
Brian & Michael Laudrup	Brothers	Denmark
Dean & David Holdsworth	Brothers	Bolton & Birmingham
Bobby & Jack Charlton	Brothers	England World Cup (1966)
Clive, Paul, Bradley & Martin Allen	Martin Allen is the uncle of Clive, Paul & Bradley!	

THE FOOTBALL TIMES

3 YEARS AGO...
OCTOBER 25, 1998: There's one red and 13 yellow cards shown when Leeds take on Chelsea at Elland Road. The red card was shown to Chelsea's Frank Leboeuf, who later had the cheek to moan about how violent the Premier League was!

4 YEARS AGO...
OCTOBER 25, 1997: Man. United destroy Premiership new boys Barnsley 7-0, with Andy Cole putting United on the road to victory with a first half hat-trick. But, as strange as it may seem, Barnsley got their revenge a few months later in the FA Cup!

11 YEARS AGO...
OCTOBER 27, 1990: Derby County score in the first half of a Premiership game for the first time this season and collect their first win of the season at Southampton. Derby are relegated seven months later.

18 YEARS AGO...
OCTOBER 22, 1983: The mighty Rangers lose 2-1 at home to Motherwell. A crowd of only 15,000 turn on the Glasgow team and voice their disapproval – it's their fifth defeat in the ninth game of the season.

31 YEARS AGO...
THIS WEEK IN 1970: Captaining QPR for the first time, Rodney Marsh shaves off his beard to look 'more dignified'. Thirty years later, he's struggling for dignity once more after dismissing Bradford's survival hopes and suggesting striker Kevin Phillips would struggle to score goals in the Premiership.

"MY CLUB DEBUT!"
BENITO CARBONE

VILLA DEBUT: October 23, 1999
GAME: Aston Villa 1 Wimbledon 1
ATTENDANCE: 27,160
MATCHFACTS RATING: 8/10

Carbone made a sparkling debut for Villa following his midweek move from Sheffield Wednesday. He could have capped his outstanding display with a hat-trick if Neil Sullivan hadn't been in inspired form. The Wimbledon No. 1 kept his team in the game but couldn't stop Dion Dublin equalising after Earle had put The Dons ahead after 27 minutes. Dublin headed in from close range after a fine far-post cross from Carbone, who was the best player on the pitch and rightly named Man Of The Match.

MONDAY 29

○ BANK HOLIDAY IN REPUBLIC OF IRELAND

Ⓑ **EDWIN VAN DER SAR** *born 1970, Voorhout, Holland*

TUESDAY 30

★ *MATCH on sale*

WEDNESDAY 31

Ⓑ **IAN WALKER** *born 1971, Watford, England*

THURSDAY 1

Ⓑ **MATT ELLIOTT** *born 1968, Wandsworth, England*

FRIDAY 2

Ⓑ **PAUL BUTLER** *born 1972, Manchester, England*

SATURDAY 3

NOVEMBER 1, 1986

Ⓑ **UGO EHIOGU** *born 1972, Hackney, England*   Ⓑ **DWIGHT YORKE** *born 1971, Canaan, Tobago*

SUNDAY 4

Ⓑ **LUIS FIGO** *born 1972, Lisbon, Portugal*   Ⓑ **MARIO MELCHIOT** *born 1976, Amsterdam, Holland*

SHARP SHOOTER
Who is Ian Harte's footballing uncle?

Last week's answer: NEIL COX

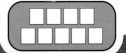

3 YEARS AGO

DID YOU KNOW?
West Ham's Stephen Bywater let in four goals on his debut – luckily The Hammers scored five!

THE FOOTBALL TIMES

29 OCTOBER – 4 NOVEMBER

2 YEARS AGO...
NOVEMBER 4, 1999: Leeds United beat Lokomotiv Moscow 7-1 on aggregate with a 3-0 away win in the UEFA Cup. A penalty from left-back Ian Harte and two strikes from Michael Bridges wrap up the tie as Leeds progress to the third round in style.

5 YEARS AGO...
OCTOBER 30, 1996: Man. United lose their 40-year unbeaten home record in Europe following a disappointing 1-0 defeat by Fenerbahce at Old Trafford.

6 YEARS AGO...
NOVEMBER 4, 1995: Juninho makes his debut for Middlesbrough in a 1-1 draw with Leeds United. It only takes the little Brazilian nine minutes to make an impact as he sets up Boro's goal with a superb 25-yard, defence-splitting pass to Fjortoft.

10 YEARS AGO...
NOVEMBER 4, 1991: Bryan Robson says he's decided to quit international football after being left out of Graham Taylor's latest England squad. Robbo's a great loss to the national team and it proves a hard task to replace the Man. United legend.

31 YEARS AGO...
NOVEMBER 1, 1970: In trying to clear a corner, England captain Bobby Moore hits a thunderous clearance from defence and accidentally knocks out the referee while playing for his club West Ham!

Pierre Van Hooijdonk ends strike and returns to Forest

PIERRE VAN HOOIJDONK ARRIVED AT THE CITY GROUND from Celtic with a big reputation and he continued his prolific form with Nottingham Forest, scoring 29 goals in Division One during their 1997-98 promotion season. The fans were jubilant at a return to the Premiership but Van Hooijdonk wasn't in the mood for celebrating. After being refused a transfer from the club he failed to turn up for pre-season training and announced he was on strike. Three months later, on October 30, 1998, he returned to the City Ground in a storm of controversy. The Dutchman scored six goals for Forest after his exile but was never forgiven by either the fans or the players and Forest were relegated in their first season back in the Premiership.

Top ten troublesome Premiership stars!

1	NICOLAS ANELKA	The sulky one has continued his excellent moaning form at Real Madrid!
2	STAN COLLYMORE	The king of football controversy is either on fire or extinguishing them!
3	PAOLO DI CANIO	Gives 100 per cent and always pushes himself, and others, to the limit!
4	PATRICK VIEIRA	Created the 'jumping spit' when sent-off against West Ham last season!
5	DENNIS WISE	Has calmed down, but still liable to snap at taxi drivers and the opposition!
6	MANNY OMOYIMNI	Forgot to tell Harry Redknapp he'd already played in the Worthington Cup!
7	ROBBIE FOWLER	The Liverpool centre-forward is fined almost every time he scores a goal.
8	GRAEME LE SAUX	Batters those who cross him, including Robbie Fowler and David Batty!
9	ERIC CANTONA	Outrageously jumped into the crowd to kung-fu kick a Crystal Palace fan!
10	SAVO MILOSEVIC	Well known in the Midlands for spitting at his own team while with Villa!

"MY RED CARD DAY!"
DAVID WEIR

DATE: October 30, 1999
GAME: Middlesbrough 2 Everton 1
SENT-OFF: 76 mins
OFFENCE(S): Professional foul
REFEREE: Andy Urso (Billericay)

Everton had a dream start when Campbell scored after just four minutes, but their luck soon ran out when Ziege equalised after 15 minutes and Deane added a second after the break. Their task was made even harder when Weir was then sent-off after 76 minutes. Middlesbrough striker Hamilton Ricard burst through the Toffees defence and Weir, the last Everton defender, brought him down, leaving the referee with no alternative.

★ *MATCH on sale*

Ⓑ **GARRY FLITCROFT** *born 1972, Bolton, England*

Ⓑ **JOE COLE** *born 1981, North London, England*

Ⓑ **GILLES GRIMANDI** *born 1970, Gap, France*

FOOTY ANAGRAM
This solid defender can now see the Light.

Last week's answer: GARY KELLY

S I R   C H A M K I N

THIS WEEK IN 1986...

15 YEARS AGO

Alex Ferguson becomes the new manager of Man. United

BY THE TIME MAN. UNITED SACKED RON ATKINSON THEY were desperate for someone who could lead the club back to winning ways. Atkinson could only win two FA Cups in his five-year spell from 1981-86 and this wasn't good enough for Man. United. Alex Ferguson had done a great job of transforming Aberdeen into a genuine power in Scotland, winning the club's first Premier League championship in 1978 and adding further titles in 1984 and 1985. Under Ferguson's astute management, Aberdeen won the European Cup-Winners' Cup, the European Super Cup and the Scottish Cup in 1983. The big clubs soon took an interest. Rangers offered him the top job at Ibrox, while Tottenham and Arsenal tried in vain to bring him to England. But there was only one job that could prise him away from Scotland and on November 6, 1986 Alex Ferguson was unveiled as the new manager of Man. United. The rebuilding process was slow, but after making some inspired signings and rejuvenating Old Trafford's youth system, Ferguson won his first trophy in 1990 by beating Crystal Palace in the FA Cup Final. And United haven't stopped winning trophies since!

Head to head – Fergie v Busby

Man. United's greatest ever managers are undoubtedly Matt Busby and Alex Ferguson. But in terms of trophies, who's the very best?

	FERGIE	BUSBY
League Championships	6	5
FA Cups	4	2
European Cups	1	1
Cup-Winners' Cups	1	0
Total	**12**	**8**

By major trophies won, it's got to be Fergie!

THE FOOTBALL TIMES

3 YEARS AGO...
THIS WEEK IN 1998: In their search for a new striker, Aston Villa state an interest in Blackburn Rovers forward Chris Sutton, who's rated at £10 million. But the transfer never goes through, which could explain why Villa have done so well recently!

7 YEARS AGO...
NOVEMBER 8, 1994: The Sun newspaper claims it has proof that goalkeeper Bruce Grobbelaar was paid to throw a number of matches in the early '90s. Many Liverpool fans disagree with the allegations, saying he just wasn't very good in the early '90s!

10 YEARS AGO...
THIS WEEK IN 1991: Blackburn manager Kenny Dalglish signs Manchester City defender Colin Hendry for £700,000, making one of the best signings of his career. Hendry was a defensive rock when Rovers won the Premier League in 1995.

17 YEARS AGO...
THIS WEEK IN 1984: England prepare to take on Turkey in a World Cup qualifier, pinning their hopes on AC Milan striker Mark Hateley! It's an inspired selection as Turkey are stuffed in an 8-0 mauling!

110 YEARS AGO...
NOVEMBER 7, 1891: At half-time in Glasgow, Rangers fans are introduced to the legendary Buffalo Bill. But the Wild West showman is greeted by shouts of 'Get your hair cut' from the Ibrox faithful!

HAPPY BIRTHDAY...
STEFFEN IVERSEN

BIRTHDATE: November 10, 1976
BIRTHPLACE: Trondheim, Norway
CLUB: Tottenham Hotspur
COUNTRY: Norway
PREVIOUS CLUBS: Rosenborg
HONOURS: 18 Norway caps

Dogged by injury since his £2.7 million move from Rosenborg in December 1996, Iversen still impresses with his skill and awareness. The popular striker finished joint top scorer with Chris Armstrong last season at White Hart Lane. Still only 25, he has a great future ahead of him for club and country, and he'll relish playing up front with new signing Sergei Rebrov.

★ *MATCH on sale*

Ⓑ **GUSTAVO POYET** *born 1967, Montevideo, Uruguay*

Ⓑ **PAUL SCHOLES** *born 1974, Salford, England*

Ⓑ **PETER SCHMEICHEL** *born 1963, Gladsaxe, Denmark*

THE EYES HAVE IT
Who is this resurgent England midfielder?

Last week's answer: CHRIS MAKIN

THIS WEEK IN 1999...

2 YEARS AGO

THE FOOTBALL TIMES

12 – 18 NOVEMBER

3 YEARS AGO...
NOVEMBER 12, 1998: At an emotional press conference, Roy Evans announces he is quitting Anfield after 34 years. After an unsuccessful period as joint-manager with Gerard Houllier, Evans leaves the Frenchman with full control of the team.

4 YEARS AGO...
NOVEMBER 18, 1997: Michael Owen scores his first ever hat-trick for Liverpool as The Reds beat Grimsby Town 3-0 in the fourth round of the League Cup at Anfield.

6 YEARS AGO...
THIS WEEK IN 1995: Norway boss Egil Olsen blames England managers past and present for the national side's decline. He responds to criticisms of his country's tactics by saying: "If England played this style they would be world champions!"

51 YEARS AGO...
NOVEMBER 15, 1950: Leslie Compton becomes the oldest player ever to make his England international debut when he plays against Wales at Roker Park at the ripe old age of 38 years and two months.

67 YEARS AGO...
NOVEMBER 14, 1934: Arsenal have seven players in the England side for the international against Italy, the record number of players to play from one club. The friendly was played at Highbury – not a ploy to get more bums on seats, then?

England and Scotland battle it out for a place in Euro 2000

IT WAS BILLED AS THE BATTLE OF BRITAIN AS SOON AS IT was revealed that England would face Scotland in a play-off to see who would progress to Euro 2000. The fans were delighted that the Auld Enemies would meet up again after both teams had failed to qualify automatically for the finals in Holland and Belgium. But things didn't go to plan for either side. In the first match at Hampden Park on November 13, 1999 a brace of goals from Paul Scholes meant Kevin Keegan's side had the advantage, but Scotland tore up the script when they came to Wembley four days later. Don Hutchison scored for Craig Brown's team and they were unfortunate not to win more convincingly as England gave a jaded performance that didn't suggest they would make much of an impression at Euro 2000. The Three Lions were through, but they'd been tamed in the process.

The biggest Auld Enemy wins in history!
There's no bigger match than when England and Scotland meet. MATCH looks at the biggest wins in the history of the oldest international fixture in the world.

BIGGEST ENGLAND WINS	BIGGEST SCOTLAND WINS
England 9 Scotland 3 (Wembley, 1963)	Scotland 7 England 2 (Glasgow, 1878)
Scotland 0 England 5 (Glasgow, 1973)	England 1 Scotland 6 (Kennington Oval, 1881)
Scotland 0 England 5 (Glasgow, 1888)	Scotland 5 England 1 (Glasgow, 1882)
England 5 Scotland 1 (Wembley, 1975)	England 1 Scotland 5 (Wembley, 1928)
Scotland 0 England 4 (Glasgow, 1958)	Scotland 4 England 1 (Glasgow, 1900)

"MY CLUB DEBUT!"
ALAN SMITH

LEEDS DEBUT: November 14, 1998
GAME: Liverpool 1 Leeds United 3
ATTENDANCE: 44,305
MATCHFACTS RATING: N/A

Making your debut at Anfield would be a dream for any player, but young Leeds striker Alan Smith went one better, scoring just two minutes after replacing Clive Wijnhard with his very first touch of the game! Receiving the ball on the edge of the area he smashed the ball into the top right-hand corner. Strike partner Jimmy Floyd Hasselbaink scored two further goals in the last ten minutes for a dramatic win in Gerard Houllier's first game in sole charge of Liverpool.

MONDAY
19

TUESDAY
20

★ *MATCH on sale*

WEDNESDAY
21

THURSDAY
22

Ⓑ **RUSSEL HOULT** *born 1972, Ashby de la Zouch, England*

FRIDAY
23

Ⓑ **ALF-INGE HAALAND** *born 1972, Stavanger, Norway*

SATURDAY
24

SUNDAY
25

Ⓑ **ALAN MOORE** *born 1974, Dublin, Republic of Ireland*

CODE BREAKER
**Can you crack the secret code to
name this Premiership star?**

Last week's answer: NICK BARMBY

10	2	15			A	

| 21 | 2 | 26 | 13 | 16 | 19 | T | | | | | |

THIS WEEK IN 1998...

3 YEARS AGO

THE FOOTBALL TIMES

6 YEARS AGO...
NOVEMBER 22, 1995: Blackburn lose 3-0 to Spartak Moscow in the Champions League. Graeme Le Saux and David Batty have a fight, Tim Sherwood and Colin Hendry exchange words and Hendry is sent-off. Not a good dressing room then!

8 YEARS AGO...
NOVEMBER 23, 1993: Graham Taylor resigns as the manager of England, seven days after failing to qualify for the 1994 World Cup. Lawrie McMenemy also leaves his post as Taylor's assistant just a week after the 7-1 victory against San Marino.

10 YEARS AGO...
NOVEMBER 20, 1991: Gary Lineker signs a lucrative deal to play for Japanese club Grampus Eight, meaning he'll bid a fond farewell to Spurs at the end of the season.

Man. United draw 3-3 with Barcelona in epic Euro battle

IN GROUP D OF THE CHAMPIONS LEAGUE, BARCELONA needed to beat Man. United at the Nou Camp on November 25, 1998 to stand a chance of qualifying for the next round of the competition. Man. United also needed a result to help them qualify as the group's winners. The scene was set for a classic encounter and neither side disappointed. Sonny Anderson struck first for Barca, driving his shot past Peter Schmeichel in the first minute, but this brought out the best in Man. United. Yorke equalised from outside the area after 25 minutes and the goal boosted United's confidence in the imposing stadium. After the break, there was a truly breathtaking move – Yorke stepped over a pass to Cole, who played a neat one-two with his strike partner and found the net in style to make it 2-1. Rivaldo, who was a class apart throughout, scored from a free-kick to equalise, but Yorke headed in a trademark Beckham cross to put United 3-2 up. It was fitting that Rivaldo scored the last goal of the game, though, chesting down a pass and scoring with a spectacular overhead kick.

19 YEARS AGO...
NOVEMBER 25, 1982: Tony Philliskirk scores five in Peterborough's 9-1 thrashing of non-league Kingstonian in the FA Cup. But the match is ordered to be replayed as the Kingstonian 'keeper is hit by an object from the crowd. The replay, behind closed doors, ends in a 3-0 win for The Posh.

32 YEARS AGO...
NOVEMBER 20, 1969: The legendary Pelé scores his 1,000th top-flight goal as he converts a penalty for Santos in their 2-1 win over Brazilian rivals Vasco da Gama.

Man. United's ten best European Cup wins

1.	MAR 2000	Group Stage **Man. United 3 Fiorentina 1** *Cole, Keane, Yorke*
2.	APR 1999	Semi-Final **Juventus 2 Man. United 3** *Keane, Yorke, Cole*
3.	MAY 1999	Final **Man. United 2 Bayern Munich 1** *Sheringham, Solskjaer*
4.	MAR 1999	Quarter-Final **Man. United 2 Inter Milan 0** *Yorke 2*
5.	MAR 1997	Quarter-Final **Man. United 4 Porto 0** *May, Cantona, Cole, Giggs*
6.	OCT 1997	Group Stage **Man. United 3 Juventus 2** *Sheringham, Scholes, Giggs*
7.	MAY 1969	Semi-Final **AC Milan 0 Man. United 1** *B Charlton*
8.	MAY 1968	Final **Benfica 1 Man. United 4** *Best, Kidd, B Charlton 2*
9.	MAR 1966	Second Round **Benfica 1 Man. United 5** *Crerand, Best 2, B Charlton, Connelly*
10.	MAY 1958	Semi-Final **Man. United 2 AC Milan 1** *Taylor, Viollet*

"MY RED CARD DAY!"
CLAUS LUNDEKVAM

DATE: November 20, 1999
GAME: Southampton 0 Tottenham 1
SENT-OFF: 90 mins
OFFENCE(s): Two bookable offences
REFEREE: Steven Bennett (Orpington)

Claus Lundekvam was dismissed for two bookable offences in the 32nd and 90th minute. It had been a closely-fought contest with referee Steven Bennett issuing eight cards in all. Oyvind Leonhardsen had given Spurs an 81st minute lead but any hopes that The Saints had of salvaging a point disappeared in injury-time when Lundekvam was given his marching orders.

★ *MATCH on sale*   Ⓑ **KASEY KELLER** *born 1969, Washington, USA*

Ⓑ **RYAN GIGGS** *born 1973, Cardiff, Wales*

Ⓑ **DAVID BATTY** *born 1968, Leeds, England*

SHARP SHOOTER
What is the name of Barcelona's famous ground?

Last week's answer: IAN TAYLOR

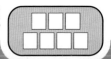

9 YEARS AGO

Eric Cantona leaves Leeds to join Ferguson's Man. United

IF ERIC CANTONA WAS SUCH A BIG FACTOR IN TURNING around Man. United's fortunes, their fans should thank the former manager of Leeds United. It was Howard Wilkinson who spotted the Frenchman in Nimes and brought him to play in the new English Premier League. Cantona was an instant success at Elland Road, scoring nine goals in 18 games and guiding Leeds to the Premiership title in 1992. Alex Ferguson noted how influential Cantona had been for Leeds as they pipped his team to the title, and he didn't want it to happen again, so he acted decisively and signed the Frenchman on November 26, 1992. Leeds fans were in uproar, especially as the fee was only £1.2 million. Now with Man. United, Cantona's creativity and masterful control gave Ferguson's team a new range of attacking options. His triumphant spell brought four Premiership titles and two FA Cups, including two doubles in 1994 and 1996. But it also had some bizarre moments, none more unbelievable than his karate-kick at a Crystal Palace fan. He even attempted philosophy when he said: "When seagulls follow ze trawler zey fink zat zey might find sardines." Or something like that – he did become detached from reality a few times! After retiring from football in 1997, Cantona turned to painting and acting in French movies – it just doesn't seem right somehow!

MATCH's five **favourite French fliers!**

1	DAVID GINOLA	Great at footy and all the girls love him. Some people have all the luck!
2	EMMANUEL PETIT	Slightly poncey, but did score the winner in the 1998 World Cup Final.
3	ERIC CANTONA	He can't act or control himself, but he's still superb on the footy pitch!
4	PATRICK VIEIRA	Classy midfielder who'll always give 110 per cent for his team-mates.
5	DIDIER DESCHAMPS	Didi may be past his best, but he's won absolutely everything in footy!

THE FOOTBALL TIMES

2 YEARS AGO...
THIS WEEK IN 1999: Chelsea's Italian midfielder Roberto di Matteo denies he is on his way to Celtic in a £4 million move. He couldn't leave Stamford Bridge anyway – what would he do with his restaurant in London if he left The Blues for Scotland?

6 YEARS AGO...
THIS WEEK IN 1995: The brother of the Sultan of Brunei (one of the richest men in the world) asks the Newcastle United team and boss Kevin Keegan to fly out to the Middle East to put his footy team in order!

11 YEARS AGO...
THIS WEEK IN 1990: The Gazza board game hits the shops just in time for the Christmas rush, but it's not a big success. Most of the unlucky people who buy it take it literally and just get bored! You have to give Gascoigne marks for effort, though.

29 YEARS AGO...
NOVEMBER 29, 1972: George Best fails to turn up for training with Man. United for an entire week. The troubled star, caught between playing and partying, is dropped from the team and rumours persist that he wants a transfer away from Old Trafford.

56 YEARS AGO...
THIS WEEK IN 1945: Dynamo Moscow are caught out during their tour of Britain when they field 12 men in a match against Rangers. The Russians had already been caught once before on the very same tour. So that's where Tranmere got the idea!

FIRST HAMMERS GOAL

JOE COLE

DATE: November 30, 1999
GAME: Birmingham 2 West Ham 3
ATTENDANCE: 17,728
MATCHFACTS RATING: 7/10

Joe Cole came on as a substitute for West Ham after 52 minutes of this Worthington Cup Fourth Round tie with The Hammers trailing 2-1. Another sub, Paul Kitson, pulled a goal back after 86 minutes to set up a dramatic finale. Then, with only a few seconds left, Cole popped up at the far post to side-foot the ball home from Paolo Di Canio's right-wing cross and win the game 3-2.

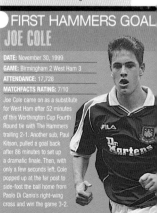

MATCH 3 - 9 DECEMBER

 MONDAY 3

 TUESDAY 4

 WEDNESDAY 5

 THURSDAY 6

 FRIDAY 7

 SATURDAY 8

SUNDAY 9

B **CHRISTIAN KAREMBEU** *born 1970, New Caledonia, South Pacific*   **B** **FRANK SINCLAIR** *born 1971, Lambeth, England*

★ *MATCH on sale*

B **CARLTON PALMER** *born 1965, West Bromwich, England*

B **COLIN HENDRY** *born 1965, Keith, Scotland*

B **STEPHEN McPHAIL** *born 1979, London, England*

FOOTY ANAGRAM
This top striker is an England legend.

Last week's answer: NOU CAMP

E R   N A S A L   H A R E

THIS WEEK IN 1998...

3 YEARS AGO

Villa new-boy Dublin bags Player Of The Month award

DION DUBLIN MADE A FANTASTIC START TO HIS ASTON Villa career after signing from Coventry City for £5.75 million. The striker revelled in his change of surroundings and hit seven goals in his first four games for Aston Villa, including a first-half brace on his debut against Tottenham and a hat-trick at Southampton. Dublin was rewarded for his stunning form on December 4, 1998 when he was named November's Carling Player of the Month. He had scored four goals for Coventry City before moving to Villa Park in November 1998 and added 11 more in the claret and blue of Villa to end the season on 15 goals. "You have a certain confidence if you've made the start that I have," he told MATCH shortly after signing. "I joined Aston Villa because it was the right move for me. There's a great set of lads here and a united spirit geared towards success." It certainly seemed like it at the time! Dublin suffered a career-threatening broken neck injury midway through last season but made a miraculous recovery to play against Bolton Wanderers in the semi-finals of the FA Cup and scored the winning spot-kick in the penalty shoot-out. He also finished the season as Villa's leading scorer with 13 Premiership goals – top man!

And the winner is...
the Premiership's award winners last season

MONTH	PLAYER	MANAGER
AUGUST	ROBBIE KEANE (Coventry City)	ALEX FERGUSON (Man. United)
SEPTEMBER	MUZZY IZZET (Leicester City)	WALTER SMITH (Everton)
OCTOBER	KEVIN PHILLIPS (Sunderland)	PETER REID (Sunderland)
NOVEMBER	SAMI HYYPIA (Liverpool)	MARTIN O'NEILL (Leicester City)
DECEMBER	ROY KEANE (Man United)	GERARD HOULLIER (Liverpool)
JANUARY	GARETH SOUTHGATE (Aston Villa)	DANNY WILSON (Sheffield Wednesday)
FEBRUARY	PAUL MERSON (Aston Villa)	BOBBY ROBSON (Newcastle United)
MARCH	DWIGHT YORKE (Man. United)	ALEX FERGUSON (Man. United)
APRIL	THIERRY HENRY (Arsenal)	ALEX FERGUSON (Man. United)

THE FOOTBALL TIMES

2 YEARS AGO...
DECEMBER 4, 1999: The Premiership goes goal-crazy, with Sunderland stuffing Chelsea 4-1 thanks to two goals apiece from 'Super' Kevin Phillips and Niall Quinn. On the same day, Man. United smash five goals past Everton at Old Trafford.

3 YEARS AGO...
DECEMBER 3, 1998: Brian Kidd leaves Man. United to become the manager of Blackburn. But after a promising start, the dream turns sour, Rovers are relegated and Kidd finds himself out of a job less than one year after taking on the role.

4 YEARS AGO...
DECEMBER 6, 1997: Spurs and Chelsea go in 1-1 at half-time, but Chelsea run riot in the second half to record a 6-1 win with Norwegian striker Tore Andre Flo bagging a hat-trick. New Spurs boss Christian Gross says he's still 'assessing' his new charges.

11 YEARS AGO...
DECEMBER 9, 1990: Bologna's Giuseppe Lorenzo sets a new world record when he is sent-off after only ten seconds of his side's crucial Serie A match with Parma.

70 YEARS AGO...
DECEMBER 5, 1931: Eddie Parris becomes the first British black player to be capped at international level when he plays for Wales against Northern Ireland. Nottingham Forest's Viv Anderson becomes England's first black player 46 years later.

HAPPY BIRTHDAY...
STEPHEN McPHAIL

BIRTHDATE: December 9, 1979
BIRTHPLACE: London, England
CLUB: Leeds United
COUNTRY: Republic of Ireland
PREVIOUS CLUBS: None
HONOURS: Three Republic of Ireland caps.

Another to come off the youth conveyor belt and into the first team at Leeds, McPhail was thrown in at the deep end when David O'Leary took over. The Irishman has a cultured left foot, superb vision and a promising future in the game. He has already made his international debut for the Republic of Ireland – against Scotland in May 2000.

14

MONDAY
10

TUESDAY
11

★ *MATCH on sale*

WEDNESDAY
12

B **GARY BREEN** *born 1973, London, England*   B **NOLBERTO SOLANO** *born 1974, Callao, Peru*

THURSDAY
13

FRIDAY
14

B **MICHAEL OWEN** *born 1979, Chester, England*

SATURDAY
15

DECEMBER 11, 1982

SUNDAY
16

B **DENNIS WISE** *born 1966, Kensington, England*

THE EYES HAVE IT
Who is this shampoo-loving wing genius?

Last week's answer: ALAN SHEARER

4 YEARS AGO

THE FOOTBALL TIMES

10-16 DECEMBER

6 YEARS AGO...
DECEMBER 13, 1995: Patrick Kluivert scores two goals for Holland against the Republic of Ireland in a Euro Championship play-off at Anfield. Their 2-0 win means the Republic don't qualify for Euro '96.

6 YEARS AGO...
DECEMBER 15, 1995: The European Court of Justice rules that clubs cannot buy and sell players once their contracts have expired. Called the 'Bosman Ruling', it means players like Steve McManaman can leave their clubs on a free transfer.

14 YEARS AGO...
DECEMBER 14, 1987: QPR defender Mark Dennis is sent off for the 11th time in his career. 'Mad Mark', as he is known, received 64 cautions in ten years. And all before referees started going card-happy!

65 YEARS AGO...
DECEMBER 12, 1936: At Elland Road, Wolves lose centre-back Stan Cullis with a broken collar bone and have 'keeper Alex Scott sent-off. Luckily, the match is abandoned because of fog and Wolves, with 11 players, win the replayed game.

109 YEARS AGO...
DECEMBER 10, 1892: Sheffield United beat Port Vale 10-0, the first double-figure away result in English football. The Port Vale 'keeper puts the score down to losing his glasses in the mud – is that the most feeble excuse in football history or what?

Ronaldo wins the World Player Of The Year award – again!

BRAZIL STRIKER RONALDO MADE HISTORY IN 1997 BY becoming the first player to retain FIFA's World Player Of The Year award. He won the same honour in 1996, beating George Weah and Alan Shearer to the most prestigious individual accolade in football. Ronaldo – real name Ronaldo Luiz Nazario da Lima – has certainly deserved his two World Player Of The Year awards. He shot to fame at PSV Eindhoven, ending the 1996 season as Holland's top scorer before winning the Spanish Super Cup with new club Barcelona. Ronaldo then won the Cup-Winners' Cup with Barca in 1997 and was also named European Player of the Year and Latin American Player of the Year in the Spanish League. At last season's glamorous awards ceremony, Barcelona's playmaker Rivaldo scooped the award ahead of Man. United's David Beckham and Fiorentina's Gabriel Batistuta.

Winners of FIFA's **World Player Of The Year** award – the complete list from 1991-1999

1991	**1st** Lothar Matthaus (Germany) **2nd** Jean-Pierre Papin (France) **3rd** Gary Lineker (England)
1992	**1st** Marco Van Basten (Holland) **2nd** Hristo Stoitchkov (Bulgaria) **3rd** Thomas Hassler (Germany)
1993	**1st** Roberto Baggio (Italy) **2nd** Romario (Brazil) **3rd** Dennis Bergkamp (Holland)
1994	**1st Romario** (Brazil) **2nd** Hristo Stoitchkov (Bulgaria) **3rd** Roberto Baggio (Italy)
1995	**1st** George Weah (Liberia) **2nd** Paolo Maldini (Italy) **3rd** Jurgen Klinsmann (Germany)
1996	**1st Ronaldo** (Brazil) **2nd** George Weah (Liberia) **3rd** Alan Shearer (England)
1997	**1st Ronaldo** (Brazil) **2nd** Roberto Carlos (Brazil) **3rd** Dennis Bergkamp (Holland) & Zinedine Zidane (France)
1998	**1st** Zinedine Zidane (France) **2nd** Ronaldo (Brazil) **3rd** Davor Suker (Croatia)
1999	**1st** Rivaldo (Brazil) **2nd** David Beckham (England) **3rd** Gabriel Batistuta (Argentina)

"MY FIRST CAP!"
GARETH SOUTHGATE

ENGLAND DEBUT: December 12, 1995
GAME: England 1 Portugal 1
ATTENDANCE: 28,592
MATCHFACTS RATING: N/A

Southgate earned his international debut for England with some fine performances at the heart of Aston Villa's impressive five-man defence. But he had to wait for 80 minutes until he finally got his chance, Terry Venables putting him on for Dennis Wise. It was Southgate's Villa team-mate Steve Stone that gave England the lead just before half-time with a low 20-yard drive from Les Ferdinand's chest down. But Portugal proved difficult opponents and scored after 59 minutes to make it 1-1.

MATCH 17 - 23 DECEMBER

MONDAY 17

TUESDAY 18

★ *MATCH Christmas issue* on sale

🅱 **LES FERDINAND** *born 1966, Acton, England*

WEDNESDAY 19

THURSDAY 20

🅱 **ED DE GOEY** *born 1966, Gouda, Holland*

FRIDAY 21

SATURDAY 22

🅱 **JODY MORRIS** *born 1978, Hamersmith, England*

SUNDAY 23

CODE BREAKER
**Can you crack the secret code to
name this Premiership star?**

Last week's answer: DAVID GINOLA

| 20 | 21 | 6 | 23 | 6 | | | T | | |
| 20 | 21 | 16 | 15 | 6 | | | | N | |

THIS WEEK IN 1997...

4 YEARS AGO

THE FOOTBALL TIMES

2 YEARS AGO...

THIS WEEK IN 1999: After months of speculation, Roy Keane signs a lucrative £50,000 a week deal with Man. United, reports MATCH. He immediately starts to repay the club by grabbing the opening goal in the next game against Valencia.

4 YEARS AGO...

THIS WEEK IN 1997: Coventry manager Gordon Strachan says he wants some new signings before Christmas, reports MATCH. "We're stuck in a rut and we need new players." Nothing new there then, Gordon!

16 YEARS AGO...

DECEMBER 21, 1985: Weird things are happening at Anfield. The linesman for Liverpool's game against Newcastle is called Mr. Everton, but he still awards some decisions in Liverpool's favour. Surely that shouldn't have happened!

18 YEARS AGO...

THIS WEEK IN 1983: Coventry City striker Terry Gibson is thrown out of his home for scoring a goal! Gibson netted past his landlord and Luton goalkeeper Les Sealey, who isn't too happy about conceding the goal and asks Gibson to leave his house!

45 YEARS AGO...

DECEMBER 22, 1956: West Bromwich Albion turn up two hours late for a league game, blaming fog for their slow journey. But none of them get to play anyway – the home team and the crowd had already left the stadium after getting bored waiting!

Goalkeeper Shilton notches up a total of 1,000 appearances

PETER SHILTON RIVALS THE LEGENDARY GORDON BANKS as the greatest 'keeper England has ever produced. Even at the age of 41, he was still playing at international level, his superb fitness and reflexes helping England to the 1990 World Cup semi-final against West Germany. That was his 125th and last cap, which was a new world record at the time. On December 22, 1997 he passed another amazing milestone to make his 1,000th appearance in the Football League. It came in the unglamorous surroundings of Brisbane Road, home of Third Division Leyton Orient. But Orient put on a great tribute for their 'keeper, with a fanfare leading him out onto the pitch and a red carpet to show him the way. Perhaps the most telling accolade was provided by Shilton himself – a clean sheet in the 2-0 win over Brighton. Shilton started his career at Leicester City and had spells with Stoke City, Nottingham Forest, Southampton, Derby County, Plymouth Argyle (where he was player-manager), Wimbledon, Bolton Wanderers and Coventry City. He's now having a well deserved rest!

Crazy **Shilts facts!**

Shilts used to spend hours at home hanging by his arms to make them longer, but it didn't work!

He played in a record 17 World Cup Finals games, despite missing the 1974 and 1978 tournaments!

Shilts learned his footballing trade under another England legend between the sticks, Gordon Banks!

He shared the England number one position with the outstanding Liverpool 'keeper Ray Clemence, meaning he could have collected even more international caps if he'd played in every game!

Shilts had such a tight bubble perm in the '80s, strikers were often laughing too much to score!

"MY RED CARD DAY!"
CHRIS ARMSTRONG

DATE: December 19, 1998
GAME: Chelsea 2 Tottenham Hotspur 0
SENT-OFF: 61 mins
REFEREE: Graham Poll (Tring)

Booked after 43 minutes for unsporting behaviour, Armstrong received his marching orders after the break for a second bookable offence. Les Ferdinand and Steve Carr joined him in the book for dissent, while Duberry, Babayaro and Vialli were cautioned for the home team. Tottenham hadn't beaten Chelsea since April 1987 and it never really looked like changing. Armstrong's dismissal gave Chelsea control and the win sent The Blues to the top of the Premiership.

MONDAY 24

○ CHRISTMAS EVE

TUESDAY 25

○ CHRISTMAS DAY

Ⓑ **GARY McALLISTER** born 1964, Motherwell, Scotland

WEDNESDAY 26

○ BOXING DAY IN UK
○ ST STEPHEN'S DAY IN REPUBLIC OF IRELAND

THURSDAY 27

Ⓑ **DUNCAN FERGUSON** born 1971, Stirling, Scotland

FRIDAY 28

SATURDAY 29

Ⓑ **KIERON DYER** born 1978, Ipswich, England

SUNDAY 30

Ⓑ **NOEL WHELAN** born 1974, Leeds, England

SHARP SHOOTER
Who came second at the 1999 World Player of the Year Awards?

Last week's answer: STEVE STONE

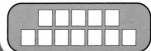

THIS WEEK IN 1998...

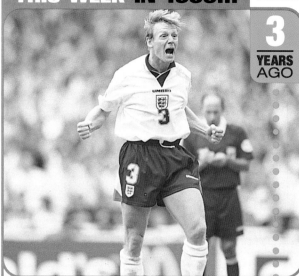

3 YEARS AGO

THE FOOTBALL TIMES

6 YEARS AGO...
DECEMBER 30, 1995: During a 7-0 win against Hibs, Gazza finds the referee's yellow card and shows it to him, as if to book the official! The ref, however, doesn't see the funny side, and decides to book the cheeky Geordie midfielder instead.

7 YEARS AGO...
DECEMBER 26, 1994: The Premiership is an away-day celebration, with none of the 11 matches ending in a win for the home side. Man. United must have been away!

22 YEARS AGO...
DECEMBER 26, 1979: A record crowd for a Third Division game – 43,309 – sees Sheffield Wednesday beat their Yorkshire rivals Sheffield United 4-0 at Hillsborough.

44 YEARS AGO...
DECEMBER 25, 1957: Football League games are played in England on Christmas Day for the last time ever, and to celebrate the fact, Chelsea debutant Jimmy Greaves scores four as The Blues beat Portsmouth 7-4. So when did they get to open all their Christmas pressies from Santa then?

52 YEARS AGO...
DECEMBER 27, 1949: The record single day attendance for Football League games is recorded in England on this day in 1949, when a total of 1,269,934 people travel to see matches in all four divisions.

'Psycho' Pearce given MBE in New Year's Honours list

STUART PEARCE WAS AWARDED AN MBE IN THE QUEEN'S New Year Honours on December 30, 1998. It was a wonderful tribute to the England left-back, whose 77 appearances for his country were full of highs and lows. The low point was his penalty miss in the 1990 World Cup semi-final shoot-out against West Germany. But England fans will always remember his stirring reaction at Wembley after he held his nerve to score from the spot six years later in Euro '96 during the quarter-final shoot-out with Spain. His clenched-fist celebration typified the way he played for both his country and his club sides. Pearce received his MBE after moving from Nottingham Forest, where he had played for 11 years, to Newcastle. He earned a recall to the England squad last season after his transfer to West Ham, but cruelly broke his leg twice to end his hopes of playing in Euro 2000.

Ten British players honoured by the Queen

PLAYER	HONOUR	REASON FOR THE QUEEN'S AWARD
STANLEY MATTHEWS	Knighted, 1965	England legend who played top-flight footy past his 50th birthday for his home-town club Stoke.
ALF RAMSEY	Knighted, 1967	Manager of England's World Cup side of 1966.
BOBBY MOORE	Awarded OBE, 1967	Captained England's winning side in 1966 and received the World Cup trophy from the Queen.
MATT BUSBY	Knighted, 1968	Created the Man. United side that became the first English team to win the European Cup.
TOM FINNEY	Knighted, 1997	Legendary England and Preston centre-forward.
MARK HUGHES	Awarded MBE, 1997	Honoured for his long and distinguished career as a top striker for club and country (Wales).
GEOFF HURST	Knighted, 1998	The hat-trick hero of England's 1966 glory.
STUART PEARCE	Awarded MBE, 1998	Hero and footballing icon for club and country.
ALEX FERGUSON	Knighted, 1999	Took Man. United to unprecedented treble of league, FA Cup and European Cup in 1999.
IAN WRIGHT	Awarded MBE, 1999	Beat Arsenal's goalscoring record of 178 goals.

"MY CLUB DEBUT!"
FRANCIS JEFFERS

EVERTON DEBUT: December 26, 1997
GAME: Man. United 2 Everton 0
ATTENDANCE: 55,167
MATCHFACTS RATING: 6/10

As far as daunting debuts go, Francis Jeffers couldn't have asked for a bigger stage to make his first appearance for The Toffees. Coming on as a second-half substitute at Old Trafford for veteran Dave Watson, Jeffers couldn't prevent Everton, who were already 2-0 down from the first half, from defeat against the rampant Red Devils.

MATCH 31 DECEMBER - 6 JANUARY

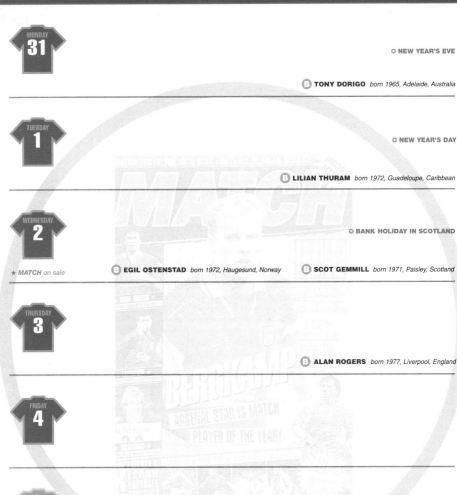

MONDAY 31

○ NEW YEAR'S EVE

Ⓑ **TONY DORIGO** *born 1965, Adelaide, Australia*

TUESDAY 1

○ NEW YEAR'S DAY

Ⓑ **LILIAN THURAM** *born 1972, Guadeloupe, Caribbean*

WEDNESDAY 2

○ BANK HOLIDAY IN SCOTLAND

★ MATCH *on sale*   Ⓑ **EGIL OSTENSTAD** *born 1972, Haugesund, Norway*   Ⓑ **SCOT GEMMILL** *born 1971, Paisley, Scotland*

THURSDAY 3

Ⓑ **ALAN ROGERS** *born 1977, Liverpool, England*

FRIDAY 4

SATURDAY 5

JANUARY 3, 1998

SUNDAY 6

FOOTY ANAGRAM
**This Moroccan superstar scores
bags of goals from midfield.**

Last week's answer: DAVID BECKHAM

A L L   H A N K   A S S   O U C H

2 YEARS AGO

Beckham named MATCH's Undisputed Player of the Year

WHEN MATCH ASKED READERS TO VOTE FOR THEIR BEST player of 1999, the response was incredible. Players from every team in the Premiership were nominated for the award, but Man. United's David Beckham emerged as the winner with 35 per cent of the votes, just beating Arsenal's Nwankwo Kanu into second place. The top five also included Roy Keane, Jaap Stam and David Ginola, but it was Beckham who succeeded 1998 winner Michael Owen as MATCH's new Undisputed Player of the Year. The England star had a fantastic season after his personal disaster at the 1998 World Cup in France. He helped United to their historic treble of Premiership, FA Cup and Champions League titles and came second at both the European and World Footballer of the Year awards. He married Victoria Adams and witnessed the birth of his first child, Brooklyn, to cap a fantastic year.

MATCH Readers' Poll results 1999
So who came top in all the other categories?

BEST NEW IMPORT: Davor Suker	BARGAIN OF THE YEAR: Davor Suker
BEST GOAL OF THE YEAR: Ryan Giggs	BEST NATIONWIDE PLAYER: Ade Akinbiyi (Wolves)
TOP BABE: Britney Spears	BEST MUSICAL ACT: Will Smith
BEST TV PUNDIT: Alan Hansen	FLASHEST KIT: Spurs Away
MOST UNDER-RATED PLAYER: Stephen Carr	BEST INTERNATIONAL PLAYER: Rivaldo
BEST YOUNG GUN: Robbie Keane	MOST EXCITING GAME: Man. United 2 Arsenal 1
MANAGER OF THE YEAR: Sir Alex Ferguson	UNDERACHIEVER OF THE YEAR: Mark Bosnich
HOTHEAD OF THE YEAR: Patrick Vieira	LOSER OF THE YEAR: Nicolas Anelka
BEST STADIUM: Nou Camp	SAVIOUR OF THE YEAR: Sweden
GOLDEN OLDIE: Tony Cottee	

THE FOOTBALL TIMES

31 DECEMBER - 6 JANUARY

3 YEARS AGO...
DECEMBER 31, 1998: Nicola Berti leaves Tottenham after a disappointing spell in England. The former Inter Milan player failed to settle at Tottenham and left for Spanish side Alaves after only 11 months.

4 YEARS AGO...
JANUARY 1, 1998: In an unprecedented move, referee Paul Danson is taken off the FA Cup Third Round tie between Lincoln and Southampton at the request of both clubs. He must have been really bad!

5 YEARS AGO...
JANUARY 6, 1997: Former Leeds United manager Howard Wilkinson is appointed as the FA's first ever technical director on a four-year contract. The position, covering a wide range of coaching issues, aims to improve the standard of football from the grass roots right up to the England squad.

6 YEARS AGO...
DECEMBER 31, 1995: QPR beat Arsenal 3-1 at Highbury. Goals from Gallen, Allen and Impey secure QPR's first league win at Highbury in 11 attempts. It looks like it'll be a while before they do it again, though!

70 YEARS AGO...
JANUARY 2, 1932: Aston Villa fans are in party mood after their 8-3 victory against Leicester City. Villa striker George Brown scores five, equalling the record for the most number of goals scored in one game.

HAPPY BIRTHDAY... LILIAN THURAM

BIRTHDATE: January 1, 1972
BIRTHPLACE: Guadeloupe, Caribbean
CLUB: Parma
COUNTRY: France
PREVIOUS CLUBS: AS Monaco
HONOURS: Italian Cup (1999), UEFA Cup (1999) World Cup winner (1998), European Championship winner (2000), 62 France caps.

After making his international debut in 1994, Thuram has become one of the most coveted defenders in the world. His formidable displays at World Cup '98 and Euro 2000 were vital in France becoming the first ever World Cup holders to win the European Championship.

The 2002 World Cup

Our teams will have their work cut out to qualify for the 2002 World Cup in Japan and North Korea, but the reward is a place at the greatest football show on earth. MATCH looks at the hopes and dreams that have been fulfilled and shattered since the famous competition began in 1930.

England's group is drawn for the 2002 World Cup qualification campaign.

THE WORLD CUP IS THE GREATEST COMPETITION IN THE history of football and a glorious showcase for the best teams and the greatest players in the world. It's no wonder that all our sides will be giving their all to qualify for the 2002 World Cup in Japan and North Korea.

Scotland, Wales, Northern Ireland and the Republic of Ireland kick-off their qualifying campaign on September 2, 2000. England play their first match against Germany a month later on October 7, just four months after beating their arch-rivals at Euro 2000.

Michael Owen was among the heroes of the last World Cup in France '98, while David Beckham was one of the villains. Brazil star Ronaldo played despite being injured before the final, continuing the controversy that is never far away from the famous tournament. There will be the usual heartbreak for those that lose at the final hurdle, but others will join the small group of great players who have won the World Cup in the past, including Bobby Moore (England 1966), Pelé (Brazil 1958, 1962, 1970) and Zinedine Zidane (France 1998).

The 2002 World Cup, jointly hosted by Japan and South Korea, will be the biggest tournament ever, with 198 nations contesting the 32 places on offer. This is a massive leap from the 13 countries that competed for the first World Cup in 1930, which was held in Uruguay and won by the hosts in their centenary year. FIFA endorsed the World Cup in 1929 after Frenchmen Henri Delaunay and Jules Rimet proposed that football needed a bigger stage than the Olympic Games. The World Cup trophy was named after Jules Rimet, who was president of FIFA from 1920 to 1954.

Our teams did not enter the first World Cup because of an argument with FIFA about player payments and the six-week boat journey to Uruguay and back. Only Belgium, France, Romania and Yugoslavia represented Europe at the finals. It was a blow for the organisers when they learned that the best team in the world at the time, England, would not be taking part.

The competition has grown and developed in many ways since then, but not every new rule has been adopted. For the 1970 World Cup in Mexico, it was decided that the quarter-final

France are the current holders of the World Cup.

and semi-final matches would be settled by the toss of a coin if the games ended in a draw after extra-time! Fortunately, all the matches produced a clear winner and the idea was abandoned.

The biggest change has been an increase in the number of finalists. In 1982 the number of qualifying teams rose from 16 to 24, and there will be 32 nations at the 2002 finals. So the tournament is bigger than ever, meaning more teams can qualify, and this is how it works. FIFA is made up of six confederations which combine to provide the 32 qualifying teams – 14 from Europe (UEFA), four from South America (CONMEBOL), three from North/Central America and the Caribbean (CONCACAF), five from Africa (CAF) and two from Asia (AFC). One further place is decided by an Oceania (OFC) versus South America play-off. Japan and South Korea qualify automatically as hosts and France are guaranteed a place after winning the last World Cup.

The European places are decided by nine groups, which our teams need to win to be assured automatic qualification. If any of our teams come second in the group, they can still progress to the World Cup, but they'll have to win a play-off match against the runner-up of another group.

The competition will be tough as always, and though we love to see the underdogs do well, some teams have an excellent pedigree in the competition. Brazil have lifted the World Cup a formidable four times (1958, 1962, 1970, 1994), while Italy (1934, 1938, 1982) and Germany (1954, 1974, 1990) have won it three times. The two-times winners are Uruguay (1930, 1950) and Argentina (1978, 1986).

World Cup and European Championship holders France will also be among the favourites. But let's hope all our teams qualify for the finals draw in December 2001, and that one of our teams can recapture the moment of England's glorious triumph at Wembley in 1966. All five teams are certainly due some success.

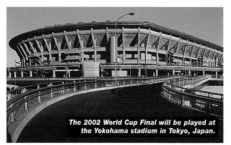

The 2002 World Cup Final will be played at the Yokohama stadium in Tokyo, Japan.

QUALIFYING FIXTURES

ENGLAND

Saturday October 7, 2000
England v Germany

Wednesday October 11, 2000
Finland v England

Saturday March 24, 2001
England v Finland

Wednesday March 28, 2001
Albania v England

Wednesday June 6, 2001
Greece v England

Saturday September 1, 2001
Germany v England

Wednesday September 5, 2001
England v Albania

Saturday October 6, 2001
England v Greece

SCOTLAND

Saturday September 2, 2000
Latvia v Scotland

Saturday October 7, 2000
San Marino v Scotland

Wednesday October 11, 2000
Croatia v Scotland

Saturday March 24, 2001
Scotland v Belgium

Wednesday March 28, 2001
Scotland v San Marino

Saturday September 1, 2001
Scotland v Croatia

Wednesday September 5, 2001
Belgium v Scotland

Saturday October 6, 2001
Scotland v Latvia

REPUBLIC OF IRELAND

Saturday September 2, 2000
Holland v Republic of Ireland

Saturday October 7, 2000
Portugal v Republic of Ireland

Wednesday October 11, 2000
Republic of Ireland v Estonia

Saturday March 24, 2001
Cyprus v Republic of Ireland

Wednesday March 28, 2001
Andorra v Republic of Ireland

Wednesday April 25, 2001
Republic of Ireland v Andorra

Saturday June 2, 2001
Republic of Ireland v Portugal

Wednesday June 6, 2001
Estonia v Republic of Ireland

Saturday September 1, 2001
Republic of Ireland v Holland

Saturday October 6, 2001
Republic of Ireland v Cyprus

NORTHERN IRELAND

Saturday September 2, 2000
Northern Ireland v Malta

Saturday October 7, 2000
Northern Ireland v Denmark

Wednesday October 11, 2000
Iceland v Northern Ireland

Saturday March 24, 2001
Northern Ireland v Czech Republic

Wednesday March 28, 2001
Bulgaria v Northern Ireland

Saturday June 2, 2001
Northern Ireland v Bulgaria

Wednesday June 6, 2001
Czech Republic v Northern Ireland

Saturday September 1, 2001
Denmark v Northern Ireland

Wednesday September 5, 2001
Northern Ireland v Iceland

Saturday October 6, 2001
Malta v Northern Ireland

WALES

Saturday September 2, 2000
Belarus v Wales

Saturday October 7, 2000
Wales v Norway

Wednesday October 11, 2000
Poland v Wales

Saturday March 24, 2001
Armenia v Wales

Wednesday March 28, 2001
Wales v Ukraine

Saturday June 2, 2001
Wales v Poland

Wednesday June 6, 2001
Ukraine v Wales

Saturday September 1, 2001
Wales v Armenia

Wednesday September 5, 2001
Norway v Wales

Saturday October 6, 2001
Wales v Belarus

GROUP 1

FAROE ISLANDS
LUXEMBOURG
RUSSIA
SLOVENIA
SWITZERLAND
YUGOSLAVIA

The table promises to be tight at the top with Russia, Yugoslavia, Slovenia and the Swiss all in with a realistic chance of qualification or a play-off place. Luxembourg and the Faroe Islands will be fighting for pride.

Qualifying fixtures

SATURDAY SEP 2, 2000
Switzerland v Russia
Faroe Islands v Slovenia
Luxembourg v Yugoslavia

SATURDAY OCT 7, 2000
Switzerland v Faroe Islands
Luxembourg v Slovenia
Yugoslavia v Russia

WEDNESDAY OCT 11, 2000
Russia v Luxembourg
Slovenia v Switzerland
Yugoslavia v Faroe Islands

SATURDAY MAR 24, 2001
Luxembourg v Faroe Islands
Yugoslavia v Switzerland
Russia v Slovenia

WEDNESDAY MAR 28, 2001
Switzerland v Luxembourg
Slovenia v Yugoslavia
Russia v Faroe Islands

SATURDAY JUN 2, 2001
Russia v Yugoslavia
Slovenia v Luxembourg
Faroe Islands v Switzerland

WEDNESDAY JUN 6, 2001
Switzerland v Slovenia

Luxembourg v Russia
Faroe Islands v Yugoslavia

SATURDAY SEP 1, 2001
Switzerland v Yugoslavia
Slovenia v Russia
Faroe Islands v Luxembourg

WEDNESDAY SEP 5, 2001
Luxembourg v Switzerland
Yugoslavia v Slovenia
Faroe Islands v Russia

SATURDAY OCT 6, 2001
Yugoslavia v Luxembourg
Russia v Switzerland
Slovenia v Faroe Islands

GROUP 2

ANDORRA
CYPRUS
ESTONIA
HOLLAND
PORTUGAL
REP. OF IRELAND

Holland and Portugal will be the favourites for the coveted two top spots, but if the Ireland team find some good form and self belief, they could well cause problems. It may come down to a very exciting last day of qualification.

Qualifying fixtures

WEDNESDAY AUG 16, 2000
Estonia v Andorra

SATURDAY SEP 2, 2000
Holland v REP. OF IRELAND
Andorra v Cyprus

SUNDAY SEP 3, 2000
Estonia v Portugal

SATURDAY OCT 7, 2000
Andorra v Estonia
Cyprus v Holland
Portugal v REP. OF IRELAND

WEDNESDAY OCT 11, 2000
REP. OF IRELAND v Estonia
Holland v Portugal

WEDNESDAY NOV 15, 2000
Cyprus v Andorra

TUESDAY FEB 14, 2001
Portugal v Andorra

SATURDAY MAR 24, 2001
Andorra v Holland
Cyprus v REP. OF IRELAND

WEDNESDAY MAR 28, 2001
Andorra v REP. OF IRELAND
Cyprus v Estonia
Portugal v Holland

WEDNESDAY APR 25, 2001
REP. OF IRELAND v Andorra
Holland v Cyprus

SATURDAY JUN 2, 2001
Estonia v Holland
REP. OF IRELAND v Portugal

WEDNESDAY JUN 6, 2001
Estonia v REP. OF IRELAND
Portugal v Cyprus

WEDNESDAY AUG 15, 2001
Estonia v Cyprus

SATURDAY SEP 1, 2001
Andorra v Portugal
REP. OF IRELAND v Holland

WEDNESDAY SEP 5, 2001
Cyprus v Portugal
Holland v Estonia

SATURDAY OCT 6, 2001
REP. OF IRELAND v Cyprus
Holland v Andorra
Portugal v Estonia

GROUP 3

BULGARIA
CZECH REPUBLIC
DENMARK
ICELAND
MALTA
N. IRELAND

Success could prove tricky for Northern Ireland, with some stiff opposition. The smart money will be going on the Czech Republic, especially after their Euro 2000 qualifying. Denmark and Bulgaria could always do it too.

Qualifying fixtures

SATURDAY SEP 2, 2000
Iceland v Denmark
Bulgaria v Czech Republic
N IRELAND v Malta

SATURDAY OCT 7, 2000
Czech Republic v Iceland
N IRELAND v Denmark
Bulgaria v Malta

WEDNESDAY OCT 11, 2000
Denmark v Bulgaria
Malta v Czech Republic
Iceland v N IRELAND

SATURDAY MAR 24, 2001
Malta v Denmark
N IRELAND v Czech Republic
Bulgaria v Iceland

WEDNESDAY MAR 28, 2001
Czech Republic v Denmark
Bulgaria v N IRELAND

WEDNESDAY APR 25, 2001
Malta v Iceland

SATURDAY JUN 2, 2001
Denmark v Czech Republic
Iceland v Malta
N IRELAND v Bulgaria

WEDNESDAY JUN 6, 2001
Denmark v Malta
Iceland v Bulgaria
Czech Republic v N IRELAND

SATURDAY SEP 1, 2001
Denmark v N IRELAND
Iceland v Czech Republic
Malta v Bulgaria

WEDNESDAY SEP 5, 2001
Bulgaria v Denmark
Czech Republic v Malta
N IRELAND v Iceland

SATURDAY OCT 6, 2001
Denmark v Iceland
Malta v N IRELAND
Czech Republic v Bulgaria

GROUP 4

AZERBAIJAN
MACEDONIA
MOLDOVA
SLOVAKIA
SWEDEN
TURKEY

Swedish and Turkish fans may already have one eye on the Finals or at least a play-off, but an often under-rated Slovakian side could do some damage if complacency creeps in. Macedonia could be the dark horses.

Qualifying fixtures

SATURDAY SEP 2, 2000
Turkey v Moldova
Azerbaijan v Sweden
Slovakia v Macedonia

SATURDAY OCT 2, 2000
Macedonia v Azerbaijan
Sweden v Turkey
Moldova v Slovakia

WEDNESDAY OCT 6, 2000
Slovakia v Sweden
Azerbaijan v Turkey
Moldova v Macedonia

SATURDAY MAR 24, 2001
Sweden v Macedonia
Turkey v Slovakia
Azerbaijan v Moldova

WEDNESDAY MAR 28, 2001
Moldova v Sweden
Slovakia v Azerbaijan
Macedonia v Turkey

SATURDAY JUN 2, 2001
Turkey v Azerbaijan
Macedonia v Moldova
Sweden v Slovakia

WEDNESDAY JUN 2, 2001
Turkey v Macedonia

Sweden v Moldova
Azerbaijan v Slovakia

SATURDAY SEP 1, 2001
Macedonia v Sweden
Slovakia v Turkey

WEDNESDAY SEP 5, 2001
Turkey v Sweden
Slovakia v Moldova
Azerbaijan v Macedonia

SUNDAY OCT 7, 2001
Macedonia v Slovakia
Moldova v Turkey
Sweden v Azerbaijan

GROUP 5

ARMENIA
BELARUS
NORWAY
POLAND
UKRAINE
WALES

Wales have progressed under Mark Hughes, but will it be enough to reach the Finals? If it is, the team will have achieved a huge feat considering the ability of Norway, Poland and Ukraine – one of whom should top the table.

Qualifying fixtures

SATURDAY SEP 2, 2000
Norway v Belarus
Norway v Armenia
Ukraine v Poland
Belarus v WALES

SATURDAY OCT 7, 2000
Armenia v Ukraine
Poland v Belarus
WALES v Norway

WEDNESDAY OCT 11, 2000
Belarus v Armenia
Norway v Ukraine
Poland v WALES

SATURDAY MAR 24, 2001
Ukraine v Belarus
Armenia v WALES
Norway v Poland

WEDNESDAY MAR 28, 2001
Belarus v Norway
Poland v Armenia
WALES v Ukraine

SATURDAY JUN 2, 2001
Armenia v Belarus
Ukraine v Norway
WALES v Poland

WEDNESDAY JUN 6, 2001
Armenia v Poland

Norway v Belarus
Ukraine v WALES

SATURDAY SEP 1, 2001
Belarus v Ukraine
Poland v Norway

WEDNESDAY SEP 5, 2001
Ukraine v Armenia
Belarus v Poland
Norway v WALES

SATURDAY OCT 6, 2001
Armenia v Norway
Poland v Ukraine
WALES v Belarus

Fixtures of every game in every group in the race for World Cup 2002!

GROUP 6

BELGIUM
CROATIA
LATVIA
SAN MARINO
SCOTLAND

Scotland should be confident of at least a play-off place, and who's to say they can't go on to secure an automatic place in the Finals? Belgium and Croatia are great sides, but Scotland aren't bad. Come on you Scots!

Qualifying fixtures

SATURDAY SEP 2, 2000
Latvia v SCOTLAND
Belgium v Croatia

SATURDAY OCT 7, 2000
Latvia v Belgium
San Marino v SCOTLAND

WEDNESDAY OCT 11, 2000
Croatia v SCOTLAND

WEDNESDAY NOV 15, 2000
San Marino v Latvia

TUESDAY FEB 14, 2001
Belgium v San Marino

SATURDAY MAR 24, 2001
Croatia v Latvia
SCOTLAND v Belgium

WEDNESDAY MAR 28, 2001
SCOTLAND v San Marino

WEDNESDAY APR 25, 2001
Latvia v San Marino

SATURDAY JUN 2, 2001
Croatia v San Marino
Belgium v Latvia

WEDNESDAY JUN 6, 2001
Latvia v Croatia
San Marino v Belgium

SATURDAY SEP 1, 2001
SCOTLAND v Croatia

WEDNESDAY SEP 5, 2001
San Marino v Croatia
Belgium v SCOTLAND

SATURDAY OCT 6, 2001
Croatia v Belgium
SCOTLAND v Latvia

GROUP 7

AUSTRIA
BOSNIA
ISRAEL
LIECHTENSTEIN
SPAIN

The big question in this group is who is going to finish second, since Spain should run away with it. Israel and Bosnia will both be pulling out all the stops to make sure Austria don't get there, and it'll be a fascinating fight.

Qualifying fixtures

SATURDAY SEP 2, 2000
Bosnia v Spain

SUNDAY SEP 3, 2000
Israel v Liechtenstein

SATURDAY OCT 7, 2000
Liechtenstein v Austria
Spain v Israel

WEDNESDAY OCT 11, 2000
Israel v Bosnia
Austria v Spain

SATURDAY MAR 24, 2001
Bosnia v Austria
Spain v Liechtenstein

WEDNESDAY MAR 28, 2001
Austria v Israel
Liechtenstein v Bosnia

SATURDAY JUN 2, 2001
Liechtenstein v Israel
Spain v Bosnia

WEDNESDAY JUN 6, 2001
Austria v Liechtenstein
Israel v Spain

SATURDAY SEP 1, 2001
Bosnia v Israel
Spain v Austria

WEDNESDAY SEP 5, 2001
Austria v Bosnia
Liechtenstein v Spain

SUNDAY OCT 7, 2001
Israel v Austria
Bosnia v Liechtenstein

GROUP 8

GEORGIA
HUNGARY
ITALY
LITHUANIA
ROMANIA

Italy and Romania stand out, although it's a tougher group than it looks. Georgia and Hungary won't roll over for anyone, and while Lithuania can be pretty safely written off, this group is an intriguing prospect for the others.

Qualifying fixtures

SATURDAY SEP 2, 2000
Romania v Lithuania

SUNDAY SEP 3, 2000
Hungary v Italy

SATURDAY OCT 7, 2000
Lithuania v Georgia
Italy v Romania

WEDNESDAY OCT 11, 2000
Lithuania v Hungary
Italy v Georgia

SATURDAY MAR 24, 2001
Hungary v Lithuania
Romania v Italy

WEDNESDAY MAR 28, 2001
Italy v Lithuania
Georgia v Romania

SATURDAY JUN 2, 2001
Romania v Hungary
Georgia v Italy

WEDNESDAY JUN 6, 2001
Lithuania v Romania
Hungary v Georgia

SATURDAY SEP 1, 2001
Georgia v Hungary
Lithuania v Italy

WEDNESDAY SEP 5, 2001
Hungary v Romania
Georgia v Lithuania

SATURDAY OCT 6, 2001
Italy v Hungary
Romania v Georgia

GROUP 9

Yet again, England are facing the old enemy Germany, and they'll be disappointed with anything less than an automatic qualification place. The Germans will push them all the way, but England will start as favourites to win it.

ALBANIA
ENGLAND
FINLAND
GERMANY
GREECE

Qualifying fixtures

SATURDAY SEP 2, 2000
Germany v Greece
Finland v Albania

SATURDAY OCT 7, 2000
ENGLAND v Germany
Greece v Finland

WEDNESDAY OCT 11, 2000
Albania v Greece
Finland v ENGLAND

SATURDAY MAR, 24 2001
Germany v Albania
ENGLAND v Finland

WEDNESDAY MAR 28, 2001
Albania v ENGLAND
Greece v Germany

SATURDAY JUN 2, 2001
Finland v Germany
Greece v Albania

WEDNESDAY JUN 6, 2001
Greece v ENGLAND
Albania v Germany

SATURDAY SEP 1, 2001
Germany v ENGLAND
Albania v Finland

WEDNESDAY SEP 5, 2001
ENGLAND v Albania
Finland v Greece

SATURDAY OCT 6, 2001
ENGLAND v Greece
Germany v Finland

THE LEAGUE CHAMPIONSHIP
THE WINNERS

2000 Man. United	1965 Man. United	1924 Huddersfield
1999 Man. United	1964 Liverpool	1923 Liverpool
1998 Arsenal	1963 Everton	1922 Liverpool
1997 Man. United	1962 Ipswich Town	1921 Burnley
1996 Man. United	1961 Tottenham	1920 WBA
1995 Blackburn	1960 Burnley	1916-19: no league
1994 Man. United	1959 Wolves	1915 Everton
1993 Man. United	1958 Wolves	1914 Blackburn
1992 Leeds United	1957 Man. United	1913 Sunderland
1991 Arsenal	1956 Man. United	1912 Blackburn
1990 Liverpool	1955 Chelsea	1911 Man. United
1989 Arsenal	1954 Wolves	1910 Aston Villa
1988 Liverpool	1953 Arsenal	1909 Newcastle
1987 Everton	1952 Man. United	1908 Man. United
1986 Liverpool	1951 Tottenham	1907 Newcastle
1985 Everton	1950 Portsmouth	1906 Liverpool
1984 Liverpool	1949 Portsmouth	1905 Newcastle
1983 Liverpool	1948 Arsenal	1904 Sheff. Wed.
1982 Liverpool	1947 Liverpool	1903 Sheff. Wed.
1981 Aston Villa	1940-46: no league	1902 Sunderland
1980 Liverpool	1939 Everton	1901 Liverpool
1979 Liverpool	1938 Arsenal	1900 Aston Villa
1978 Nott'm Forest	1937 Man. City	1899 Aston Villa
1977 Liverpool	1936 Sunderland	1898 Sheff. United
1976 Liverpool	1935 Arsenal	1897 Aston Villa
1975 Derby County	1934 Arsenal	1896 Aston Villa
1974 Leeds United	1933 Arsenal	1895 Sunderland
1973 Liverpool	1932 Everton	1894 Aston Villa
1972 Derby County	1931 Arsenal	1893 Sunderland
1971 Arsenal	1930 Sheff. Wed.	1892 Sunderland
1970 Everton	1929 Sheff. Wed.	1891 Everton
1969 Leeds United	1928 Everton	1890 Preston
1968 Man. City	1927 Newcastle	1889 Preston
1967 Man. United	1926 Huddersfield	
1966 Liverpool	1925 Huddersfield	

THE RECORD HOLDERS

MOST LEAGUE CHAMPIONSHIPS

Liverpool	18
Man. United	13
Arsenal	11
Everton	9

BIGGEST WIN

WBA 12 Darwen 0 — April 4, 1892
Nott'm Forest 12 Leicester Fosse 0 — April 21, 1909

HIGHEST ATTENDANCE

Man. United v Arsenal 83,260
at Maine Road, January 17, 1948

LOWEST ATTENDANCE

West Brom v Derby County 405
at Stoney Lane, November 29, 1890

RECORD LEAGUE GOALSCORERS

Total League goals
Arthur Rowley 434
WBA, Fulham, Leicester, Shrewsbury

League goals in one season
Dixie Dean Everton 1927-28 60

League goals in one game
Ted Drake Arsenal 7
v Aston Villa, December 14, 1935
James Ross Preston 7
v Stoke City, October 6, 1888

THE FA CUP

THE F.A. CUP SPONSORED BY AXA — WINNERS 2000

FA CUP WINNERS

2000	Chelsea	1	Aston Villa	0	1974	Liverpool	3	Newcastle	0
1999	Man. United	2	Newcastle	0	1973	Sunderland	1	Leeds United	0
1998	Arsenal	2	Newcastle	0	1972	Leeds United	1	Arsenal	0
1997	Chelsea	2	Middlesbrough	0	1971	Arsenal	2	Liverpool	1
1996	Man. United	1	Liverpool	0	1970	Chelsea	2	Leeds United	2
1995	Everton	1	Man. United	0	replay	Chelsea	2	Leeds United	1
1994	Man. United	4	Chelsea	0	1969	Man. City	1	Leicester City	0
1993	Arsenal	1	Sheff. Wed.	1	1968	West Brom	1	Everton	0
replay	Arsenal	2	Sheff. Wed.	1	1967	Tottenham	2	Chelsea	1
1992	Liverpool	2	Sunderland	0	1966	Everton	3	Sheff. Wed.	2
1991	Tottenham	2	Nott'm Forest	1	1965	Liverpool	2	Leeds United	1
1990	Man. United	3	Crystal Palace	3	1964	West Ham	3	Preston	2
replay	Man. United	1	Crystal Palace	0	1963	Man. United	3	Leicester City	1
1989	Liverpool	3	Everton	2	1962	Tottenham	3	Burnley	1
1988	Wimbledon	1	Liverpool	0	1961	Tottenham	2	Leicester City	0
1987	Coventry	3	Tottenham	2	1960	Wolves	3	Blackburn	0
1986	Liverpool	3	Everton	1	1959	Nott'm Forest	2	Luton Town	1
1985	Man. United	1	Everton	0	1958	Bolton	2	Man. United	0
1984	Everton	2	Watford	0	1957	Aston Villa	2	Man. United	1
1983	Man. United	2	Brighton	2	1956	Man. City	3	Birmingham City	1
replay	Man. United	4	Brighton	0	1955	Newcastle	3	Man. City	1
1982	Tottenham	1	QPR	1	1954	West Brom	3	Preston	2
replay	Tottenham	1	QPR	0	1953	Blackpool	4	Bolton	3
1981	Tottenham	1	Man. City	1	1952	Newcastle	1	Arsenal	0
replay	Tottenham	3	Man. City	2	1951	Newcastle	2	Blackpool	0
1980	West Ham	1	Arsenal	0	1950	Arsenal	2	Liverpool	0
1979	Arsenal	3	Man. United	2	1949	Wolves	3	Leicester City	1
1978	Ipswich	1	Arsenal	0	1948	Man. United	4	Blackpool	2
1977	Man. United	2	Liverpool	1	1947	Charlton	1	Burnley	0
1976	Southampton	1	Man. United	0	1946	Derby	4	Charlton Athletic	1
1975	West Ham	2	Fulham	0				Games since the war only	

FA CUP STATS

RECORD FA CUP GOALSCORERS

Total FA Cup goals
Henry Cursham Notts County 48
Ian Rush Chester City, Liverpool, Newcastle United 42

Cup goals in one season
Sandy Brown Tottenham 1900-01 15

Cup goals in one game
Ted MacDougall Bournemouth 9
v Margate, November 20, 1971

MOST FA CUP FINAL WINS

Man. United	10
Tottenham	8
Arsenal, Aston Villa	7

MOST FA CUP FINAL DEFEATS

Everton, Newcastle	7
Liverpool	6

BIGGEST WIN

Preston North End 26 Hyde FC 0
October 15, 1887

HIGHEST ATTENDANCE

Bolton v West Ham 126,047*
Wembley, April 28, 1923
*Estimated to be nearer 200,000

LOWEST ATTENDANCE

Bradford City v Norwich 200
1915 (at Lincoln)

Ted Drake

THE LEAGUE CUP

WINNERS 1999-2000

LEAGUE CUP WINNERS

Year	Winner		Runner-up	
2000	Leicester City	2	Tranmere	1
1999	Tottenham	1	Leicester City	0
1998	Chelsea	2	Middlesbrough	0
1997	Leicester City	1	Middlesbrough	1
replay	Leicester City	1	Middlesbrough	0
1996	Aston Villa	3	Leeds United	0
1995	Liverpool	2	Bolton	1
1994	Aston Villa	3	Man. United	1
1993	Arsenal	2	Sheff. Wed.	1
1992	Man. United	1	Nott'm Forest	0
1991	Sheff. Wed.	1	Man. United	0
1990	Nott'm Forest	1	Oldham Athletic	0
1989	Nott'm Forest	3	Luton Town	1
1988	Luton Town	3	Arsenal	2
1987	Arsenal	2	Liverpool	1
1986	Oxford United	3	QPR	0
1985	Norwich	1	Sunderland	0
1984	Liverpool	0	Everton	0
replay	Liverpool	1	Everton	0
1983	Liverpool	2	Man. United	1
1982	Liverpool	3	Tottenham	1
1981	Liverpool	1	West Ham	1
replay	Liverpool	2	West Ham	1
1980	Wolves	1	Nott'm Forest	0
1979	Nott'm Forest	3	Southampton	2
1978	Nott'm Forest	0	Liverpool	0
replay	Nott'm Forest	1	Liverpool	0
1977	Aston Villa	0	Everton	0
replay	Aston Villa	1	Everton	1
replay	Aston Villa	3	Everton	2

Year	Winner		Runner-up	
1976	Man. City	2	Newcastle	1
1975	Aston Villa	1	Norwich	0
1974	Wolves	2	Man. City	1
1973	Tottenham	1	Norwich	0
1972	Stoke City	2	Chelsea	1
1971	Tottenham	2	Aston Villa	0
1970	Man. City	2	West Brom	1
1969	Swindon	3	Arsenal	1
1968	Leeds United	1	Arsenal	0
1967	QPR	3	West Brom	2

Final played over two legs from 1961-66

1966	West Ham	2	West Brom	1
	West Brom	4	West Ham	1
	West Brom won 5-3 on agg			
1965	Chelsea	3	Leicester	2
	Leicester City	0	Chelsea	0
	Chelsea won 3-2 on agg			
1964	Stoke City	1	Leicester	1
	Leicester	3	Stoke City	2
	Leicester won 4-3 on agg			
1963	Birmingham	3	Aston Villa	1
	Aston Villa	0	Birmingham	0
	Birmingham won 3-1 on agg			
1962	Rochdale	0	Norwich	3
	Norwich	1	Rochdale	0
	Norwich won 4-0 on agg			
1961	Rotherham	2	Aston Villa	0
	Aston Villa	3	Rotherham	0
	Aston Villa won 3-2 on agg			

LEAGUE CUP STATS

Geoff Hurst

RECORD GOALSCORERS

Total League Cup goals
Geoff Hurst West Ham, Stoke City 49
Ian Rush Chester City, Liverpool,
Newcastle United 49

Goals in one season
Clive Allen Tottenham 1986-87 12

Goals in one game
Frankie Bunn Oldham Athletic 6
v Scarborough, October 25, 1989

MOST WINS
Aston Villa, Liverpool	5
Nottingham Forest	4
Tottenham, Leicester City	3

MOST DEFEATS IN FINALS
Arsenal, Man. United	3
Eight teams have lost two finals	

BIGGEST WIN
West Ham 10 Bury 0	Oct. 25, 1983
Liverpool 10 Fulham 0	Sept. 23, 1986

HIGHEST ATTENDANCE
Norwich v Sunderland 100,000
Wembley March 24, 1985

GOLDEN BOOT WINNERS

Year	Player	Goals
2000	**Kevin Phillips** Sunderland	30
1999	**Michael Owen** Liverpool	18
	Jimmy Floyd Hasselbaink Leeds	
	Dwight Yorke Man. United	
1998	**Michael Owen** Liverpool	18
	Chris Sutton Blackburn	
	Dion Dublin Coventry	
1997	**Alan Shearer** Newcastle	25
1996	**Alan Shearer** Blackburn	31
1995	**Alan Shearer** Blackburn	34
1994	**Andy Cole** Newcastle	34
1993	**Teddy Sheringham** Forest & Spurs	22
1992	**Ian Wright** C. Palace & Arsenal	29
1991	**Alan Smith** Arsenal	23
1990	**Gary Lineker** Tottenham	24
1989	**Alan Smith** Arsenal	23
1988	**John Aldridge** Liverpool	26
1987	**Clive Allen** Tottenham	33
1986	**Gary Lineker** Everton	30
1985	**Kerry Dixon** Chelsea	24
	Gary Lineker Leicester	
1984	**Ian Rush** Liverpool	32
1983	**Luther Blissett** Watford	27
1982	**Kevin Keegan** Southampton	26
1981	**Steve Archibald** Tottenham	20
	Peter Withe Aston Villa	
1980	**Phil Boyer** Southampton	23
1979	**Frank Worthington** Bolton	24
1978	**Bob Latchford** Everton	30
1977	**Malcolm McDonald** Arsenal	25
	Andy Gray Aston Villa	
1976	**Ted MacDougall** Norwich	23
1975	**Malcolm McDonald** Newcastle	21
1974	**Mick Channon** Southampton	21
1973	**Bryan 'Pop' Robson** West Ham	28
1972	**Francis Lee** Man. City	33
1971	**Tony Brown** West Brom	28
1970	**Jeff Astle** West Brom	25
1969	**Jimmy Greaves** Tottenham	27
1968	**Ron Davies** Southampton	28
	George Best Man. United	
1967	**Ron Davies** Southampton	37
1966	**Roger Hunt** Liverpool	30
1965	**Jimmy Greaves** Tottenham	29
	Andy McEvoy Blackburn	
1964	**Jimmy Greaves** Tottenham	35
1963	**Jimmy Greaves** Tottenham	37
1962	**Ray Crawford** Ipswich	33
	Derek Kevan West Brom	
1961	**Jimmy Greaves** Chelsea	41
1960	**Dennis Viollet** Man. United	32
1959	**Jimmy Greaves** Chelsea	32
1958	**Bobby Smith** Tottenham	36
1957	**John Charles** Leeds	38
1956	**Nat Lofthouse** Bolton	33
1955	**Ronnie Allen** West Brom	27

Year	Player	Goals
1954	**Jimmy Glazzard** Huddersfield	29
1953	**Charlie Wayman** Preston	24
1952	**George Robledo** Newcastle	33
1951	**Stan Mortensen** Blackpool	30
1950	**Dickie Davis** Sunderland	25
1949	**Willie Moir** Bolton	25
1948	**Ronnie Rooke** Arsenal	33
1947	**Dennis Westcott** Wolves	38
1940-46: *no league*		
1939	**Tommy Lawton** Everton	34
1938	**Tommy Lawton** Everton	28
1937	**Freddie Steele** Stoke City	33
1936	**Ginger Richardson** West Brom	39
1935	**Ted Drake** Arsenal	42
1934	**Jack Bowers** Derby	34
1933	**Jack Bowers** Derby	35
1932	**Dixie Dean** Everton	45
1931	**Pongo Waring** Aston Villa	49
1930	**Vic Watson** West Ham	42
1929	**Dave Halliday** Sunderland	43
1928	**Dixie Dean** Everton	60
1927	**Jimmy Trotter** Sheff. Wed.	37
1926	**Ted Harper** Blackburn	43
1925	**Fred Roberts** Man. City	31
1924	**Wilf Chadwick** Everton	28
1923	**Charlie Buchan** Sunderland	30
1922	**Andy Wilson** Middlesbrough	31
1921	**Joe Smith** Bolton	38
1920	**Fred Morris** West Brom	37
1915-18: *no league*		
1915	**Bobby Parker** Everton	36
1914	**George Elliot** Middlesbrough	31
1913	**Dave McLean** Sheff. Wed.	30
1912	**Harold Hampton** Aston Villa	25
	George Holley Sunderland	
	Dave McLean Sheff. Wed.	
1911	**Albert Shepherd** Newcastle	25
1910	**John Parkinson** Liverpool	30
1909	**Bert Freeman** Everton	36
1908	**Enoch West** Nott'm Forest	27
1907	**Alec Young** Everton	28
1906	**Bullet Jones** Birmingham	26
	Albert Shepherd Bolton	
1905	**Arthur Brown** Sheff. United	23
1904	**Steve Bloomer** Derby	20
1903	**Alec Raybould** Liverpool	31
1902	**James Settle** Everton	18
	Fred Priest Sheff. United	
1901	**Steve Bloomer** Derby	24
1900	**Bill Garrett** Aston Villa	27
1899	**Steve Bloomer** Derby	24
1898	**Fred Wheldon** Aston Villa	21
1897	**Steve Bloomer** Derby	24
1896	**Steve Bloomer** Derby	22
1895	**John Campbell** Sunderland	22
1894	**Jack Southworth** Everton	27
1893	**John Campbell** Sunderland	31
1892	**John Campbell** Sunderland	32

Jimmy Greaves

THE CHARITY SHIELD

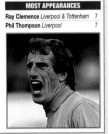

CHARITY SHIELD WINNERS

Year	Winner		Runner-up	
1999	Arsenal	2	Man. United	1
1998	Arsenal	3	Man. United	0
1997	Man. United	1	Chelsea	1
	United win 4-2 on pens			
1996	Man. United	4	Newcastle	0
1995	Everton	1	Blackburn	0
1994	Man. United	2	Blackburn	0
1993	Man. United	1	Arsenal	1
	United win 5-4 on pens			
1992	Leeds United	4	Liverpool	3
1991	Arsenal	0	Tottenham	0
1990	Liverpool	1	Man. United	1
1989	Liverpool	1	Arsenal	0
1988	Liverpool	2	Wimbledon	1
1987	Everton	1	Coventry	0
1986	Everton	1	Liverpool	1
1985	Everton	2	Man. United	0
1984	Everton	1	Liverpool	0
1983	Man. United	2	Liverpool	0
1982	Liverpool	1	Tottenham	0
1981	Aston Villa	2	Tottenham	2
1980	Liverpool	1	West Ham	0
1979	Liverpool	3	Arsenal	1
1978	Nott'm Forest	5	Ipswich	0
1977	Liverpool	0	Man. United	0
1976	Liverpool	1	Southampton	0
1975	Derby	2	West Ham	0
1974	Liverpool	1	Leeds	1
	Liverpool win 6-5 on pens			
1973	Burnley	1	Man. City	0
1972	Man. City	1	Aston Villa	0
1971	Leicester	1	Liverpool	0
1970	Everton	2	Chelsea	1
1969	Leeds	2	Man. City	1
1968	Man. City	6	West Brom	1
1967	Man. United	3	Tottenham	3
1966	Liverpool	1	Everton	0
1965	Man. United	2	Liverpool	2
1964	Liverpool	2	West Ham	2
1963	Everton	4	Man. United	0
1962	Tottenham	5	Ipswich	1
1961	Tottenham	3	FA XI	2
1960	Burnley	2	Wolves	2
1959	Wolves	3	Nott'm Forest	1
1958	Bolton	4	Wolves	1
1957	Man. United	4	Aston Villa	0
1956	Man. United	1	Man. City	0
1955	Chelsea	3	Newcastle	0
1954	Wolves	4	West Brom	4
1953	Arsenal	3	Blackpool	1
1952	Man. United	4	Newcastle	2
1951	Tottenham	2	Newcastle	1
1950	World Cup Team	4	Canadian Team	2
1949	Portsmouth	1	Wolves	1
1948	Arsenal	4	Man. United	3
1939-47:	no trophy			
1938	Arsenal	2	Preston	1
1937	Man. City	2	Sunderland	0
1936	Sunderland	2	Arsenal	1
1935	Sheff. Wed.	1	Arsenal	0
1934	Arsenal	4	Man. City	0
1933	Arsenal	3	Everton	0
1932	Everton	5	Newcastle	3
1931	Arsenal	1	West Brom	0
1930	Arsenal	2	Sheff. Wed.	1
1929	Professionals	3	Amateurs	0
1928	Everton	2	Blackburn	1
1927	Cardiff	2	Corinthians	1
1926	Amateurs	6	Professionals	3
1925	Amateurs	6	Professionals	1
1924	Professionals	3	Amateurs	1
1923	Professionals	2	Amateurs	0
1922	Huddersfield	1	Liverpool	0
1921	Tottenham	2	Burnley	0
1920	West Brom	2	Tottenham	0
1914-19:	no trophy			
1913	Professionals	7	Amateurs	2
1912	Blackburn	2	QPR	1
1911	Man. United	8	Swindon	4
1910	Brighton	1	Aston Villa	0
1909	Newcastle	2	Northampton	0
1908	Man. United	1	QPR	1
replay	Man. United	4	QPR	0

CHARITY SHIELD STATS

MOST WINS	
Man. United	12
Arsenal, Liverpool	10
Everton	9
Tottenham	4

MOST DEFEATS	
Arsenal, Liverpool, Newcastle	5
Man. United, Man. City	4
Aston Villa, Blackburn	3

BIGGEST WIN	
Man. United 8 Swindon Town 4	1911
Man. City 6 West Brom 1	1968
Nott'm Forest 5 Ipswich Town 0	1978

MOST APPEARANCES	
Ray Clemence Liverpool & Tottenham	7
Phil Thompson Liverpool	7

PFA PLAYER OF THE YEAR

PLAYER OF THE YEAR

2000	Roy Keane Man. United
1999	David Ginola Tottenham
1998	Dennis Bergkamp Arsenal
1997	Alan Shearer Newcastle
1996	Les Ferdinand Newcastle
1995	Alan Shearer Blackburn
1994	Eric Cantona Man. United
1993	Paul McGrath Aston Villa
1992	Gary Pallister Man. United
1991	Mark Hughes Man. United
1990	David Platt Aston Villa
1989	Mark Hughes Man. United
1988	John Barnes Liverpool
1987	Clive Allen Tottenham
1986	Gary Lineker Everton
1985	Peter Reid Everton
1984	Ian Rush Liverpool
1983	Kenny Dalglish Liverpool
1982	Kevin Keegan Southampton
1981	John Wark Ipswich Town
1980	Terry McDermott Liverpool
1979	Liam Brady Arsenal
1978	Peter Shilton Nottingham Forest
1977	Andy Gray Aston Villa
1976	Pat Jennings Tottenham
1975	Colin Todd Bolton Wanderers
1974	Norman Hunter Leeds United

YOUNG PLAYER OF THE YEAR

2000	Harry Kewell Leeds United
1999	Nicolas Anelka Arsenal
1998	Michael Owen Liverpool
1997	David Beckham Man. United
1996	Robbie Fowler Liverpool
1995	Robbie Fowler Liverpool
1994	Andy Cole Newcastle
1993	Ryan Giggs Man. United
1992	Ryan Giggs Man. United
1991	Lee Sharpe Man. United
1990	Matt Le Tissier Southampton
1989	Paul Merson Arsenal
1988	Paul Gascoigne Tottenham
1987	Tony Adams Arsenal
1986	Tony Cottee West Ham United
1985	Mark Hughes Man. United
1984	Paul Walsh Luton Town
1983	Ian Rush Liverpool
1982	Steve Moran Southampton
1981	Gary Shaw Aston Villa
1980	Glenn Hoddle Tottenham
1979	Cyrille Regis West Bromwich Albion
1978	Tony Woodcock Nottingham Forest
1977	Andy Gray Aston Villa
1976	Peter Barnes Man. City
1975	Mervyn Day West Ham United
1974	Kevin Beattie Ipswich Town

FOOTBALL WRITERS' PLAYER OF THE YEAR

2000	Roy Keane Man. United
1999	David Ginola Tottenham
1998	Dennis Bergkamp Arsenal
1997	Gianfranco Zola Chelsea
1996	Eric Cantona Man. United
1995	Jurgen Klinsmann Tottenham
1994	Alan Shearer Blackburn
1993	Chris Waddle Sheff. Wed.
1992	Gary Lineker Tottenham
1991	Gordon Strachan Leeds United
1990	John Barnes Liverpool
1989	Steve Nicol Liverpool
1988	John Barnes Liverpool
1987	Clive Allen Tottenham
1986	Gary Lineker Everton
1985	Neville Southall Everton
1984	Ian Rush Liverpool
1983	Kenny Dalglish Liverpool
1982	Steve Perryman Tottenham
1981	Frans Thijssen Ipswich Town
1980	Terry McDermott Liverpool
1979	Kenny Dalglish Liverpool
1978	Kenny Burns Nottingham Forest
1977	Emlyn Hughes Liverpool
1976	Kevin Keegan Liverpool
1975	Alan Mullery Fulham
1974	Ian Callaghan Liverpool
1973	Pat Jennings Tottenham
1972	Gordon Banks Stoke City
1971	Frank McLintock Arsenal
1970	Billy Bremner Leeds United
1969	Dave Mackay Derby County
	Tony Book Manchester City (shared)
1968	George Best Man. United
1967	Jack Charlton Leeds United
1966	Bobby Charlton Man. United
1965	Bobby Collins Leeds United
1964	Bobby Moore West Ham United
1963	Stanley Matthews Stoke City
1962	Jimmy Adamson Burnley
1961	Danny Blanchflower Tottenham
1960	Bill Slater Wolverhampton Wanderers
1959	Syd Owen Luton Town
1958	Danny Blanchflower Tottenham
1957	Tom Finney Preston North End
1956	Bert Trautmann Man. City
1955	Don Revie Leeds United
1954	Tom Finney Preston North End
1953	Nat Lofthouse Bolton Wanderers
1952	Billy Wright Wolverhampton Wanderers
1951	Harry Johnston Blackpool
1950	Joe Mercer Arsenal
1949	Johnny Carey Man. United
1948	Stanley Matthews Stoke City

FA CARLING PREMIERSHIP SEASON 1999-2000

		P	W	D	L	F	A	Pts	Top Scorer	Average Att.
1	Man. United	38	28	7	3	97	45	91	Yorke, Cole 20	58,017
2	Arsenal	38	22	7	9	73	43	73	Henry, 18	38,033
3	Leeds	38	21	6	11	58	43	69	Bridges 19	39,154
4	Liverpool	38	19	10	9	51	30	67	Owen 12	44,073
5	Chelsea	38	18	11	9	53	44	65	Flo, Poyet 10	34,584
6	Aston Villa	38	15	13	10	46	35	58	Dublin 13	31,696
7	Sunderland	38	16	10	12	57	56	58	Phillips 30	41,375
8	Leicester	38	16	7	15	55	55	55	Cottee 14	19,827
9	West Ham	38	15	10	13	52	53	55	di Canio, Wanchope 15	25,093
10	Tottenham	38	15	8	15	57	49	53	Armstrong, Iversen 15	34,911
11	Newcastle	38	14	10	14	63	54	52	Shearer 23	36,316
12	Middlesbrough	38	14	10	14	46	52	52	Ricard 12	33,919
13	Everton	38	12	14	12	59	49	50	Campbell 12	34,880
14	Coventry	38	12	8	18	46	54	44	Keane, McAllister 12	20,808
15	Southampton	38	12	8	18	45	62	44	Pahars 14	15,131
16	Derby	38	9	11	18	44	57	38	Delap 8	29,351
17	Bradford	38	9	9	20	38	68	36	Windass 10	18,030
18	Wimbledon	38	7	12	19	46	74	33	Cort, Hartson 9	17,115
19	Sheff. Wed.	38	8	7	23	38	70	31	de Bilde 11	24,885
20	Watford	38	6	6	26	35	77	24	Helguson 6	18,510

NATIONWIDE DIVISION ONE SEASON 1999-2000

		P	W	D	L	F	A	Pts	Top Scorer	Average Att.
1	Charlton	46	27	10	9	79	45	91	Hunt 24	19,557
2	Man. City	46	26	11	9	78	40	89	Goater 22	32,522
3	Ipswich	46	25	12	9	71	42	87	Johnson 24	18,523
4	Barnsley	46	24	10	12	88	67	82	Hignett 20	15,412
5	Birmingham	46	22	11	13	65	44	77	Furlong 11	21,938
6	Bolton	46	21	13	12	69	50	76	Gudjohnson 13	14,244
7	Wolves	46	21	11	14	64	48	74	Akinbiyi 16	21,470
8	Huddersfield	46	21	11	14	62	49	74	Wijnhard 16	14,028
9	Fulham	46	17	16	13	49	41	67	Clark 10	13,090
10	QPR	46	16	18	12	62	53	66	Kiwomya 12	12,591
11	Blackburn	46	15	17	14	55	51	62	Carsley 11	19,183
12	Norwich	46	14	15	17	45	50	57	Roberts 18	15,538
13	Tranmere	46	15	12	19	57	68	57	Allison 16	7,273
14	Nott'm Forest	46	14	14	18	53	55	56	Freedman, Rogers 9	17,195
15	Crystal Palace	46	13	15	18	57	67	54	Morrison 12	15,662
16	Sheff. United	46	13	15	18	59	71	54	Bent 15	13,717
17	Stockport	46	13	15	18	55	67	54	Dinning 12	7,410
18	Portsmouth	46	13	12	21	55	66	51	Claridge 14	13,906
19	Crewe	46	14	9	23	46	67	51	Rivers 8	6,221
20	Grimsby	46	13	12	21	41	67	51	Ashcroft 10	6,156
21	West Brom	46	10	19	17	43	60	49	Hughes 11	14,583
22	Walsall	46	11	13	22	52	77	46	Ricketts 11	6,778
23	Port Vale	46	7	15	24	48	69	36	Rougier 8	5,996
24	Swindon	46	8	12	26	38	77	36	Hay 10	6,976

*Ipswich promoted via the play-offs

NATIONWIDE DIVISION TWO SEASON 1999-2000

		P	W	D	L	F	A	Pts	Top Scorer	Average Att.
1	Preston	46	28	11	7	74	37	95	Macken 23	12,818
2	Burnley	46	25	13	8	69	47	88	Payton 27	12,941
3	Gillingham	46	25	10	11	79	48	85	Taylor 14	7,087
4	Wigan	46	22	17	7	72	38	83	Barlow 17	7,006
5	Millwall	46	23	13	10	76	50	82	Harris 28	9,259
6	Stoke	46	23	13	10	68	42	82	Thorne 24	11,426
7	Bristol Rovers	46	23	11	12	69	45	80	Cureton, Roberts 22	8,402
8	Notts County	46	18	11	17	61	55	65	Stallard 13	5,667
9	Bristol City	46	15	19	12	59	57	64	Thorpe 12	9,803
10	Reading	46	16	14	16	57	63	62	Caskey 17	8,985
11	Wrexham	46	17	11	18	52	61	62	Connolly 9	3,952
12	Wycombe	46	16	13	17	56	53	61	Devine 23	5,100
13	Luton	46	17	10	19	61	65	61	George 13	5,657
14	Oldham	46	16	14	16	50	55	60	Allott, Whitehall 9	5,390
15	Bury	46	13	18	15	61	64	57	Lawson, Preece 8	4,024
16	Bournemouth	46	16	9	21	59	62	57	Stein 9	4,917
17	Brentford	46	13	13	20	47	61	52	Owusu 11	5,742
18	Colchester	46	14	10	22	59	62	52	McGavin 16	3,803
19	Cambridge	46	12	12	22	64	65	48	Benjamin 19	4,403
20	Oxford	46	12	9	25	43	73	45	Murphy 12	5,789
21	Cardiff	46	9	17	20	45	67	44	Bowen 12	6,895
22	Blackpool	46	8	17	21	49	77	41	Murphy 9	4,840
23	Scunthorpe	46	9	12	25	40	74	39	Hodges, Ipoua 6	4,063
24	Chesterfield	46	7	15	24	34	63	36	Reeves 14	2,935

*Gillingham promoted via the play-offs

NATIONWIDE DIVISION THREE SEASON 1999-2000

		P	W	D	L	F	A	Pts	Top Scorer	Average Att.
1	Swansea	46	24	13	9	51	30	85	Cusack, Boyd, Watkin 7	5,895
2	Rotherham	46	24	12	10	72	36	84	Fortune-West 17	4,427
3	Northampton	46	25	7	14	63	45	82	Corazzin 13	5,459
4	Darlington	46	21	16	9	66	36	79	Gabbiadini 24	5,531
5	Peterborough	46	22	12	12	63	54	78	Clarke 16	6,548
6	Barnet	46	21	12	13	59	53	75	Charlery 13	2,743
7	Hartlepool	46	21	9	16	60	49	72	Miller 15	2,981
8	Cheltenham	46	20	10	16	50	42	70	Grayson, Milton 9	4,124
9	Torquay	46	19	12	15	62	52	69	Bedeau 16	2,526
10	Rochdale	46	18	14	14	57	54	68	Ellis 12	2,687
11	Brighton	46	17	16	13	64	46	67	Freeman 12	5,733
12	Plymouth	46	16	18	12	55	51	66	McGregor 13	5,371
13	Macclesfield	46	18	11	17	66	61	65	Barker 16	2,304
14	Hull City	46	15	14	17	43	43	59	Eyre 8	5,736
15	Lincoln	46	15	11	17	67	69	59	Thorpe 15	3,404
16	Southend	46	15	11	20	53	61	56	Carruthers 16	4,137
17	Mansfield	46	16	8	22	50	65	56	Greenacre 9	2,593
18	Halifax	46	15	9	22	44	58	54	Painter 8	2,536
19	Leyton Orient	46	13	13	20	47	52	52	Christie 7	4,358
20	York	46	13	12	21	39	53	51	Conlon 11	2,811
21	Exeter	46	11	11	24	46	72	44	Alexander 16	3,014
22	Shrewsbury	46	9	13	24	40	67	40	Steele 11	2,832
23	Carlisle	46	9	12	25	42	75	39	Soley 8	3,191
24	Chester	46	10	9	27	44	79	39	Beckett 14	2,642

*Peterborough promoted via the play-offs

THE SCOTTISH FOOTBALL LEAGUE
THE WINNERS

2000 Rangers	1965 Kilmarnock	1924 Rangers
1999 Rangers	1964 Rangers	1923 Rangers
1998 Celtic	1963 Rangers	1922 Celtic
1997 Rangers	1962 Dundee	1921 Rangers
1996 Rangers	1961 Rangers	1920 Rangers
1995 Rangers	1960 Hearts	1919 Celtic
1994 Rangers	1959 Rangers	1918 Rangers
1993 Rangers	1958 Hearts	1917 Celtic
1992 Rangers	1957 Rangers	1916 Celtic
1991 Rangers	1956 Rangers	1915 Celtic
1990 Rangers	1955 Aberdeen	1914 Celtic
1989 Rangers	1954 Celtic	1913 Rangers
1988 Celtic	1953 Rangers	1912 Rangers
1987 Rangers	1952 Hibernian	1911 Rangers
1986 Celtic	1951 Hibernian	1910 Celtic
1985 Aberdeen	1950 Rangers	1909 Celtic
1984 Aberdeen	1949 Rangers	1908 Celtic
1983 Dundee United	1948 Hibernian	1907 Celtic
1982 Celtic	1947 Rangers	1906 Celtic
1981 Celtic	1940-46: *no league*	1905 Celtic (play-off)
1980 Aberdeen	1939 Rangers	1904 Third Lanark
1979 Celtic	1938 Celtic	1903 Hibernian
1978 Rangers	1937 Rangers	1902 Rangers
1977 Celtic	1936 Celtic	1901 Rangers
1976 Rangers	1935 Rangers	1900 Rangers
1975 Rangers	1934 Rangers	1899 Rangers
1974 Celtic	1933 Rangers	1898 Celtic
1973 Celtic	1932 Motherwell	1897 Hearts
1972 Celtic	1931 Rangers	1896 Celtic
1971 Celtic	1930 Rangers	1895 Hearts
1970 Celtic	1929 Rangers	1894 Celtic
1969 Celtic	1928 Rangers	1893 Celtic
1968 Celtic	1927 Rangers	1892 Dumbarton
1967 Celtic	1926 Celtic	1891 Band Rangers
1966 Celtic	1925 Rangers	

SCOTTISH LEAGUE STATS

MOST WINS IN A SEASON

1986-87 Rangers	31
1987-88 Celtic	31

FEWEST WINS IN A SEASON

1975-76 St Johnstone	3
1982-83 Kilmarnock	3

MOST DEFEATS IN A SEASON

1991-92 Dunfermline	29

FEWEST DEFEATS IN A SEASON

1995-96 Rangers	3

MOST POINTS IN A SEASON

1999-00 Rangers	90

MOST GOALS SCORED IN A SEASON

1999-00 Rangers	96

FEWEST GOALS SCORED IN A SEASON

1988-89 Hamilton	19

MOST GOALS CONCEDED IN A SEASON

1984-85 Morton	100

LEAST GOALS CONCEDED IN A SEASON

1989-90 Rangers	19

BIGGEST EVER WIN

Celtic 11 Dundee 0 *October 26, 1895*

RECORD GOALSCORING FEATS

Total goals scored
Jimmy McGrory 410
Celtic, Clydebank, 1922-38

Goals in one season
Bill McFadyen 52
Motherwell, 1931-32

Goals in one game
Jimmy McGrory 8
Celtic v Dunfermline, January 14, 1928

THE SCOTTISH CUP

TENNENTS SCOTTISH CUP WINNERS SEASON 99/2000

SCOTTISH CUP WINNERS

Year	Winner		Runner-up			Year	Winner		Runner-up	
2000	Rangers	4	Aberdeen	0		1971	Celtic	1	Rangers	1
1999	Rangers	1	Celtic	0		replay	Celtic	2	Rangers	1
1998	Hearts	2	Rangers	1		1970	Aberdeen	3	Celtic	1
1997	Kilmarnock	1	Falkirk	0		1969	Celtic	4	Rangers	0
1996	Rangers	5	Hearts	1		1968	Dunfermline	3	Hearts	1
1995	Celtic	1	Airdrie	0		1967	Celtic	2	Aberdeen	0
1994	Dundee United	1	Rangers	0		1966	Rangers	0	Celtic	0
1993	Rangers	2	Aberdeen	1		replay	Rangers	1	Celtic	0
1992	Rangers	2	Airdrie	1		1965	Celtic	3	Dunfermline	2
1991	Motherwell	4	Dundee United	3		1964	Rangers	3	Dundee	1
1990	Aberdeen	0	Celtic	0		1963	Rangers	1	Celtic	1
	Aberdeen won 9-8 on pens					replay	Rangers	3	Celtic	0
1989	Celtic	1	Rangers	0		1962	Rangers	2	St Mirren	0
1988	Celtic	2	Dundee United	1		1961	Dunfermline	0	Celtic	0
1987	St Mirren	1	Dundee United	0		replay	Dunfermline	2	Celtic	0
1986	Aberdeen	3	Hearts	0		1960	Rangers	2	Kilmarnock	0
1985	Celtic	2	Dundee United	1		1959	St Mirren	3	Aberdeen	1
1984	Aberdeen	2	Celtic	1		1958	Clyde	1	Hibernian	0
1983	Aberdeen	1	Rangers	0		1957	Falkirk	1	Kilmarnock	1
1982	Aberdeen	4	Rangers	1		replay	Falkirk	2	Kilmarnock	1
1981	Rangers	0	Dundee United	0		1956	Hearts	3	Celtic	1
replay	Rangers	4	Dundee United	1		1955	Clyde	1	Celtic	1
1980	Celtic	1	Rangers	0		replay	Clyde	1	Celtic	0
1979	Rangers	0	Hibernian	0		1954	Celtic	2	Aberdeen	1
replay	Rangers	0	Hibernian	0		1953	Rangers	1	Aberdeen	1
replay	Rangers	3	Hibernian	2		replay	Rangers	1	Aberdeen	0
1978	Rangers	2	Aberdeen	1		1952	Motherwell	4	Dundee	0
1977	Celtic	1	Rangers	0		1951	Celtic	1	Motherwell	0
1976	Rangers	3	Hearts	1		1950	Rangers	3	East Fife	0
1975	Celtic	3	Airdrie	1		1949	Rangers	4	Clyde	1
1974	Celtic	3	Dundee United	0		1948	Rangers	1	Greenock Morton	1
1973	Rangers	3	Celtic	2		replay	Rangers	1	Greenock Morton	0
1972	Celtic	6	Hibernian	1		1947	Aberdeen	2	Hibernian	1

SCOTTISH CUP STATS

MOST APPEARANCES IN A FINAL

Celtic	48
Rangers	46
Aberdeen	15
Queens Park	12
Hearts	12
Hibernian	10
Kilmarnock	8
Vale of Leven	7
Dundee United	7

MOST SCOTTISH CUP FINAL WINS

Celtic	30
Rangers	29
Queens Park	10

MOST SCOTTISH CUP FINAL DEFEATS

Rangers, Celtic	17
Hibernian, Aberdeen	8

BIGGEST WIN IN A FINAL

Arbroath 36   Bon Accord 0
September 12, 1885

HIGHEST FINAL ATTENDANCE

Celtic v Aberdeen   147,365
1937 Final

LOWEST FINAL ATTENDANCE

Queens Park v Clydesdale   2,500*
1874 Final
*approximate figure

THE SCOTTISH LEAGUE CUP

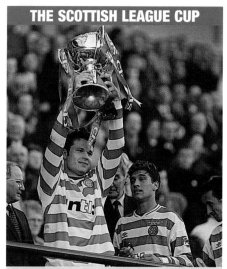

SCOTTISH PLAYER OF THE YEAR

PLAYER OF THE YEAR

2000	**Barry Ferguson** *Rangers*
1999	**Henrik Larsson** *Celtic*
1998	**Jackie McNamara** *Celtic*
1997	**Paolo di Canio** *Celtic*
1996	**Paul Gascoigne** *Rangers*
1995	**Brian Laudrup** *Rangers*
1994	**Mark Hateley** *Rangers*
1993	**Andy Goram** *Rangers*
1992	**Ally McCoist** *Rangers*
1991	**Paul Elliott** *Celtic*
1990	**Jim Bett** *Aberdeen*
1989	**Theo Snelders** *Aberdeen*
1988	**Paul McStay** *Celtic*
1987	**Brian McClair** *Celtic*
1986	**Richard Gough** *Dundee United*
1985	**Jim Duffy** *Morton*
1984	**Willie Miller** *Aberdeen*
1983	**Charlie Nicholas** *Celtic*
1982	**Sandy Clark** *Airdrie*
1981	**Mark McGhee** *Aberdeen*
1980	**Davie Provan** *Celtic*
1979	**Paul Hegarty** *Dundee United*
1978	**Derek Johnstone** *Rangers*

YOUNG PLAYER OF THE YEAR

2000	**Kenny Miller** *Hibernian*
1999	**Barry Ferguson** *Rangers*
1998	**Gary Naysmith** *Hearts*
1997	**Alex Burke** *Kilmarnock*
1996	**Jackie McNamara** *Celtic*
1995	**Charlie Miller** *Rangers*
1994	**Phil O'Donnell** *Motherwell*
1993	**Eoin Jess** *Aberdeen*
1992	**Phil O'Donnell** *Motherwell*
1991	**Eoin Jess** *Aberdeen*
1990	**Scott Crabbe** *Hearts*
1989	**Billy McKinlay** *Dundee United*
1988	**John Collins** *Hibernian*
1987	**Robert Fleck** *Rangers*
1986	**Craig Levein** *Hearts*
1985	**Craig Levein** *Hearts*
1984	**John Robertson** *Hearts*
1983	**Pat Nevin** *Clyde*
1982	**Charlie Nicholas** *Celtic*
1981	**Frank McAvennie** *St Mirren*
1980	**John McDonald** *Rangers*
1979	**Graham Stewart** *Dundee United*
1978	**Graeme Payne** *Dundee United*

SCOTTISH LEAGUE CUP WINNERS

Year	Winner	Score	Runner-up	Score		Year	Team 1	Score	Team 2	Score
2000	**Celtic**	2	Aberdeen	0		1973	Hibernian	2	Celtic	1
1999	**Rangers**	2	St Johnstone	1		1972	Partick Thistle	4	Celtic	1
1998	**Celtic**	3	Dundee United	0		1971	Rangers	1	Celtic	0
1997	**Rangers**	4	Hearts	3		1970	Celtic	1	St Johnstone	0
1996	**Aberdeen**	2	Dundee	0		1969	Celtic	6	Hibernian	2
1995	**Raith Rovers**	2	Celtic	2		1968	Celtic	5	Dundee	3
	Raith won 6-5 penalties					1967	Celtic	1	Rangers	0
1994	**Rangers**	2	Hibernian	1		1966	Celtic	2	Rangers	1
1993	**Rangers**	2	Aberdeen	1		1965	Rangers	2	Celtic	1
1992	**Hibernian**	2	Dunfermline	0		1964	Rangers	5	Morton	0
1991	**Rangers**	2	Celtic	1		1963	Hearts	1	Kilmarnock	0
1990	**Aberdeen**	2	Rangers	1		1962	Rangers	1	Hearts	1
1989	**Rangers**	3	Aberdeen	2		replay	Rangers	3	Hearts	1
1988	**Rangers**	3	Aberdeen	3		1961	Rangers	2	Kilmarnock	0
	Rangers won 5-3 penalties					1960	Hearts	2	Third Lanark	1
1987	**Rangers**	2	Celtic	1		1959	Hearts	5	Partick Thistle	1
1986	**Aberdeen**	3	Hibernian	0		1958	Celtic	7	Rangers	1
1985	**Rangers**	1	Dundee United	0		1957	Celtic	0	Partick Thistle	0
1984	**Rangers**	3	Celtic	2		replay	Celtic	3	Partick Thistle	0
1983	**Celtic**	2	Rangers	1		1956	Aberdeen	2	St Mirren	1
1982	**Rangers**	2	Dundee United	1		1955	Hearts	4	Motherwell	2
1981	**Dundee United**	3	Dundee	0		1954	East Fife	3	Partick Thistle	2
1980	**Dundee United**	0	Aberdeen	0		1953	Dundee	2	Kilmarnock	0
replay	**Dundee United**	3	Aberdeen	0		1952	Dundee	3	Rangers	2
1979	**Rangers**	2	Aberdeen	1		1951	Motherwell	3	Hibernian	0
1978	**Rangers**	2	Celtic	1		1950	East Fife	3	Dunfermline	0
1977	**Aberdeen**	2	Celtic	1		1949	Rangers	2	Raith Rovers	0
1976	**Rangers**	1	Celtic	0		1948	East Fife	0	Falkirk	0
1975	**Celtic**	6	Hibernian	3		replay	East Fife	4	Falkirk	1
1974	**Dundee**	1	Celtic	0		1947	Rangers	4	Aberdeen	0

SCOTTISH LEAGUE CUP STATS

MOST APPEARANCES IN A FINAL

Rangers	27
Celtic	23
Aberdeen	12
Hibernian	7
Dundee	6
Hearts	6
Dundee United	5
Partick Thistle	4
East Fife	3
Kilmarnock	3

MOST LEAGUE CUP FINAL WINS

Rangers	21
Celtic	11
Aberdeen	5

MOST LEAGUE CUP FINAL DEFEATS

Celtic	12
Aberdeen	7
Rangers	6

BIGGEST LEAGUE CUP FINAL WIN

Celtic 7   Rangers 1
1956-57

MOST GOALS SCORED IN A FINAL

Celtic 6   Hibernian 3
1974-75

BANK OF SCOTLAND PREMIER LEAGUE SEASON 1999-2000

		P	W	D	L	F	A	Pts	Top Scorer	Ave. Att.
1	Rangers	36	28	6	2	96	26	90	Dodds 19*	48,116
2	Celtic	36	21	6	9	90	38	69	Viduka 25	53,889
3	Hearts	36	15	9	12	47	47	54	McSwegan 13	14,246
4	Motherwell	36	14	10	12	49	63	52	McCulloch 9	7,360
5	St Johnstone	36	10	12	14	36	44	42	Lowndes 11	6,114
6	Hibernian	36	10	11	15	49	61	41	Latapy 9	11,870
7	Dundee	36	12	5	19	45	64	41	Falconer 12	6,938
8	Dundee United	36	11	6	19	34	57	39	Dodds 10	7,499
9	Kilmarnock	36	8	13	15	38	52	37	Cocard 7	9,419
10	Aberdeen	36	9	6	21	44	83	33	Stavrum 8	12,646

*includes 10 goals for Dundee United

SCOTTISH FIRST DIVISION SEASON 1999-2000

		P	W	D	L	F	A	Pts	Top Scorer	Ave. Att.
1	St Mirren	36	23	7	6	75	39	76	Yardley 19	4,942
2	Dunfermline	36	20	11	5	66	33	71	Crawford 16	5,067
3	Falkirk	36	20	8	8	67	40	68	Crabbe 14	3,344
4	Livingston	36	19	7	10	60	45	64	Bingham 15	3,974
5	Raith	36	17	8	11	55	40	59	Dargo 12	3,126
6	Inverness CT	36	13	10	13	60	55	49	Sheerin 11	2,283
7	Ayr	36	10	8	18	42	52	38	Hurst 14	2,180
8	Morton	36	10	6	20	45	61	36	Curran 9	1,468
9	Airdrie	36	7	8	21	29	69	29	Neil, Thompson 5	1,819
10	Clydebank	36	1	7	28	17	82	10	Cameron 5	602

INTERNATIONAL APPEARANCES

MOST INTERNATIONAL CAPS

LOTHAR MATTHAUS GERMANY

With an international career spanning over 20 years following his debut in 1980 against Holland, Lothar Matthaus has amassed a record of appearances that is unlikely to be beaten for a considerable time. A veteran of five World Cups and four European Championships, the articulate German captained his country's World Cup-winning side of 1990.

1.	**Lothar Matthaus** *Germany 1980-2000*	**150**
2.	Tomas Ravelli *Sweden 1981-97*	143
3.	Majed Abdullah *Saudi Arabia 1978-95*	140
4.	Andoni Zubizarreta *Spain 1985-99*	126
5.	Peter Shilton *England 1970-90*	125
=	Marcelo Balboa *USA 1988-98*	125
7.	Gheorghe Hagi *Romania 1983-2000*	125
8.	Peter Schmeichel *Denmark 1988-*	123
9.	Masami Ihara *Japan 1988-98*	121
10	Pat Jennings *N. Ireland 1964-86*	119

MOST ENGLAND CAPS

PETER SHILTON ENGLAND

Peter Shilton made his international debut against East Germany at the age of just 21. His last cap, in the 1990 World Cup third place play-off against Italy, aged 40, was the end of a remarkable international career.

ENGLAND

1.	**Peter Shilton** *1970-90*	**125**
2.	Bobby Moore *1962-73*	108
3.	Bobby Charlton *1958-70*	106
4.	Billy Wright *1946-59*	105
5.	Bryan Robson *1980-91*	90
6.	Kenny Sansom *1979-88*	86
7.	Ray Wilkins *1976-86*	84
8.	Gary Lineker *1984-92*	80
9.	John Barnes *1983-95*	79
10.	Terry Butcher *1980-90*	77

SCOTLAND

1.	**Kenny Dalglish** *1971-86*	**102**
2.	Jim Leighton *1983-98*	91
3.	Alex McLeish *1980-93*	77
4.	Paul McStay *1984-97*	76
5.	Willie Miller *1975-90*	65

WALES

1.	**Neville Southall** *1982-97*	**92**
=	Peter Nicholas *1979-92*	73
2.	Ian Rush *1980-97*	73
4.	Mark Hughes *1984-99*	72
5.	Joey Jones *1976-86*	72

REPUBLIC OF IRELAND

1.	**Steve Staunton** *1990-2000*	**84**
2.	Paul McGrath *1982-98*	83
3.	Pat Bonner *1981-96*	80
4.	Niall Quinn *1986-*	79
5.	Tony Cascarino *1986-*	77

NORTHERN IRELAND

1.	**Pat Jennings** *1964-86*	**119**
2.	Mal Donaghy *1980-95*	91
3.	Sammy McIlroy *1972-87*	88
4.	Jimmy Nicholl *1976-86*	73
5.	David McCreery *1976-90*	67

INTERNATIONAL GOALS

MOST INTERNATIONAL GOALS

FERENC PUSKAS HUNGARY

One of the all-time greats, Ferenc Puskas earned his reputation with a lethal left foot and a strike ratio to match. In 84 games for his country he scored 83 goals, including two when Hungary became the first ever foreign team to beat England on home soil in 1953. Puskas was also a World Cup runner-up in 1952 and represented Spain after fleeing Hungary in 1956.

1.	**Ferenc Puskas** *Hungary 1945-56*	**83**
2.	Pelé *Brazil 1957-71*	77
3.	Sandor Kocsis *Hungary 1948-56*	75
4.	Gerd Müller *W. Germany 1966-74*	68
5.	Imre Schlosser *Hungary 1906-27*	60
6.	Joachim Streich *E. Germany 1969-84*	55
7.	Kazuyoshi Miura *Japan 1990-98*	54
8.	Poul Nielsen *Denmark 1910-25*	52
9.	Kunishige Mumamoto *Japan 1964-77*	51
10.	Bobby Charlton *England 1958-70*	49

MOST ENGLAND GOALS

BOBBY CHARLTON ENGLAND

Sir Bobby Charlton played 106 games for England, scoring a record 49 goals in the process. The Man. United hero was a key member of England's 1966 World Cup-winning side and is highly respected all over the world.

ENGLAND

1.	**Bobby Charlton** *1958-70*	**49**
2.	Gary Lineker *1984-92*	48
3.	Jimmy Greaves *1959-67*	44
4.	Tom Finney *1946-58*	30
=	Nat Lofthouse *1950-58*	30
=	Alan Shearer *1992-2000*	30
7.	Vivian Woodward *1903-11*	29
8.	Steve Bloomer *1895-1907*	28
9.	David Platt *1989-96*	27
10.	Bryan Robson *1980-91*	26

SCOTLAND

1.	**Denis Law** *1959-74*	**30**
=	Kenny Dalglish *1971-86*	30
3.	Hughie Gallacher *1924-35*	23
4.	Lawrie Reilly *1949-57*	22
5.	Ally McCoist *1986-99*	19

WALES

1.	**Ian Rush** *1980-97*	**28**
2.	Ivor Allchurch *1951-66*	23
=	Trevor Ford *1947-57*	23
4.	Dean Saunders *1986-*	21
5.	Mark Hughes *1984-99*	16

REPUBLIC OF IRELAND

1.	**Frank Stapleton** *1977-90*	**20**
=	Niall Quinn *1986-*	20
3.	John Aldridge *1986-97*	19
=	Tony Cascarino *1986-*	19
=	Don Givens *1969-82*	19

NORTHERN IRELAND

1.	**Colin Clarke** *1986-93*	**13**
2.	Iain Dowie *1990-99*	12
=	Gerry Armstrong *1977-86*	12
=	Joe Bambrick *1929-38*	12
=	Billy Gillespie *1913-31*	12

WORLD PLAYER OF THE YEAR

THE WINNERS AND ENGLISH CONTENDERS

A World Cup Finalist with Brazil in 1998, Rivaldo took his form back with him to club side Barcelona and reproduced some stunning displays in 1999. His sublime skill, creativity and goalscoring ability took the Catalan side through to the latter stages of the Champions League.

1999	**Rivaldo**	*Brazil*
1998	**Zinedine Zidane**	*France*
1997	**Ronaldo**	*Brazil*
1996	**Ronaldo**	*Brazil*
1995	**George Weah**	*Liberia*
1994	**Romario**	*Brazil*
1993	**Roberto Baggio**	*Italy*
1992	**Marco Van Basten**	*Holland*
1991	**Lothar Matthaus**	*Germany*

ENGLISH CONTENDERS

1999 David Beckham *Man. United (2nd)*
Superb creative player, ball distribution and free-kicks as Man. United won their historic treble in 1999.

1996 Alan Shearer *Newcastle United (3rd)*
Became Europe's top marksman after winning the Golden Boot at Euro '96 with five goals for England.

1991 Gary Lineker *Tottenham Hotspur (3rd)*
An FA Cup winner with Spurs after leading England to the World Cup semi-finals in the previous year.

WORLD CLUB CUP

THE WINNERS

1999	**Man. United**	1	Palmeiras	0	1980	**Nacional**	1	Nott'm Forest	0
1998	**Real Madrid**	2	Vasco da Gama	1	1979	**Olimpia**	3	Malmo	1*
1997	**B. Dortmund**	2	Cruzeiro	0	1978	*Not contested*		
1996	**Juventus**	1	River Plate	0	1977	**Boca Juniors**	5	B. M'gladbach	2*
1995	**Ajax**	0	Gremio	0	1976	**Bayern Munich**	2	Cruzeiro	0*
	(Ajax won 4-3 on penalties)				1975	*Not contested*		
1994	**Velez Sarsfield**	2	AC Milan	0	1974	**Atletico Madrid**	2	Independiente	1*
1993	**Sao Paulo**	3	AC Milan	2	1973	**Independiente**	1	Juventus	0
1992	**Sao Paulo**	2	Barcelona	1	1972	**Ajax**	4	Independiente	1*
1991	**Red Star Belgrade**	3	Colo Colo	0	1971	**Nacional**	3	Panathinaikos	2*
1990	**AC Milan**	3	Olimpia	0	1970	**Feyenoord**	2	Estudiantes	2*
1989	**AC Milan** *(aet)*	1	Atletico Nacional	0	1969	**AC Milan**	4	Estudiantes	2*
1988	**Nacional**	1	PSV Eindhoven	1	1968	**Estudiantes**	2	Man. United	1*
	Nacional won 7-6 on penalties				1967	**Racing Club**	2	Celtic	1*
1987	**FC Porto** *(aet)*	2	Penarol	1	1966	**Penarol**	4	Real Madrid	0*
1986	**River Plate**	1	Steaua Bucharest	0	1965	**Inter Milan**	3	Independiente	0
1985	**Juventus**	2	Argentinos Jnrs	2	1964	**Inter Milan**	3	Independiente	1*
	(Juventus won 4-2 on penalties)				1963	**Santos**	7	AC Milan	6*
1984	**Independiente**	1	Liverpool	0	1962	**Santos**	8	Benfica	4*
1983	**Gremio**	2	SV Hamburg	1	1961	**Penarol**	7	Benfica	2*
1982	**Penarol**	2	Aston Villa	0	1960	**Real Madrid**	5	Penarol	1*
1981	**Flamengo**	3	Liverpool	0					

* *Denotes aggregate scores where finals were contested over two legs or more.*

CLUB WORLD CHAMPIONSHIP

The Club World Championship is a new eight-team tournament featuring the biggest clubs in the world.

2000	**Corinthians**	0	Vasco da Gama	0

Corinthians win 4-3 on penalties aet

THE WORLD CUP

THE FINALS

1998 FRANCE　FINAL **FRANCE 3 BRAZIL 0**
Venue: St Denis Attendance: 75,000
Top scorer: Davor Suker Croatia 6
Second Round: England; Group stages: Scotland;
Did not qualify: Wales, N. Ireland, Rep. Of Ireland.

1994 USA　FINAL **BRAZIL 0 ITALY 0** Brazil won 3-2 on pens
Venue: Los Angeles Attendance: 94,800
Top scorer: Oleg Salenko Russia 6
　　　　　　Hristo Stoichkov Bulgaria 6
Second Round: Rep. Of Ireland;
Did not qualify: England, Scotland, Wales, N. Ireland.

1990 ITALY　FINAL **WEST GERMANY 1 ARGENTINA 0**
Venue: Rome Attendance: 73,600
Top scorer: Salvatore Schillaci Italy 6
Semi-finals: England; Quarter-finals: Rep. Of Ireland; Group stages:
Scotland; Did not qualify: Wales, N. Ireland.

1986 MEXICO　FINAL **ARGENTINA 3 WEST GERMANY 2**
Venue: Mexico City Attendance: 114,800
Top scorer: Gary Lineker England 6
Quarter-finals: England; Group stages: Scotland, N. Ireland;
Did not qualify: Wales, Rep. Of Ireland.

1982 SPAIN　FINAL **ITALY 3 WEST GERMANY 1**
Venue: Madrid Attendance: 90,000
Top scorer: Paolo Rossi Italy 6
Second Round: England, N. Ireland; Group stages: Scotland;
Did not qualify: Wales, Rep. Of Ireland.

1978 ARGENTINA　FINAL **ARGENTINA 3 HOLLAND 1**
Venue: Buenos Aires Attendance: 77,000
Top scorer: Mario Kempes Argentina 6
Group stages: Scotland;
Did not qualify: England, Wales, N. Ireland, Rep. Of Ireland.

1974 W. GERMANY　FINAL **WEST GERMANY 2 HOLLAND 1**
Venue: Munich Attendance: 180,000
Top scorer: Gregorz Lato Poland 7
Group stages: Scotland;
Did not qualify: England, Wales, N. Ireland, Rep. Of Ireland.

1970 MEXICO　FINAL **BRAZIL 4 ITALY 1**
Venue: Mexico City Attendance: 110,000
Top scorer: Gerd Muller West Germany 10
Quarter-finals: England;
Did not qualify: Scotland, Wales, N. Ireland, Rep. Of Ireland.

1966 ENGLAND　FINAL **ENGLAND 4 WEST GERMANY 2**
Venue: London Attendance: 93,000
Top scorer: Eusebio Portugal 9
Winners: England;
Did not qualify: Scotland, Wales, N. Ireland, Rep. Of Ireland.

1962 CHILE　FINAL **BRAZIL 3 CZECHOSLOVAKIA 1**
Venue: Santiago Attendance: 69,068
Top scorer: Drazen Jerkovic Yugoslavia 5
Quarter-finals: England;
Did not qualify: Scotland, Wales, N. Ireland, Rep. Of Ireland.

1958 SWEDEN　FINAL **BRAZIL 5 SWEDEN 2**
Venue: Stockholm Attendance: 49,737
Top scorer: Just Fontaine France 13
Quarter-finals: N. Ireland, Wales; Group stages: England;
Scotland; Did not qualify: Rep. Of Ireland.

1954 SWITZERLAND　FINAL **WEST GERMANY 3 HUNGARY 2**
Venue: Berne Attendance: 55,000
Top scorer: Sandor Kocsis Hungary 11
Quarter-finals: England; Group stages: Scotland;
Did not qualify: Wales, N. Ireland, Rep. Of Ireland

1950 BRAZIL　FINAL **URUGUAY 2 BRAZIL 1**
Venue: Rio de Janeiro Attendance: 199,854
Top scorer: Ademir Brazil 9
First Round: England Withdrew: Scotland;
Did not qualify:
Rep. Of Ireland Did not enter: N. Ireland, Wales

1938 FRANCE　FINAL **ITALY 4 HUNGARY 2**
Venue: Paris Attendance: 65,000
Top scorer: Da Silva Leonidas Brazil 8
Did not qualify: Rep. Of Ireland
Did not enter: England, Scotland, N. Ireland, Wales

1934 ITALY　FINAL **ITALY 2 CZECHOSLOVAKIA 1**
Venue: Rome Attendance: 55,000
Top scorer: Angelo Schiavio Italy 4
　　　　　　Oldrich Nejedly Czechoslovakia 4
　　　　　　Edmund Conen Germany 4
Did not enter: England, Scotland, Wales,
N Ireland, Rep. Of Ireland

1930 URUGUAY　FINAL **URUGUAY 4 ARGENTINA 2**
Venue: Montevideo Attendance: 90,000
Top scorer: Guillermo Stabile Argentina 8
Did not qualify: Wales, Rep. Of Ireland
Did not enter: England, Scotland, N Ireland

THE EUROPEAN CHAMPIONSHIP

France won Euro 2000 in dramatic fashion.

ALL-TIME WINNERS

2000 HOLLAND & BELGIUM FINAL **FRANCE 2 ITALY 1**
Venue: Rotterdam Attendance: 50,000
Top Scorer: Patrick Kluivert *Holland* 5
Savo Milosevic *Yugoslavia* 5
Group stages: **England;**
Did not qualify: **Scotland, Wales, N. Ireland, Rep. Of Ireland**

1996 FINAL **GERMANY 2 CZECH REPUBLIC 1**
Venue: London Attendance: 73,611
Top Scorer: Alan Shearer *England* 5
Semi-finals: **England;** *Group stages:* **Scotland;**
Did not qualify: **Wales, N. Ireland, Rep. Of Ireland**

1992 SWEDEN FINAL **DENMARK 2 GERMANY 0**
Venue: Stockholm Attendance: 37,000
Top Scorer: Henrik Larsen *Denmark* 3
Karlheinz Riedle *Germany* 3
Dennis Bergkamp *Holland* 3
Tomas Brolin *Sweden* 3
Group stages: **England, Scotland;**
Did not qualify: **Wales, N. Ireland, Rep. Of Ireland**

1988 W GERMANY FINAL **HOLLAND 2 USSR 0**
Venue: Munich Attendance: 72,000
Top Scorer: Marco Van Basten *Holland* 5
Group stages: **England, Rep. Of Ireland;**
Did not qualify: **Scotland, Wales, N. Ireland**

1984 FRANCE FINAL **FRANCE 2 SPAIN 0**
Venue: Paris Attendance: 47,000
Top Scorer: Michel Platini *France* 9
Did not qualify: **England, Scotland, Wales, N. Ireland, Rep. Of Ireland**

1980 ITALY FINAL **WEST GERMANY 2 BELGIUM 1**
Venue: Rome Attendance: 48,000
Top Scorer: Klaus Allofs *West Germany* 3
Group stages: **England;**
Did not qualify: **Scotland, Wales, N. Ireland, Rep. Of Ireland**

1976 YUGOSLAVIA FINAL **CZECHOSLOVAKIA 2 WEST GERMANY 2**
(Czechoslovakia won 5-3 on penalties)
Venue: Belgrade Attendance: 45,000
Top Scorer: Don Givens *Rep. Of Ireland* 8
Quarter-finals: **Wales;** *Group stages:* **England, Scotland,**
N. Ireland, Rep. Of Ireland

1972 BELGIUM FINAL **WEST GERMANY 3 USSR 0**
Venue: Brussels Attendance: 65,000
Top Scorer: Gerd Muller *West Germany* 11
Quarter-finals: **England;** *Group stages:* **Scotland, Wales,**
N. Ireland, Rep. Of Ireland

1968 ITALY FINAL **ITALY 1 YUGOSLAVIA 1** rply: ITALY 2 YUGOSLAVIA 0
Venue: Rome Attendance: 85,000
Top Scorer: Luigi Riva *Italy* 7
Semi-finals: **England;** *Group stages:* **Scotland, Wales,**
N. Ireland, Rep. Of Ireland

1964 SPAIN FINAL **SPAIN 2 USSR 1**
Venue: Madrid Attendance: 105,000
Top Scorer: Ole Madsen *Denmark* 11
Quarter-finals: **Rep. Of Ireland;** *Second round:* **N. Ireland;**
First round: **Wales;** *Did not qualify:* **Scotland**

1960 FRANCE FINAL **USSR 2 YUGOSLAVIA 0**
Venue: Paris Attendance: 18,000
Top Scorer: Just Fontaine *France* 6
Did not qualify: **Rep. Of Ireland;** *Did not enter:* **England,**
Scotland, Wales, N. Ireland

THE EUROPEAN CUP

Real Madrid lifted the 2000 Champions League trophy in the Stade De France.

EUROPEAN CUP WINNERS

Year	Winner		Runner-up	
2000	Real Madrid	3	Valencia	0
1999	Man. United	2	Bayern Munich	1
1998	Real Madrid	1	Juventus	0
1997	B. Dortmund	2	Juventus	1
1996	Juventus	1	Ajax	1
	Juventus won 4-2 on penalties			
1995	Ajax	1	AC Milan	0
1994	AC Milan	4	Barcelona	0
1993	Marseille	1	AC Milan	0
1992	Barcelona	1	Sampdoria	0
1991	Red Star Belgrade	0	Marseille	0
	Red Star won 5-3 on penalties			
1989	AC Milan	4	Steaua Bucharest	0
1988	PSV Eindhoven	0	Benfica	0
	PSV won 6-5 on penalties			
1987	Porto	2	Bayern Munich	1
1986	Steaua Bucharest	0	Barcelona	0
	Steaua won 2-0 on penalties			
1985	Juventus	1	Liverpool	0
1984	Liverpool	1	AS Roma	1
	Liverpool won 4-2 on penalties			
1983	SV Hamburg	1	Juventus	0
1982	Aston Villa	1	Bayern Munich	0
1981	Liverpool	1	Real Madrid	0
1980	Nott'm Forest	1	SV Hamburg	0
1979	Nott'm Forest	1	Malmo	0
1978	Liverpool	1	FC Bruges	0
1977	Liverpool	3	B.M'gladbach	1
1976	Bayern Munich	1	St Etienne	0
1975	Bayern Munich	2	Leeds United	0
1974	Bayern Munich	1	Atletico Madrid	1
1973	Ajax	1	Juventus	0
1972	Ajax	2	Inter Milan	0
1971	Ajax	2	Panathinaikos	0
1970	Feyenoord	2	Celtic	1
1969	AC Milan	4	Ajax	1
1968	Man. United	4	Benfica	0
1967	Celtic	2	Inter Milan	1
1966	Real Madrid	2	Partizan Belgrade	1
1965	Inter Milan	1	Benfica	0
1964	Inter Milan	3	Real Madrid	1
1963	AC Milan	2	Benfica	1
1962	Benfica	5	Real Madrid	3
1961	Benfica	3	Barcelona	2
1960	Real Madrid	7	Eintracht Frankfurt	3
1959	Real Madrid	2	Reims	0
1958	Real Madrid	3	AC Milan	2
1957	Real Madrid	2	Fiorentina	0
1956	Real Madrid	4	Reims	3

EUROPEAN CUP STATS

Phil Neal

MOST WINNERS MEDALS
Francisco Gento	Real Madrid	6
Alfredo di Stefano	Real Madrid	5
Jose Maria Zarraga	Real Madrid	5
Jose-Hector Rial	Real Madrid	4
Marquitos	Real Madrid	4
Phil Neal	Liverpool	4

WINNERS WITH DIFFERENT CLUBS
Miodrag Belodedici	Steaua '86, Red Star '91
Ronald Koeman	PSV '88, Barcelona '92
Dejan Savicevic	Red Star '91, AC Milan '94
Marcel Desailly	Marseille '93, AC Milan '94
Frank Rijkaard	AC Milan '89, '90, Ajax '95
Vladimir Jugovic	Red Star '91, Juventus '96
Didier Deschamps	Marseille '93, Juventus '96
Paulo Sousa	Juventus '96, B. Dortmund '97
Christian Panucci	AC Milan '94, Real Madrid '98
Clarence Seedorf	Ajax '95, Real Madrid '98

RECORD EUROPEAN CUP SCORER
Alfredo di Stefano, Real Madrid **49**
1955-64

RECORD EUROPEAN CUP WIN
Feyenoord 12 Reykjavik 2
September 17, 1969

RECORD AGGREGATE WIN
Benfica v Stade Dudelange **18-0**
(8-0 & 10-0) 1965

RECORD EUROPEAN CUP FINAL WIN
Real Madrid 7 Eintracht Frankfurt 3
May 18, 1960

THE UEFA CUP
THE WINNERS

2000	Galatasaray	0	Arsenal	0

Galatasaray won 4-1 on penalties

1999	Parma	3	Marseille	0
1998	Inter Milan	3	Lazio	0
1997	FC Schalke	1	Inter Milan	0
	Inter Milan	1	FC Schalke	0

Schalke won 4-1 on penalties

| 1996 | Bayern Munich | 2 | Bordeaux | 0 |
| | Bordeaux | 1 | Bayern Munich | 3 |

Bayern Munich win 5-1

| 1995 | Parma | 1 | Juventus | 0 |
| | Juventus | 1 | Parma | 1 |

Parma win 2-1

| 1994 | Casino Salzburg | 0 | Inter Milan | 1 |
| | Inter Milan | 1 | Salzburg | 0 |

Inter Milan win 2-0

| 1993 | B. Dortmund | 1 | Juventus | 3 |
| | Juventus | 3 | B. Dortmund | 0 |

Juventus win 6-1

| 1992 | Torino | 2 | Ajax | 2 |
| | Ajax | 0 | Torino | 0 |

Ajax win on away goals

| 1991 | Inter Milan | 2 | Roma | 0 |
| | Roma | 1 | Inter Milan | 0 |

Inter Milan win 2-1

| 1990 | Juventus | 3 | Fiorentina | 1 |
| | Fiorentina | 0 | Juventus | 0 |

Juventus win 3-1

| 1989 | Napoli | 2 | VfB Stuttgart | 1 |
| | VfB Stuttgart | 3 | Napoli | 3 |

Napoli win 5-4

| 1988 | Espanyol | 3 | Bayer Leverkusen | 0 |
| | Bayer Leverkusen | 3 | Espanyol | 0 |

Leverkusen win 3-2 on penalties

| 1987 | IFK Gothenburg | 1 | Dundee United | 0 |
| | Dundee United | 1 | IFK Gothenburg | 1 |

IFK Gothenburg win 2-1

| 1986 | Real Madrid | 5 | Cologne | 1 |
| | Cologne | 2 | Real Madrid | 0 |

Real Madrid win 5-3

| 1985 | Videoton | 0 | Real Madrid | 3 |
| | Real Madrid | 1 | Videoton | 0 |

Real Madrid win 3-1

| 1984 | Anderlecht | 1 | Tottenham | 1 |
| | Tottenham | 1 | Anderlecht | 1 |

Tottenham win 4-3 on penalties

| 1983 | Anderlecht | 1 | Benfica | 0 |
| | Benfica | 1 | Anderlecht | 1 |

Anderlecht win 2-1

| 1982 | IFK Gothenburg | 1 | Hamburg | 0 |
| | Hamburg | 0 | IFK Gothenburg | 3 |

IFK Gothenburg win 4-0

| 1981 | Ipswich Town | 3 | AZ 67 Alkmaar | 0 |
| | AZ 67 Alkmaar | 4 | Ipswich Town | 2 |

Ipswich Town win 5-4

| 1980 | B. M'gladbach | 3 | Eintracht Frankfurt | 2 |
| | Eintracht Frankfurt | 1 | b.m'gladbach | 0 |

Eintracht Frankfurt win on away goals

| 1979 | Crvena Zvezda | 1 | B. M'gladbach | 1 |

| | B. M'gladbach | 1 | Crvena Zvezda | 0 |

B. M'gladbach win 2-1

| 1978 | Bastia | 0 | PSV Eindhoven | 0 |
| | PSV Eindhoven | 3 | Bastia | 0 |

PSV Eindhoven win 3-0

| 1977 | Juventus | 1 | Athletic Bilbao | 0 |
| | Athletic Bilbao | 2 | Juventus | 1 |

Athletic Bilbao win on away goals

| 1976 | Liverpool | 3 | Club Brugge | 2 |
| | Club Brugge | 1 | Liverpool | 1 |

Liverpool win 4-3

| 1975 | B. M'gladbach | 0 | Twente Enschede | 0 |
| | Twente Enschede | 1 | B. M'gladbach | 5 |

B. M'gladbach win 5-1

| 1974 | Tottenham | 2 | Feyenoord | 2 |
| | Feyenoord | 2 | Tottenham | 0 |

Feyenoord win 4-2

| 1973 | Liverpool | 3 | B.M'gladbach | 0 |
| | B.M'gladbach | 2 | Liverpool | 0 |

Liverpool win 3-2

| 1972 | Wolves | 1 | Tottenham | 2 |
| | Tottenham | 1 | Wolves | 1 |

Tottenham win 3-2

| 1971 | Juventus | 2 | Leeds United | 2 |
| | Leeds United | 1 | Juventus | 1 |

Leeds United win on away goals

| 1970 | Anderlecht | 3 | Arsenal | 1 |
| | Arsenal | 3 | Anderlecht | 0 |

Arsenal win 4-3

| 1969 | Newcastle United | 3 | Ujpest Dozsa | 0 |
| | Ujpest Dozsa | 2 | Newcastle United | 3 |

Newcastle United win 6-2

| 1968 | Leeds United | 1 | Ferencvaros | 0 |
| | Ferencvaros | 0 | Leeds United | 0 |

Leeds United win 1-0

| 1967 | Dinamo Zagreb | 2 | Leeds United | 0 |
| | Leeds United | 0 | Dinamo Zagreb | 0 |

Dinamo Zagreb win 2-0

| 1966 | Barcelona | 0 | Real Zaragoza | 1 |
| | Real Zaragoza | 2 | Barcelona | 4 |

Barcelona win 4-3

1965	Ferencvaros	1	Juventus	0
1964	Real Zaragoza	2	Valencia	1
1963	Dinamo Zagreb	1	Valencia	2
	Valencia	2	Dinamo Zagreb	0

Valencia win 4-1

| 1962 | Valencia | 6 | Barcelona | 2 |
| | Barcelona | 1 | Valencia | 1 |

Valencia win 7-3

| 1961 | Birmingham City | 2 | Roma | 2 |
| | Roma | 2 | Birmingham City | 0 |

Roma win 4-2

| 1960 | Birmingham City | 0 | Barcelona | 0 |
| | Barcelona | 4 | Birmingham City | 1 |

Barcelona win 4-1

| 1959 | London XI | 2 | Barcelona | 2 |
| | Barcelona | 6 | London XI | 0 |

Barcelona win 8-2

UEFA CUP STATS

MOST UEFA CUP WINS	
Borussia M'gladbach, Inter Milan	3
Barcelona, IFK Gothenburg, Liverpool, Leeds United, Real Madrid, Tottenham, Real Zaragoza	2

RECORD CUP WIN (ONE LEG)	
Cologne 13 Union Luxembourg 0	
First Round	October 5, 1965

RECORD AGGREGATE WIN	
Feyenoord 21 US Rumelange 0	
First Round	Sept.13 & 27, 1972 9-0 &12-0

RECORD UEFA CUP FINAL WIN (ONE LEG)	
Parma 3 Marseille 0	May 12, 1999
Inter Milan 3 Lazio 0	May 6, 1998

RECORD CUP FINAL WIN (TWO LEGS)	
Barcelona 8 London 1	(2-2 and 6-0)
	March 5 and May 1, 1958

EUROPEAN PLAYER OF THE YEAR
THE WINNERS

1999	Rivaldo	*Brazil*
1998	Zinedine Zidane	*France*
1997	Ronaldo	*Brazil*
1996	Matthias Sammer	*Germany*
1995	George Weah	*Liberia*
1994	Hristo Stoichkov	*Bulgaria*
1993	Roberto Baggio	*Italy*
1992	Marco Van Basten	*Holland*
1991	Jean-Pierre Papin	*France*
1990	Lothar Matthaus	*Germany*

1989	Marco Van Basten	*Holland*
1988	Marco Van Basten	*Holland*
1987	Ruud Gullit	*Holland*
1986	Igor Belanov	*USSR*
1985	Michel Platini	*France*
1984	Michel Platini	*France*
1983	Michel Platini	*France*
1982	Paolo Rossi	*Italy*
1981	Karl-Heinz Rummenigge	*West Germany*
1980	Karl-Heinz Rummenigge	*West Germany*
1979	Kevin Keegan	*England*
1978	Kevin Keegan	*England*
1977	Allan Simonsen	*Denmark*
1976	Franz Beckenbauer	*West Germany*
1975	Oleg Blokhin	*USSR*

1974	Johan Cruyff	*Holland*
1973	Johan Cruyff	*Holland*
1972	Franz Beckenbauer	*West Germany*
1971	Johan Cruyff	*Holland*
1970	Gerd Muller	*West Germany*
1969	Gianni Rivera	*Italy*
1968	George Best	*Northern Ireland*
1967	Florian Albert	*Hungary*
1966	Bobby Charlton	*England*
1965	Eusebio	*Portugal*
1964	Denis Law	*Scotland*
1963	Lev Yashin	*USSR*
1962	Josef Masopust	*Czechoslovakia*
1961	Omar Enrique Sivori	*Argentina/Italy*
1960	Luis Suarez	*Spain*
1959	Alfredo di Stefano	*Argentina/Spain/Colombia*
1958	Raymond Kopa	*France*
1957	Alfredo di Stefano	*Argentina/Spain/Colombia*
1956	Stanley Matthews	*England*

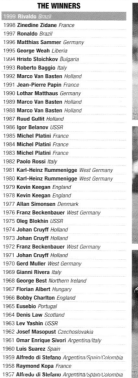

CUP-WINNERS' CUP STATS

1999	Lazio	2	Real Mallorca	1
1998	Chelsea	1	Stuttgart	0
1997	Barcelona	1	Paris St Germain	0
1996	Paris St Germain	1	Rapid Vienna	0
1995	Real Zaragoza	2	Arsenal	1
1994	Arsenal	1	Parma	0
1993	Parma	3	Antwerp	1
1992	Werder Bremen	2	Monaco	0
1991	Man. United	2	Barcelona	1
1990	Sampdoria	2	Anderlecht	0
1989	Barcelona	2	Sampdoria	0
1988	Mechelen	1	Ajax	0
1987	Ajax	1	Locomotiv Leipzig	0
1986	Dynamo Kiev	3	Atletico Madrid	0
1985	Everton	3	Rapid Vienna	1
1984	Juventus	2	Porto	1
1983	Aberdeen	2	Real Madrid *(aet)*	1
1982	Barcelona	2	Standard Liege	1
1981	Dynamo Tbilisi	2	Carl Zeiss Jena	1
1980	Valencia	0	Arsenal	0

(aet. Valencia won 5-4 on penalties)

1979	Barcelona	4	F. Dusseldorf *(aet)*	3
1978	Anderlecht	4	Austria/WAC	0
1977	Hamburg	2	Anderlecht	0
1976	Anderlecht	4	West Ham United	2

1975	Dynamo Kiev	3	Ferencvaros	0
1974	Magdeburg	2	AC Milan	0
1973	AC Milan	1	Leeds United	0
1972	Rangers	3	Moscow Dynamo	2
1971	Chelsea	1	Real Madrid *(aet)*	1
1971	Chelsea	2	Real Madrid	1

(replay, aet.)

1970	Man. City	2	Gornik Zabrze	1
1969	Slovan Bratislava	3	Barcelona	2
1968	AC Milan	2	Hamburg	0
1967	Bayern Munich	1	Rangers *(aet)*	0
1966	B. Dortmund	2	Liverpool *(aet)*	1
1965	West Ham United	2	Munich 1860	0
1964	Sporting Lisbon	3	MTK Budapest *(aet)*	3
1964	Sporting Lisbon	1	MTK Budapest	0

(replay)

1963	Tottenham	5	Atletico Madrid	1
1962	Atletico Madrid	1	Fiorentina	1
1962	Atletico Madrid	3	Fiorentina	0

(replay)

| 1961 | Fiorentina | 2 | Rangers *(2nd leg)* | 1 |
| 1961 | Fiorentina | 2 | Rangers *(1st leg)* | 0 |

The Cup-Winners' Cup ran from 1961-1999

EUROPEAN ROUND-UP 1999-2000 SEASON

AUSTRIA
League winners: FC Tirol
Austrian Cup winners: Grazer AK
Top scorer: Ivica Vastic (Sturm Graz) 32

BELGIUM
League winners: Anderlecht
Belgian Cup winners: Genk
Top scorers: Ole-Martin Aarst (Gent) 30
Toni Brogno (Westerlo) 30

BULGARIA
League winners: Lev Sofia
Bulgarian Cup winners: LVSKI Sofia
Top scorer: Svetoslav Todorov (Lovech) 18

CROATIA
League winners: Dinamo Zagreb
Croatian Cup winners: Hajduk Split
Top scorer: Tomo Sokota (Dinamo) 21

CZECH REPUBLIC
League winners: Sparta Prague
Czech Republic Cup winners: Liberec
Top scorer: Radek Drulak (Drnovice) 23

DENMARK
League winners: Herfolge BK
Danish Cup winners: Viborg FF
Top scorer: Peter Lassen (Silkeborg) 16

FRANCE
League winners: Monaco
French Cup winners: Nantes
League Cup winners: Gueugnon
Top scorer: Sonny Anderson (Lyon) 23

GERMANY
League winners: Bayern Munich
German Cup winners: Bayern Munich
Top scorer: Martin Max (1860 Munich) 19

GREECE
League winners: Olympiakos
Greek Cup winners: AEK Athens
Top scorer: Dimitris Nalitzis (PAOK) 24

HOLLAND
League winners: PSV Eindhoven
Dutch Cup winners: Roda JC
Top scorer: Ruud Van Nistelrooy (PSV) 29

HUNGARY
League winners: Dunaferr
Hungary Cup winners: MTK
Top scorer: Attila Tokoli (Dunaferr) 22

ITALY
League winners: Lazio
Italian Cup winners: Lazio
Top scorer: Andriy Shevchenko (Milan) 24

Ruud Van Nistelrooy was Holland's top goalscorer as PSV won another title.

Bayern Munich were again champions of Germany.

Lazio snatched the Scudetto from under the noses of Juventus.

Deportivo La Coruna won the Primera Liga for the first time ever.

NORTHERN IRELAND

League winners: Linfield
Irish Cup winners: Glentoran
Irish League Cup winners: Linfield
Top scorer: Vinney Arkins (Portadown) 34

POLAND

League winners: Polonia Warszawa
League Cup winners: Polonia Warszawa
Polish Cup winners: Amica Wronki
Top scorer: Adam Kompala (Gornik) 19

PORTUGAL

League winners: Sporting Lisbon
Portuguese Cup winners: FC Porto
Top scorer: Mario Jardel (FC Porto) 38

REPUBLIC OF IRELAND

League winners: Shelbourne
Irish League Cup winners: Derry City
Top scorer: Pat Morley (Cork City) 20

ROMANIA

League winners: Spartak Moscow
Romanian Cup winners: Dinamo Bucharest
Top scorer: Marian Savu (N. Bucharest) 20

RUSSIA

League winners: Spartak Moscow
Russian Cup winners: Lokomotiv Moskow
Top scorer: Kovalenko (Chernomorets) 8

SLOVENIA

League winners: Maribor
Slovenian Cup winners: Olimpija Ljubljana
Top scorer: Klitan Bozgo (Maribor) 24

SPAIN

League winners: Deportivo La Coruna
Spanish Cup winners: Espanyol
Top scorer: Salva Ballesta (R. Santander) 27

SWITZERLAND

League winners: St Gallen
Swiss Cup winners: FC Zurich
Top scorer: Charles Rmoah (St Gallen) 23

TURKEY

League Cup winners: Galatasaray
Turkish Cup winners: Galatasaray
Top scorer: Serkan Aykut (Samsun) 30

UKRAINE

League winners: Dynamo Kiev
Ukranian Cup winners: Dynamo Kiev
Top scorer: Ivan Hetsko (Karpaty) 22

YUGOSLAVIA

League winners: Crvcna Zvezda Belgrade
Yugoslavian Cup winners: Crvena Zvezda Belgrade
Top scorer: Mateja Kezman (P. Belgrade) 27

Peter Schmeichel was a title winner again with Portugal's Sporting Lisbon.

ARSENAL

Arsenal FC, Avenall Road, Highbury, London N5 1BU
Tel: 0207 7044000 **Tickets:** 0207 4133366 **Clubcall:** 0906 4744000
Official website: www.arsenal.co.uk

Ground Capacity: 38,500
Record Victory: **12-0 v Loughborough**, March 12, 1900
Record Defeat: **0-8 v Loughborough**, December 12, 1896
Most League Goals: **Cliff Bastin 150**, 1930-1947
Most Aggregate Goals: **Ian Wright 185**, 1991-1998
Record Fee In: **Thierry Henry** (Juventus £10.5 million, 1999)
Record Fee Out: **Nicolas Anelka** (Real Madrid £21 million, 1999)

ASTON VILLA

Aston Villa FC, Villa Park, Trinity Road, Birmingham B6 6HE
Tel: 0121 3272299 **Tickets:** 09068 121848 **Clubcall:** 09068 121148
Official website: www.avfc.co.uk

Ground Capacity: 39,217
Record Victory: **13-0 Wednesbury Old Ath**, October 30, 1886
Record Defeat: **1-8 v Blackburn**, February 16, 1889
Most League Goals: **Harry Hampton 215**, 1904-1915
Most Aggregate Goals: **Billy Walker 244**, 1919-1934
Record Fee In: **Stan Collymore** (Liverpool £7 million, 1997)
Record Fee Out: **Dwight Yorke** (Man. United £12.6 million, 1998)

COVENTRY CITY

Coventry City FC, Highfield Road Stadium, King Richard Street,
Coventry CV2 4FW **Tel:** 01203 234000 **Tickets:** 01203 234020
Clubcall: 09068 121166 **Official website:** www.ccfc.co.uk

Ground Capacity: 23,650
Record Victory: **9-0 v Bristol City**, April 28, 1934
Record Defeat: **2-10 v Norwich**, March 15, 1930
Most League Goals: **Clarrie Broughton 171**, 1931-1937
Most Aggregate Goals: **Clarrie Broughton 181**, 1931-1937
Record Fee In: **Robbie Keane** (Wolves £6 million, 1999)
Record Fee Out: **Dion Dublin** (Aston Villa £5.75 million, 1998)

BRADFORD CITY

Bradford City FC, Valley Parade, Bradford, BD8 7DY
Tel: 01274 773355 **Tickets:** 01274 770022 **Clubcall:** 09068 888640
Official website: www.bradfordcityfc.co.uk

Ground Capacity: 21,634
Record Victory: **13-0 Peterhead**, February 9, 1923
Record Defeat: **0-8 v Celtic**, January 30, 1965
Most League Goals: **Bobby Campbell 121**, 1981-1986
Most Aggregate Goals: **Bobby Campbell 143**, 1979-1986
Record Fee In: **David Wetherall** (Leeds £2 million, 1999)
Record Fee Out: **Des Hamilton** (Newcastle £2 million, 1997)

DERBY COUNTY

Derby County FC, Pride Park Stadium, Derby DE24 8XL
Tel: 01332 202202 **Tickets:** 01332 209999 **Clubcall:** 09068 121187
Official website: www.dcfc.co.uk

Ground Capacity: 33,597
Record Victory: **12-0 v Finn Harps**, September 16, 1976
Record Defeat: **2-11 v Everton**, 1889-90
Most League Goals: **Steve Bloomer 292**, 1892-1914
Most Aggregate Goals: **Steve Bloomer 331**, 1892-1914
Record Fee In: **Seth Johnson** (Crewe Alexandra £3 million, 1999)
Record Fee Out: **Christian Dailly** (Blackburn £5.75 million, 1998)

CHARLTON ATHLETIC

Charlton Athletic FC, The Valley, Floyd Road, Charlton, SE7 8BL
Tel: 0208 3334000 **Tickets:** 0208 3334010 **Clubcall:** 09068 121146
Official website: www.charlton-athletic.co.uk

Ground Capacity: 20,043
Record Victory: **8-1 v Middlesbrough**, September 12, 1953
Record Defeat: **1-11 v Aston Villa**, November 14, 1959
Most League Goals: **Stuart Leary 153**, 1953-1962
Most Aggregate Goals: **Stuart Leary 153**, 1953-1962
Record Fee In: **Neil Redfearn** (Barnsley £1.02 million, 1998)
Record Fee Out: **Lee Bowyer** (Leeds United £2.8 million, 1996)

EVERTON

Everton FC, Goodison Park, Goodison Road, Liverpool L4 4EL
Tel: 0151 3302200 **Tickets:** 0151 3302300 **Clubcall:** 09068 121199
Official website: www.evertonfc.com

Ground Capacity: 40,200
Record Victory: **11-2 v Derby County**, January 18, 1890
Record Defeat: **4-10 v Tottenham**, October 11, 1958
Most League Goals: **Dixie Dean 349**, 1925-1937
Most Aggregate Goals: **Dixie Dean 377**, 1925-1937
Record Fee In: **Nick Barmby** (Middlesbrough £5.75 million, 1996)
Record Fee Out: **Andrei Kanchelskis** (Fiorentina £8 million, 1997)

CHELSEA

Chelsea FC, Fulham Road, London, SW6 1HS
Tel: 0207 3855545 **Tickets:** 0207 3867799 **Clubcall:** 09068 121159
Official website: www.chelseafc.co.uk

Ground Capacity: 41,000
Record Victory: **13-0 v Jeunesse Hautcharage**, Sept 29, 1971
Record Defeat: **1-8 v Wolverhampton Wanderers**, Sept 26, 1953
Most League Goals: **Bobby Tampling 164**, 1958-1970
Most Aggregate Goals: **Bobby Tampling 202**, 1958-1970
Record Fee In: **JF Hasselbaink** (Atletico Madrid £15 million, 2000)
Record Fee Out: **Michael Duberry** (Leeds £4.5 million, 1999)

IPSWICH TOWN

Ipswich Town FC, Portman Road, Ipswich IP1 2DA
Tel: 01473 400500 **Tickets:** 01473 400555 **Clubcall:** 09068 121068
Official website: www.itfc.co.uk

Ground Capacity: 22,600
Record Victory: **10-0 v Floriana**, September 25, 1962
Record Defeat: **1-10 v Fulham**, December 26, 1963
Most League Goals: **Ray Crawford 203**, 1958-1969
Most Aggregate Goals: **Ray Crawford 227**, 1958-1969
Record Fee In: **Marcus Stewart** (Huddersfield £2.5 million, 2000)
Record Fee Out: **Kieron Dyer** (Tottenham £6 million, 1999)

LEEDS UNITED

Leeds United FC, Elland Road, Leeds, LS11 0ES
Tel: 0113 2266000 **Tickets:** 0891 121680 **Clubcall:** 09068 121180
Official website: www.lufc.co.uk

Ground Capacity: 40,204
Record Victory: **10-0 v Lyn**, September 17, 1969
Record Defeat: **1-8 v Stoke City**, August 27, 1934
Most League Goals: **Peter Lorimer, 168**, 1965-1986
Most Aggregate Goals: **Peter Lorimer, 238**, 1965-1986
Record Fee In: **Olivier Dacourt** (Lens £7.2 million, 2000)
Record Fee Out: **JF Hasselbaink** (Atletico Madrid £12m, 1999)

NEWCASTLE UNITED

 Newcastle United FC, St James' Park, Newcastle-Upon-Tyne NE1 4ST **Tel:** 0191 2018400 **Tickets:** 0191 2611571 **Clubcall:** 0891 121190 **Official website:** www.nufc.co.uk

 Ground Capacity: 36,834
Record Victory: **13-0 v Newport County**, October 5, 1946
Record Defeat: **0-9 v Burton Wanderers**, April 15, 1895
Most League Goals: **Jackie Milburn 177**, 1946-1957
Most Aggregate Goals: **Jackie Milburn 200**, 1946-1957
Record Fee In: **Alan Shearer** (Blackburn £15 million, 1996)
Record Fee Out: **Dietmar Hamann** (Liverpool £8 million, 1999)

LEICESTER CITY

 Leicester City FC, Filbert Street, Leicester LE2 7FL
Tel: 0116 2915000 **Tickets:** 0116 2915232 **Clubcall:** 0891 121185
Official website: www.lcfc.co.uk

 Ground Capacity: 22,000
Record Victory: **10-0 v Portsmouth**, October 20, 1928
Record Defeat: **0-12 v Nottingham Forest**, April 21, 1909
Most League Goals: **Arthur Chandler 259**, 1923-1935
Most Aggregate Goals: **Arthur Chandler 273**, 1923-1935
Record Fee In: **Darren Eadie** (Norwich City £3 million, 1999)
Record Fee Out: **Emile Heskey** (Liverpool £11 million, 2000)

SOUTHAMPTON

 Southampton FC, The Dell, Milton Road, Southampton, Hants SO15 2XH **Tel:** 01703 220505 **Tickets:** 01703 228575 **Clubcall:** 0891 121178 **Official website:** www.saintsfc.co.uk

 Ground Capacity: 15,000
Record Victory: **9-3 v Wolves**, September 18, 1965
Record Defeat: **0-8 v Everton**, November 20, 1971
Most League Goals: **Mike Channon 185**, 1966-1982
Most Aggregate Goals: **Mike Channon 185**, 1966-1982
Record Fee In: **David Hirst** (Sheffield Wednesday £2 million, 1997)
Record Fee Out: **Kevin Davies** (Blackburn £7.25 million, 1998)

LIVERPOOL

 Liverpool FC, Anfield Road, Liverpool L4 0TH
Tel: 0151 2632361 **Tickets:** 0151 2608680 **Clubcall:** 0891 121184
Official website: www.liverpoolfc.net

 Ground Capacity: 45,370
Record Victory: **11-0 v Stromsgodset**, September 17, 1974
Record Defeat: **1-9 v Birmingham City**, December 11, 1954
Most League Goals: **Roger Hunt 245**, 1959-1969
Most Aggregate Goals: **Ian Rush 344**, 1980-1997
Record Fee In: **Emile Heskey** (Leicester City £11 million, 2000)
Record Fee Out: **Stan Collymore** (Aston Villa £7 million, 1997)

SUNDERLAND

 Sunderland AFC, Stadium Of Light, Sunderland SR5 1SU
Tel: 0191 5515000 **Tickets:** 0191 5515151 **Clubcall:** 0891 121140
Official website: www.sunderland-afc.com

 Ground Capacity: 48,000
Record Victory: **11-1 v Fairfield**, February 2, 1895
Record Defeat: **0-8 v Watford**, September 25, 1982
Most League Goals: **Charlie Buchan 209**, 1911-1925
Most Aggregate Goals: **Bob Gurney 228**, 1926-1939
Record Fee In: **Stefan Schwarz** (Valencia £4 million, 1999)
Record Fee Out: **Michael Bridges** (Leeds United £5 million, 1999)

MANCHESTER CITY

 Man. City FC, Maine Road, Moss Side, Manchester M14 7WN
Tel: 0161 2323000 **Tickets:** 0161 2262224 **Clubcall:** 0891 121191
Official website: www.mcfc.co.uk

 Ground Capacity: 33,000
Record Victory: **10-1 v Huddersfield**, November 7, 1987
Record Defeat: **1-9 v Everton**, September 3, 1906
Most League Goals: **Tommy Johnson 158**, 1919-1930
Most Aggregate Goals: **Eric Brook 178**, 1928-1939
Record Fee In: **Lee Bradbury** (Portsmouth £3 million, 1997)
Record Fee Out: **Georgi Kinkladze** (Ajax £5 million, 1998)

TOTTENHAM HOTSPUR

 Tottenham Hotspur FC, White Hart Lane, Bill Nicholson Way, Tottenham, London N17 0AP **Tel:** 0208 3655000 **Tickets:** 0208 3655050 **Clubcall:** 0891 100500 **Official website:** www.spurs.co.uk

 Ground Capacity: 36,236
Record Victory: **13-2 v Crewe Alexandra**, February 3, 1960
Record Defeat: **0-8 v Cologne**, July 22, 1995
Most League Goals: **Jimmy Greaves 220**, 1961-1970
Most Aggregate Goals: **Jimmy Greaves 266**, 1961-1970
Record Fee In: **Sergei Rebrov** (Dynamo Kiev £11 million, 2000)
Record Fee Out: **Paul Gascoigne** (Lazio £5.5 million, 1992)

MAN. UNITED

 Man. United FC, Old Trafford, Sir Matt Busby Way, Manchester M16 0RA **Tel:** 0161 8688000 **Tickets:** 0161 8688668 **Clubcall:** 0891 121161 **Official website:** www.manutd.com

 Ground Capacity: 68,500
Record Victory: **10-0 v Anderlecht**, September 26, 1956
Record Defeat: **0-7 v Blackburn**, April 10, 1926
Most League Goals: **Bobby Charlton 199**, 1956-1973
Most Aggregate Goals: **Bobby Charlton 199**, 1956-1973
Record Fee In: **Dwight Yorke** (Aston Villa £12.6 million, 1998)
Record Fee Out: **Paul Ince** (Inter Milan £7 million, 1995)

WEST HAM UNITED

 West Ham United FC, Boleyn Ground, Green Street, Upton Park, London E13 9AZ **Tel:** 0208 5482748 **Tickets:** 0208 5482700 **Clubcall:** 0891 121165 **Official website:** www.whufc.co.uk

 Ground Capacity: 26,054
Record Victory: **10-0 v Bury**, October 25, 1983
Record Defeat: **2-8 v Blackburn**, December 26, 1963
Most League Goals: **Vic Watson 298**, 1929-1935
Most Aggregate Goals: **Vic Watson 326**, 1920-1935
Record Fee In: **Marc-Vivien Foe** (Lens £4.2 million, 1999)
Record Fee Out: **John Hartson** (Wimbledon £7.5 million, 1999)

MIDDLESBROUGH

 Middlesbrough FC, Riverside Stadium, Middlesbrough TS3 6RS
Tel: 01642 877700 **Tickets:** 01642 877745 **Clubcall:** 0891 121181
Official website: www.boro.co.uk

 Ground Capacity: 35,059
Record Victory: **9-0 v Brighton**, August 23, 1923
Record Defeat: **0-9 v Blackburn**, November 6, 1954
Most League Goals: **George Camsell 326**, 1925-1939
Most Aggregate Goals: **George Camsell 326**, 1925-1939
Record Fee In: **Fabrizio Ravanelli** (Juventus £7 million, 1996)
Record Fee Out: **Juninho** (Atletico Madrid £12 million, 1997)

ENGLISH LEAGUE & SCOTTISH PREMIER ADDRESSES

DIVISION ONE CONTACTS

BARNSLEY
Barnsley FC, Oakwell Ground, Grove Street, Barnsley, South Yorkshire S71 1ET
Tel: 01226 211211 Tickets: 01226 211211
Clubcall: 0891 121152
Official website: www.barnsleyfc.com

BIRMINGHAM CITY
Birmingham City FC, St Andrews Ground, Birmingham B9 4NH
Tel: 0121 7720101 Tickets: 0121 7720101
Clubcall: 0891 121188
Official website: www.bcfc.com

BLACKBURN ROVERS
Blackburn Rovers FC, Ewood Park, Blackburn, Lancashire BB2 4JF
Tel: 01254 698888 Tickets: 01254 698888
Clubcall: 0891 121179
Official website: www.rovers.co.uk

BOLTON WANDERERS
Bolton Wanderers FC, Reebok Stadium, Lostock, Bolton BL6 6JW
Tel: 01204 673601
Tickets: 01204 673601
Clubcall: 0891 121164
Official website: www.boltonwfc.co.uk

BURNLEY
Burnley FC, Turf Moor, Brunshaw Road, Burnley BB10 4BX
Tel: 01282 700000 Tickets: 01282 700010
Clubcall: 0891 121153
Official website: www.clarets.co.uk

CREWE ALEXANDRA
Crewe Alexandra FC, Gresty Road, Crewe, Cheshire CW2 6EB
Tel: 01270 213014 Tickets: 01270 252610
Clubcall: 0891 121647
Unofficial web: www.crewealex.u-net.com

CRYSTAL PALACE
Crystal Palace FC, Selhurst Park Stadium, London SE25 6PU
Tel: 0208 7686000 Tickets: 0208 7686000
Clubcall: 09068 400333
Official website: www.cpfc.co.uk

FULHAM
Fulham FC, Craven Cottage, Stevenage Road, London SW6 6HT
Tel: 0207 8938383 Tickets: 0207 3844710
Clubcall: 09068 440044
Official website: www.fulhamfc.co.uk

GILLINGHAM FC
Gillingham FC, Priestfield Stadium, Gillingham, Kent ME7 4DD
Tel: 01634 851854 Tickets: 01634 576828
Clubcall: 0891 332211
Official website: www.gillinghamfc.co.uk

GRIMSBY TOWN
Grimsby Town FC, Blundell Park, Cleethorpes, NE Lincolnshire DN35 7PY
Tel: 01472 605050 Tickets: 01472 605050
Clubcall: 09068 555855
Official website: www.gtfc.co.uk

HUDDERSFIELD TOWN
Huddersfield Town FC, The Alfred McAlpine Stadium, Huddersfield HD1 6PX
Tel: 01484 484100 Tickets: 01484 484123
Clubcall: 01484 121638 Official website: www.huddersfield-town.co.uk

NORWICH CITY
Norwich City FC, Carrow Road, Norwich NR1 1JE
Tel: 01603 760760 Tickets: 01603 760760
Clubcall: 09068 121144
Official website: www.canaries.co.uk

NOTTINGHAM FOREST
Nottingham Forest FC, The City Ground, Notttingham NG2 5FJ
Tel: 0115 9824444 Tickets: 0115 9844445
Clubcall: 09068 121174
Official website: www.nottinghamforest.co.uk

PORTSMOUTH
Portsmouth FC, Fratton Park, Frogmore Road, Portsmouth PO4 8RA
Tel: 01705 731204 Tickets: 01705 618777
Clubcall: 0891 121182
Official website: www.pompeyfc.co.uk

PRESTON NORTH END
Preston North End FC, Deepdale, Preston, Lancs PR1 6RU
Tel: 01772 902020 Tickets: 01772 909229
Clubcall: 0891 121173
Official website: www.prestonnorthend.co.uk

QUEENS PARK RANGERS
Queens Park Rangers FC, Loftus Road Stadium, London W12 7PA
Tel: 0208 7430206 Tickets: 0208 7402575
Clubcall: 09068 121162
Official website: www.qpr.co.uk

SHEFFIELD UNITED
Sheffield United FC, Bramall Lane, Sheffield, S2 4SU
Tel: 0114 2215757 Tickets: 0114 2211889
Clubcall: 0891 888650
Official website: www.sufc.co.uk

SHEFFIELD WEDNESDAY
Sheffield Wednesday FC, Hillsborough, Sheffield S6 1SW
Tel: 0114 2212121 Tickets: 0114 2212400
Clubcall: 0891 121186
Official website: www.swfc.co.uk

STOCKPORT COUNTY
Stockport County FC, Edgeley Park, Hardcastle Road, Stockport SK3 9DD
Tel: 0161 2868888 Tickets: 0161 2868888
Clubcall: 0891 121638 Official website: www.stockportmbc.gov.uk/scfc.com

TRANMERE ROVERS
Tranmere Rovers FC, Prenton Park, Prenton, Wirrall CH42 9PY
Tel: 0151 6084385 Tickets: 0151 6090137
Clubcall: 0891 121646
Official website: www.tranmererovers.co.uk

WATFORD
Watford FC, Vicarage Road Stadium, Watford WD1 8ER
Tel: 01923 496000 Tickets: 01923 496010
Clubcall: 09068 104104
Official website: www.watfordfc.co.uk

WEST BROMWICH ALBION
West Bromwich Albion FC, The Hawthorns, West Bromwich B71 4LF
Tel: 0121 5258888 Tickets: 0121 5535472
Clubcall: 0891 121193
Official website: www.wba.co.uk

WIMBLEDON
Wimbledon FC, Selhurst Park Stadium, London SE25 6PY
Tel: 0208 7712233 Tickets: 0208 7718841
Clubcall: 0891 121175
Official website: www.wimbledon-fc.co.uk

WOLVERHAMPTON WANDERERS
Wolverhampton Wanderers FC, Molineux Stadium, Wolverhampton WV1 4QR
Tel: 01902 655000 Tickets: 01902 653653
Clubcall: 0891 121823

DIVISION TWO CONTACTS

BOURNEMOUTH
Bournemouth FC, Dean Court Ground, Bournemouth BH7 7AF
Tel: 01202 397777 Tickets: 01202 397939
Clubcall: 09068 121163
Official website: www.afcb.co.uk

BRENTFORD
Brentford Football and Sports Club PLC, Braemer Road, Brentford, Middx TW8 0NT
Tel: 0208 8472511 Tickets: 0208 8472511
Clubcall: 0891 121108
Official website: www.brentfordfc.co.uk

BRISTOL CITY
Bristol City FC, Ashton Gate, Ashton Road, Bristol BS3 2JE
Tel: 0117 9630630 Tickets: 0117 9666666
Clubcall: 0891 121176
Official website: www.bcfc.co.uk

BRISTOL ROVERS
Bristol Rovers FC, The Memorial Ground, Filton Avenue, Bristol BS7 0AQ
Tel: 0117 9096648 Tickets: 0117 9243200
Clubcall: 0891 121131
Official website: www.bristolrovers.co.uk

BURY
Bury FC, Gigg Lane, Bury, Lancashire BL9 9HR
Tel: 0161 7644881 Tickets: 0161 7052144
Clubcall: 0930 190003
Official website: www.buryfc.co.uk

CAMBRIDGE UNITED
Cambridge United FC, Abbey Stadium, Newmarket Road, Cambridge CB5 8LN
Tel: 01223 566500 Tickets: 01223 566500
Clubcall: 09068 555885
Official website: www.cambridgeunited.com

COLCHESTER UNITED
Colchester United FC, Layer Road Ground, Colchester CO2 7JJ
Tel: 01206 508800 Tickets: 01206 508802
Clubcall: 09068 400222
Official website: www.cufc.co.uk

LUTON TOWN
Luton Town FC, Kenilworth Road Stadium, 1 Maple Road, Luton LU4 8AW
Tel: 01582 411622 Tickets: 01582 416976
Clubcall: 09068 121123
Unofficial web: www.btinternet.com/~ben.w

MILLWALL
Millwall FC, The Den, Zampa Road, Bermondsey, London SE16 3LN
Tel: 0207 2321222 Tickets: 0207 2319999
Clubcall: 0891 400300
Official website: www.millwallfc.co.uk

NORTHAMPTON TOWN
Northampton Town FC, Sixfields Stadium, Northampton NN5 50A
Tel: 01604 757773 Tickets: 01604 588338
Clubcall: 0930 555970
Official website: www.ntfc.co.uk

NOTTS COUNTY
Notts County FC, Meadow Lane Stadium, Nottingham NG2 3HJ
Tel: 0115 9529000 Tickets: 0115 9557210
Clubcall: 09068 443131
Official website: www.nottscountyfc.co.uk

OLDHAM ATHLETIC
Oldham Athletic FC, Boundary Park, Oldham OL1 2PA
Tel: 07000 528427 Tickets: 07000 528427
Clubcall: 0891 121142
Official website: www.oldhamathletic.co.uk

OXFORD UNITED
Oxford United FC, Manor Ground, London Road, Headington, Oxford OX3 7RS
Tel: 01865 761503 Tickets: 01865 761503
Clubcall: 0891 440055
Official website: www.oufc.co.uk

PETERBOROUGH UNITED
Peterborough United FC, London Road Ground, Peterborough PE2 8ZL
Tel: 01733 563947 Tickets: 01733 563947
Clubcall: 0891 121654
Official website: www.theposh.com

PORT VALE
Port Vale FC, Vale Park, Burslem, Stoke-on-Trent ST6 1AW
Tel: 01782 655800 Tickets: 01782 811707
Clubcall: 0891 121636
Official website: www.port-vale.co.uk

READING
Reading FC, Madejski Stadium, Bennet Road, Reading RG2 0FL
Tel: 0118 9681100 Tickets: 0118 9681100
Clubcall: 0891 121000
Official website: www.readingfc.co.uk

ROTHERHAM UNITED
Rotherham FC, Millmoor Ground, Rotherham S60 1HR
Tel: 01709 512434 Tickets: 01709 512434
Clubcall: 09068 121637
Official website: www.themillers.co.uk

STOKE CITY
Stoke City FC, Stanley Matthews Way, Stoke-on-Trent, Staffs ST4 4EG
Tel: 01782 592200 Tickets: 01782 592200
Clubcall: 0891 121040
Official website: www.stokecity.co.uk

SWANSEA CITY
Swansea City FC, Vetch Field, Swansea SA1 3SU
Tel: 01792 474114 Tickets: 01792 462584
Clubcall: 0891 121639
Official website: www.swansfc.co.uk

SWINDON TOWN
Swindon Town FC, County Ground, Swindon, SN1 2EP
Tel: 01793 333700 Tickets: 01793 333777
Clubcall: 0891 121640
Unofficial web: www.swindonfc.co.uk

WALSALL
Walsall FC, Bescot Stadium, The Bescot Crescent, Walsall WS1 4SA
Tel: 01922 622791 Tickets: 01922 613202
Clubcall: 0891 555800
Official website: www.saddlers.co.uk

WIGAN ATHLETIC
Wigan Athletic FC, JJB Stadium, Robin Park, Wigan WN5 0UZ
Tel: 01942 774000 Tickets: 01942 244433
Clubcall: 0891 121655
Official website: www.wiganlatics.co.uk

WREXHAM
Wrexham FC, The Racecourse Ground, Wrexham LL11 2AH
Tel: 01978 262129 Tickets: 01978 262163
Clubcall: 0891 121642
Official website: www.wrexhamafc.co.uk

WYCOMBE WANDERERS
Wycombe Wanderers FC, Adams Park, High Wycombe Bucks HP12 4HJ
Tel: 01494 472100 Tickets: 01494 441118
Clubcall: 09003 446855 Official website: www.wycombewanderers.co.uk

Contact details for all English league and Scottish Premier clubs!

DIVISION THREE CONTACTS

BARNET
Barnet FC, Underhill Stadium, Barnet, Hertfordshire EN5 2BE
Tel: 0208 4416932 Tickets: 0208 4496325
Clubcall: 0891 121544
Unofficial website: www.netbees.co.uk

BLACKPOOL
Blackpool FC, Bloomfield Road Ground, Blackpool FY1 6JJ
Tel: 01253 405331 Tickets: 01253 404331
Clubcall: 0891 121648
Official website: www.blackpoolfc.co.uk

BRIGHTON & HOVE ALBION
Brighton & Hove Albion FC, Whitdean Stadium, Tongdean Lane, Brighton, Sussex.
Tel: 01273 778855 Tickets: 01273 778855
Clubcall: 09068 800609
Official website: www.seagulls.co.uk

CARDIFF CITY
Cardiff City FC, Sloper Road, Cardiff CF1 8SX Tel: 01222 221001 Tickets: 01222 221001 Clubcall: 09068 121171
Official website: www.cardiffcity.com

CARLISLE UNITED
Carlisle United FC, Brunton Park Stadium, Carlisle, Cumbria CA1 1LL
Tel: 01228 526237 Tickets: 01228 526237
Clubcall: 0891 230011
Unofficial website: www.cufconline.org.uk

CHELTENHAM TOWN
Cheltenham Town FC, Whaddon Road, Cheltenham, Gloucestershire GL52 5NA
Tel: 01242 573558 Tickets: 01242 573558
Clubcall: 09066 555 833
Official website: www.cheltenhamtown.co.uk

CHESTERFIELD
Chesterfield FC, Recreation Ground, Saltergate, Chesterfield S40 4SX
Tel: 01246 209765 Tickets: 01246 209760
Clubcall: 09068 555818
website: None

DARLINGTON
Darlington Town FC, Feethams, Darlington DL1 5JB Tel: 01325 240240 Tickets: 01325 240240 Clubcall: 0891 443100
Official web: www.darlingtonfc.force9.co.uk

EXETER CITY
Exeter City FC, St James' Park, Exeter, Devon EX4 6PX Tel: 01392 254073
Tickets: 01392 254073
Clubcall: 0891 121634
Unofficial website: www.ecfc.demon.co.uk

HALIFAX TOWN
Halifax Town FC, Shay Grounds, Halifax, West Yorkshire HX1 2YS
Tel: 01422 353423 Tickets: 01422 353423
Clubcall: 0891 227328 website: None

HARTLEPOOL UNITED
Hartlepool United FC, Victoria Park, Clarence Road, Hartlepool TS24 8B2
Tel: 01429 272584 Tickets: 01429 272589
Clubcall: 0891 664447
Official website: www.hartlepoolunited.co.uk

HULL CITY
Hull City FC, Boothferry Park, Boothferry Road, Hull, East Yorkshire HU4 6EU
01482 575263 Tickets: 01482 575263
Clubcall: 09068 888688 Unofficial website: www.hullcity.org.uk

KIDDERMINSTER HARRIERS
Kidderminster Harriers FC, Aggborough Stadium, Kidderminster DY10 1NB
Tel: 01562 823931 Tickets: 01562 823931
Clubcall: 09066 555815
Official website: www.harriers.co.uk

LEYTON ORIENT
Leyton Orient FC, Brisbane Road, London E10 5NG Tel: 0208 926 1111 Tickets: 0208 926 1111 Clubcall: 0891 121150
Official website: www.leytonorient.com

LINCOLN CITY
Lincoln City FC, Sincil Bank Stadium, Lincoln LN5 8LD Tel: 01522 880011
Tickets: 01522 880011 Clubcall: 09066 555900 Official website: www.redimps.com

MACCLESFIELD TOWN
Macclesfield Town FC, Moss Rose Ground, London Road, Macclesfield, Cheshire SK11 7SP Tel: 01625 264686 Tickets: 01625 264686 Clubcall: 0930 555835
Official website: www.mtfc.co.uk

MANSFIELD TOWN
Mansfield Town FC, Field Mill Ground, Quarry Lane, Mansfield, Notts NG18 5DA
Tel: 01623 658000 Tickets: 01623 658070
Clubcall: 09068 121311
Official website: www.stagsnet.co.uk

PLYMOUTH ARGYLE
Plymouth Argyle FC, Home Park Stadium, Plymouth, Devon PL2 3DQ Tel: 01752 562561 Tickets: 01752 562561 Clubcall: 09067 090090 Official web: www.pafc.co.uk

ROCHDALE
Rochdale FC, Spotland Stadium, Sand Lane, Rochdale, Lancashire OL11 5DS
Tel: 01706 644648 Tickets: 01706 644648
Clubcall: 0891 555 858 Official website: www.rochdale-football-club.co.uk

SCUNTHORPE UNITED
Scunthorpe United FC Glanford Park, Doncaster Road, Scunthorpe, DN15 8TD
Tel: 01724 848077 Tickets: 01724 848077
Clubcall: 09068 121652
Official web: www.scunthorpe-united.co.uk

SHREWSBURY TOWN
Shrewsbury Town FC, Gay Meadow, Shrewsbury SY2 6AB
Tel: 01743 360111 Tickets: 01743 360111
Clubcall: 0891 888611
Official website: www.shrewsburytown.co.uk

SOUTHEND UNITED
Southend United FC, Roots Hall, Victoria Avenue, Southend-On-Sea, Essex SS2 6NQ
Tel: 01224 650400 Tickets: 01224 632328
Clubcall: 0891 121551
Unofficial web: www.alcatraz.demon.co.uk

TORQUAY UNITED
Torquay United FC, Plainmoor Ground, Torquay, Devon TQ1 3PS
Tel: 01803 328666 Tickets: 01803 328666
Clubcall: None
Official website: www.torquayunited.com

SCOTTISH PREMIER LEAGUE CONTACTS

ABERDEEN
Pittodrie Stadium, Pittodrie Street, Aberdeen AB24 5HQ
Tel: 01224 650400 Tickets: 01224 632328
Official website: www.afc.co.uk

CELTIC
Celtic Park, Glasgow G40 3RE Tel: 0141 556 2611 Tickets: 0141 5518653 Clubcall: 0891 196721 Official website: www.celticfc.co.uk

DUNDEE
Dens Park, Sandeman Street, Dundee DD3 7JY Tel: 01382 889966
Tickets: 01382 204777 Clubcall: None
Official website: www.dundeefc.co.uk

DUNDEE UNITED
Tannadice Park, Tannadice Street, Dundee DD3 7JW Tel: 01382 833166 Tickets: 01382 833166 Clubcall: 0891 881909
Unofficial website: www.gloryyears.co.uk

DUNFERMLINE
East End Park, Halbeath Rd, Dunfermline KY12 7RB. Tel: 01383 724295. Tickets: 01383 724295 Clubcall: 09066 555060
Official website: www.fife.co.uk/pars

HEART OF MIDLOTHIAN
Tynecastle Stadium, Gorgie Rd, Edinburgh EH11 2NL Tel: 0131 2007200 Tickets: 0131 200 7201 Official web: www.heartsfc.co.uk

HIBERNIAN
Easter Road Stadium, Albion Rd, Edinburgh EH7 5QG Tel: 0131 6612159 Tickets: 0131 6567088 Clubcall: 0891 121555
Official website: www.hibs.co.uk

KILMARNOCK
Rugby Park, Kilmarnock KA1 2DP
Tel: 01563 525184 Tickets: 01563 525184
Clubcall: 0891 633249
Official website: www.kilmarnockfc.co.uk

MOTHERWELL
Fir Park, Motherwell ML1 2QN Tel: 01698 333333 Tickets: 01698 333333 Clubcall: 0891 121553 Official web: motherwellfc.co.uk

RANGERS
Ibrox, 150 Edmiston Drive, Glasgow G51 2XD Tel: 0141 42785000 Tickets: 0870 6001993 Clubcall: 0891 121 555
Official website: www.rangers.co.uk

ST JOHNSTONE
McDiarmid Park, Crieff Road, Perth PH1 2SJ Tel: 01738 459090 Tickets: 01224 632328 Clubcall: 0898 121559
Official website: www.stjohnstonefc.co.uk

ST MIRREN
St Mirren Park, Love St, Paisley PA3 2EJ
Tel: 0141 889 2558 Tickets: 0141 8892558
Unofficial web: http://Fp.Davemacd.f9.co.uk

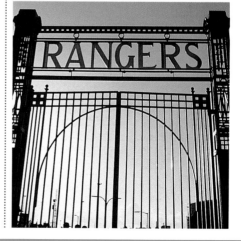

USEFUL CONTACT NUMBERS

THE FOOTBALL ASSOCIATION

The Secretary
16 Lancaster Gate
London
W2 3LW

Tel: 020 7262 4542
Fax: 020 7402 0486
www.the-fa.org

THE PREMIER LEAGUE

The Secretary
11 Connaught Place
London
W2 2ET

Tel: 020 7298 1600
Fax: 020 7298 1601
www.fa-premier.com

THE FOOTBALL LEAGUE

Unit 5
Edward VII Quay
Navigation Way
Preston
Lancashire
PR2 2YF

Tel: 01772 325 800
Fax: 01772 325 801
www.footballleague.co.uk

THE SCOTTISH FOOTBALL ASSOCIATION

6 Park Gardens
Glasgow
G3 7YF

Tel: 0141 332 6372
Fax: 0141 332 7559
www.scottishfa.co.uk

SCOTTISH PREMIER LEAGUE

The National Stadium
Hampden Park
Glasgow
G42 9BA

Tel: 0141 649 6962
Fax: 0141 649 6963
www.scotprem.com

THE SCOTTISH LEAGUE

188 West Regent Street
Glasgow
G2 4RY

Tel: 0141 248 3844
Fax: 0141 221 7450
www.scottishfa.co.uk

SCOTTISH JUNIOR FOOTBALL ASSOCIATION

46 St. Vincent Crescent
Glasgow
G3 8NG

Tel: 0141 248 1095
Fax: 0141 248 1130

SCOTTISH YOUTH FOOTBALL ASSOCIATION

4 Park Gardens
Glasgow

Tel: 0141 332 7106
Fax: 0141 332 5865

THE IRISH FOOTBALL ASSOCIATION

20 Windsor Avenue
Belfast
BT9 6EE

Tel: 01232 669458

FOOTBALL LEAGUE OF IRELAND

80 Merrion Square South
Dublin 2

Tel: 0035 3 1676 5120
Fax: 0035 3 1676 8906

FIFA

FIFA House
Hitzigweg 11
PO Box 85
8030
ZURICH
Switzerland

Tel: +41 1 384 9595
(Dialling code from UK)
Fax: +41 1 384 9696
(Dialling code from UK)
www.fifa.com

UEFA

Union Of European Football
Associations
Chemin de Redoute 54
Case postale 303
ch-1260 Nyon
Switzerland

Tel: +41 22 994 4444
(Dialling code from UK)
Fax: +41 22 994 448890
(Dialling code from UK)
www.uefa.com

ENGLISH SCHOOLS FA

1/2 Eastgate Street
Stafford
ST16 2NQ

Tel: 01785 251 142
Fax: 01785 255 485

BRITISH UNIVERSITIES SPORTS ASSOCIATION

BUSA
8 Union Street
London
SE1 1SZ

Tel: 020 7357 8555
Fax: 020 7403 1218

NATIONAL FEDERATION OF FOOTBALL SUPPORTERS' CLUBS

'The Stadium'
14 Coombe Close
Lordswood
Chatham
Kent
ME5 8NU

Tel and Fax: 0163 319 461

PROFESSIONAL FOOTBALLERS' ASSOCIATION

2 Oxford Court
Bishopsgate
Off Lower Mosley Street
Manchester
M2 3WQ

Tel: 0161 236 0575
Fax: 0161 228 7229
www.thepfa.co.uk

REFEREES' ASSOCIATION

1 Westhill Road
Coundon
Coventry
CV6 2AD

Tel: 01203 601 701
Fax: 02476 601 556
www.referee.u-k.org

WOMENS' FOOTBALL ALLIANCE

9 Wyllyotts Place
Potters Bar
Herts
EN6 2JD

Tel: 01707 651 840

NATIONAL PLAYING FIELDS ASSOCIATION

578B Catherine Place
London
SW1

Tel: 020 7584 6445
Fax: 020 7581 2402

THE ASSOCIATION OF FOOTBALL STATISTICIANS

18 St Philip Square
London
SW8 3RS

Tel: 020 7498 8906
Fax: 020 7498 8906
www.the-afs.com

THE FOOTBALL PROGRAMME DIRECTORY

'The Beeches'
66 Southend Road
Wickford
Essex
SS11 8EN

Tel: 01268 732 041

THE FOOTBALL FOUNDATION

Second Floor
Walkden House
10 Melton Street
London
NW1 2EJ

Tel: 020 7832 0100
Fax: 020 7832 0119

FOOTBALL POSTCARDS COLLECTORS' CLUB

275 Overdown Road
Tilehurst
Reading
RG31 6NX

Tel: 0118 942 4448

UK PROGRAMME COLLECTORS' CLUB

46 Milton Road
Kirkcaldy
Fife
KY1 1TL

Tel: 01592 595069

FOOTBALL RESEARCH UNIT

University of Liverpool
8-10 Abercromby Square
Liverpool
L69 7ZW

Tel: 0151 794 2401
Fax: 0151 794 2402
http://fru.merseyside.org

KICK IT OUT (ANTI-RACISM CAMPAIGN)

PO Box 29544
London
N1 0ZG

www.kickitout.org

FA WOMENS' PREMIER LEAGUE

The FA
16 Lancaster Gate
London
W2 3LW

Tel: 020 7314 5210
Fax: 020 7314 5379

SPORT ENGLAND

16 Upper Woburn Place
London
WC1H 0QP

Tel: 020 7273 1500
Fax: 020 7383 5740

AMATEUR FOOTBALL ALLIANCE

55 Islington
Park Street
London

Tel: 020 7359 3493
Fax: 00 7359 507

MATCH